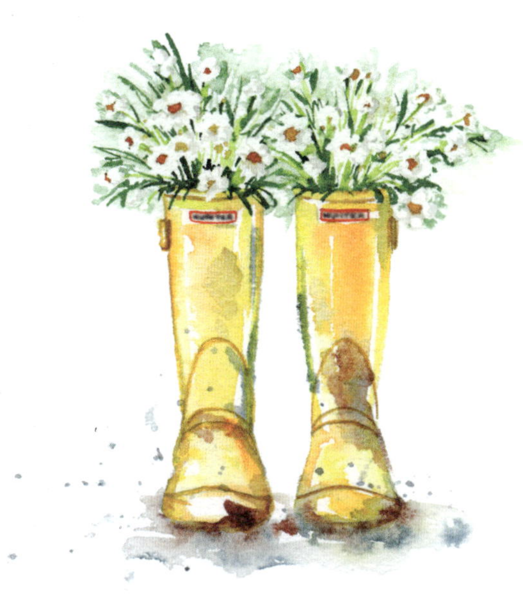

First published in Great Britain in 2025 by
ILEX, an imprint of Octopus Publishing Group Ltd
Carmelite House
50 Victoria Embankment
London, EC4Y 0DZ
www.octopusbooks.co.uk
www.octopusbooksusa.com

An Hachette UK Company
www.hachette.co.uk

The authorized representative in the EEA is
Hachette Ireland, 8 Castlecourt Centre, Dublin 15, D15 XTP3, Ireland
(email: info@hbgi.ie)

Distributed in the US by Hachette Book Group
1290 Avenue of the Americas, 4th and 5th Floors, New York, NY 10104

Distributed in Canada by Canadian Manda Group
664 Annette St., Toronto, Ontario, Canada M6S 2C8

ISBN 978-1-84091-919-6
eISBN 978-1-84091-920-2

A CIP catalogue record for this book
is available from the British Library

Printed and bound in China

Publishing Director: Alison Starling
Consultant Editorial Director: Ellie Corbett
Assistant Editor: Ellen Sleath
Managing Editor: Rachel Silverlight
Art Director: Ben Gardiner
Design: JC Lanaway
Production Managers: Lucy Carter and Nic Jones

YOU WILL BE ABLE TO **PAINT** *with* **WATERCOLOUR** BY THE END OF THIS BOOK

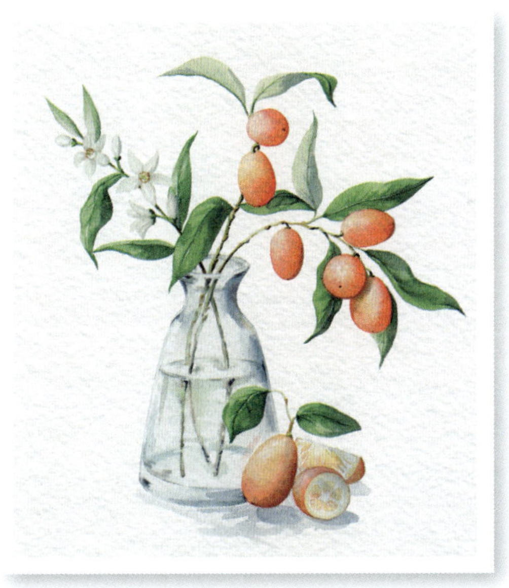

HARRIET DE WINTON

ilex

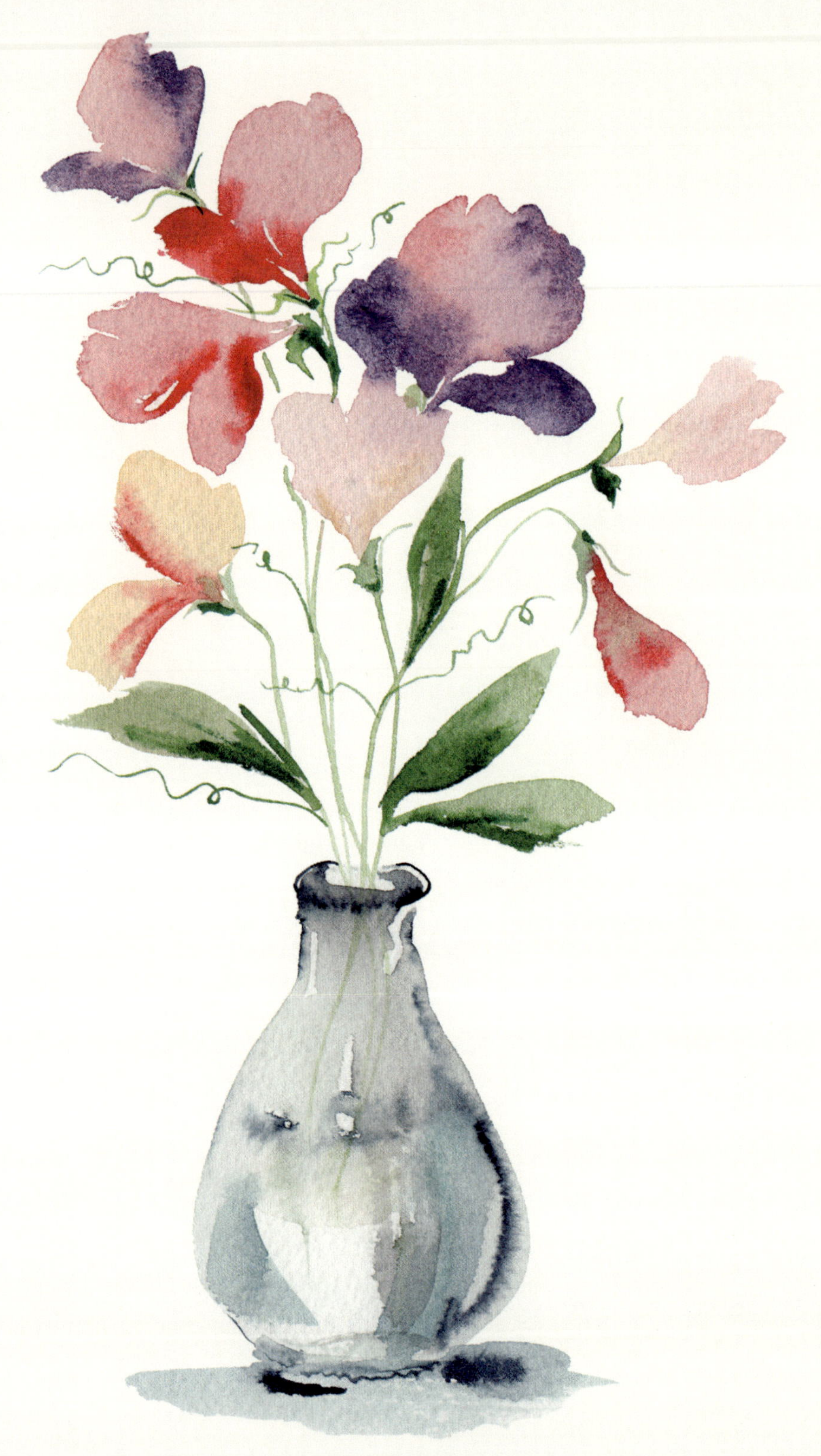

Contents

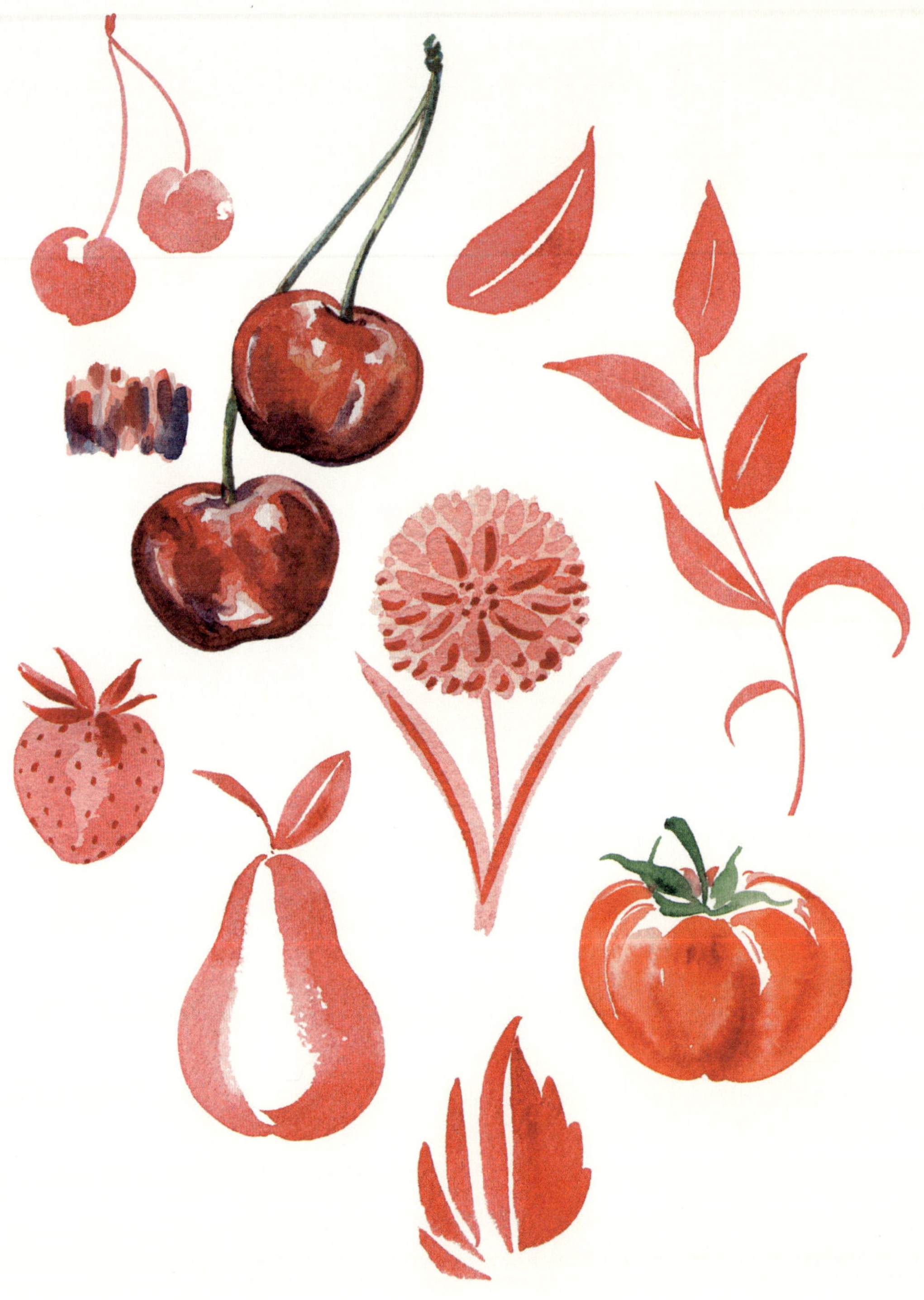

Introduction

Watercolour is the kindest art form I've ever come across. It welcomes you in with the simple requirement of a few art supplies and shows you amazing things almost immediately. It's relaxing in its process and breathtaking in its results. I'm so glad you've decided to try it.

For those of you right at the start of your watercolour journey, the sight of a long kit list could put you off before you've even started. That's why in the opening pages of this book I've stripped back our watercolour kit to the bare essentials so we can focus on simply learning to paint; consider it a first date with watercolour. Once you've got the basics and are excited to proceed, on page 63 you will find a fully comprehensive art supplies list that will open up an amazing range of materials to try.

Each page guides you through the process of watercolour with key techniques disguised as fun illustration projects. I've taken inspiration from a wide range of topics: flowers, fruit, trees, buildings, birds and much more. Get ready to fill pages with both lovely artworks and mindless scribbles while equipping yourself with a plethora of skills. Those skills can then be applied to the more detailed tutorials and inspiration pages that come later in the book.

Watercolour isn't all about proficiently following tutorials; it's also about joy, risk taking and a huge sense of satisfaction and surprise! This book will awaken your artistic confidence with prompts and little challenges in addition to the step-by-step guides. Making more of your own choices and additions to each piece will help you find your unique watercolour style, ready to paint your own pieces by the end of this book.

You will be able to paint with watercolour by the end of this book, and whatever road you take in terms of style, scale and subject matter, consider this the trusty map in your pocket that guides you down many creative paths.

How to Use This Book

I'm a self-taught artist who has painted nearly every day in my creative career. The techniques I've described in this book are tried and tested but they are not the only way to do things. Other artists and teachers have different approaches, but I'd like to think there is no wrong answer when the ultimate goal is creative curiosity.

This book is for beginners as well as intermediate artists who want to shore up their skills and get inspired. Alongside all the learning I hope you will enjoy the therapeutic qualities of painting watercolours and finish each session feeling both relaxed and also excited to turn to the next skill.

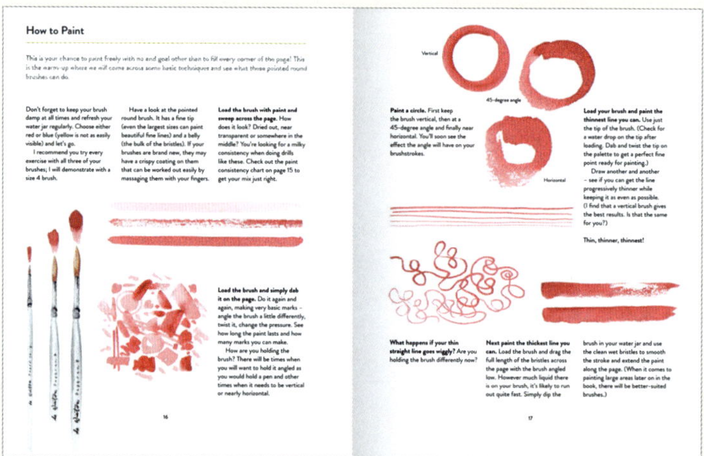

Essentials: The first half of the book covers the essentials, with a limited kit list and tutorials based around the fundamentals of watercolour. The second half of the book goes into more depth about every aspect of watercolour painting, and we end with a springboard of inspirational pages for painting beyond this book.

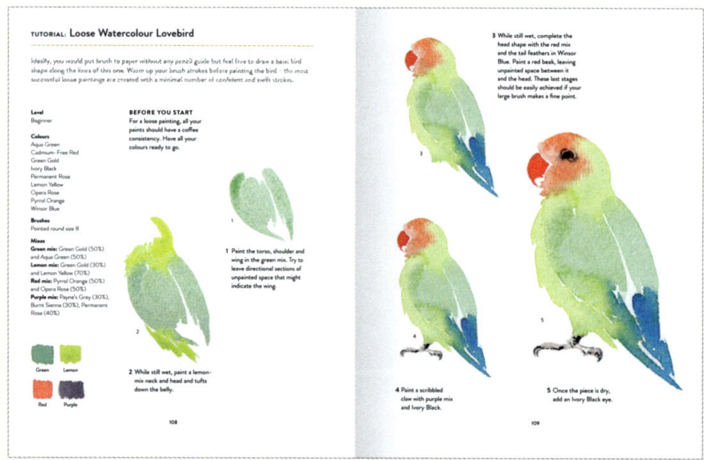

Tutorials: This book has detailed step-by-step tutorials showing you exactly what colours and brushes to use, alongside sections with looser inspirational guidelines, encouraging you to forge your own creative path. I have found that a combination of the two approaches is the best way to improve both technical skills and creative confidence.

Colour swatches: There is a full colour palette for you to refer to on the back flap of the book, and each tutorial also features colour swatches of the mixes I'm using. That being said, we all have different colours in our palette. Feel free to incorporate your own shades, similar or otherwise, using the swatches as a guide.

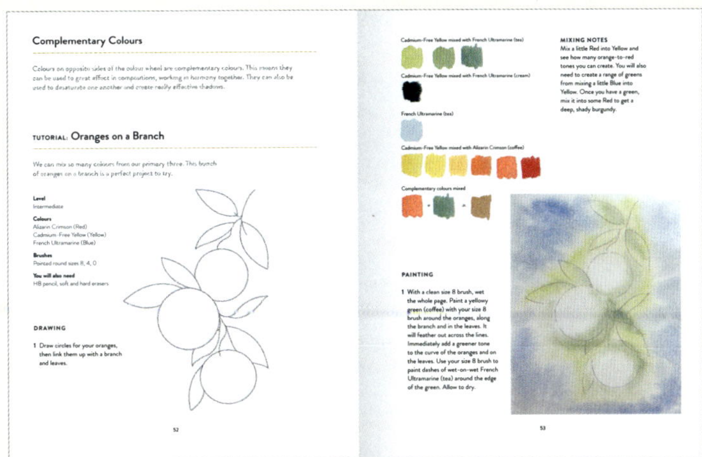

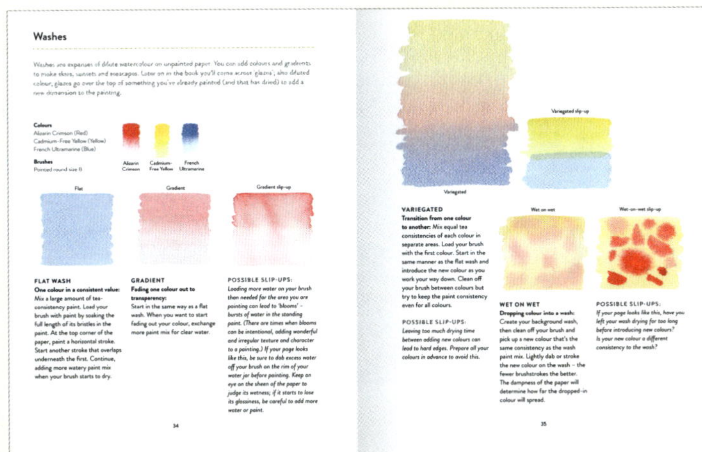

Slip-ups: In striving to get things right first time it's easy to skip valuable lessons we can learn from trial and error. We make discoveries through getting things wrong – I have enough practice pages to fill another book! Congratulate yourself every time something goes a bit wobbly, and remember that you've banked up a bit more watercolour knowledge for next time.

Prompts: Once you're pleased with your tutorial paintings, the best thing you can do is try your own variations on the theme. Don't worry, I'm not deserting you – there are suggestions and prompts throughout the book for how you can develop the tutorials and make them your own.

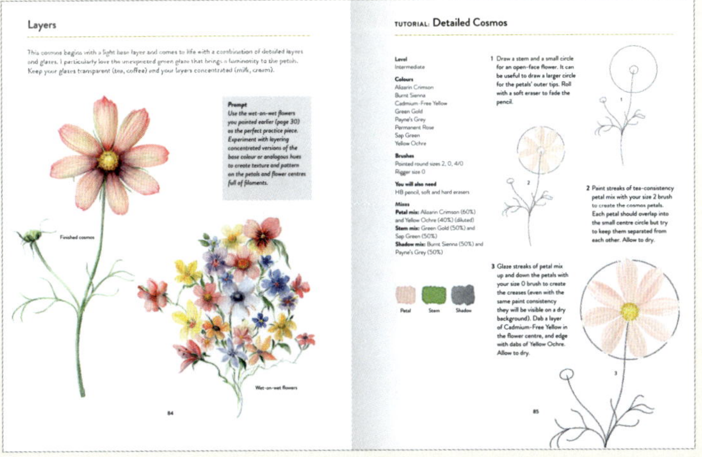

But for now, grab your paints, and let's get started!

Essential Materials

As you progress through the book there will be scope to experiment with a broader palette of colour, brushes and other watercolour materials but for now we're keeping it really simple with a small handful of pointed round brushes and the primary colours.

Colours

You can use tubes or pans of paint. I've always preferred tubes so I can squeeze some paint onto a palette and have as much space as I need to wake up and mix the colour. A common mistake by beginners is to buy the cheaper student-quality paints. I recommend buying the best you can afford; the higher-quality paint will last longer and your paintings will have a beautiful vibrancy. I love Daniel Smith, Winsor & Newton and Daler Rowney.

There are many different shades of red, yellow and blue, which means you could mix a variety of colours beyond what my chosen three will do. Our primary colours for this part of the book are Alizarin Crimson, Cadmium-Free Yellow and French Ultramarine. Where I have capitalised Red, Yellow and Blue in the book, I am referring to these specific primary colours.

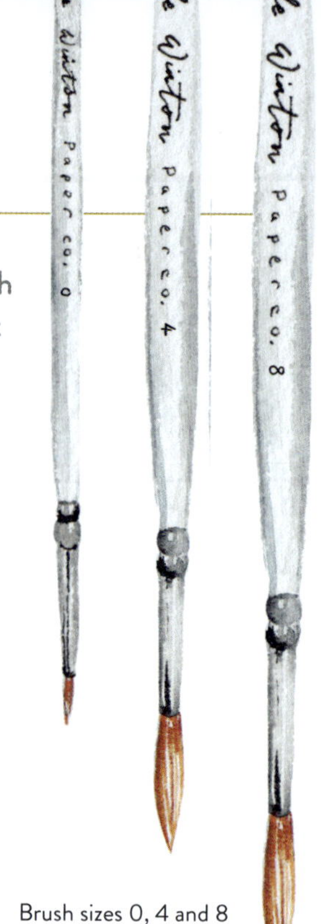

Brush sizes 0, 4 and 8

Brushes

I began with Pro Arte series 60 synthetic pointed round brushes and I still prefer them over the many different types I've experimented with over the years.

Anatomy of a brush: Watercolour brushes are made up of a handle, metal ferrule and bristles. Bristles can be formed of animal hair or can be a synthetic version that mimics it. Animal-hair brushes hold more water, and synthetic brushes are cheaper, are cruelty-free and have more stiffness (otherwise known as 'snap'), which is great for detail painting.

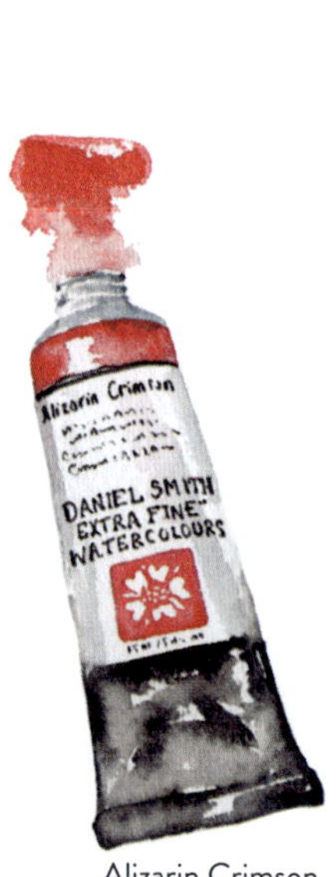

Alizarin Crimson

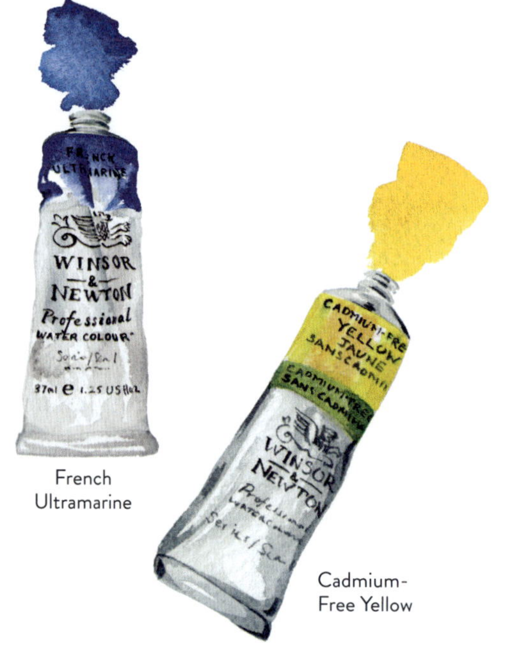

French Ultramarine

Cadmium-Free Yellow

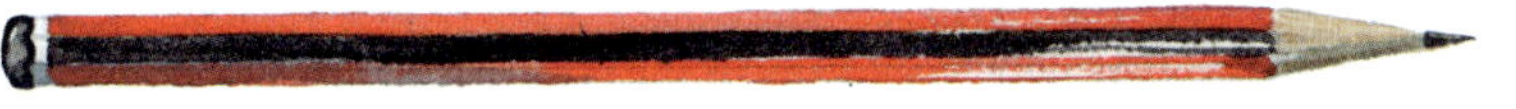

HB pencil

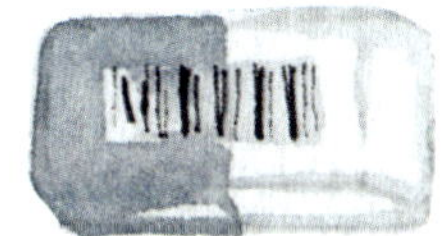

Hard eraser

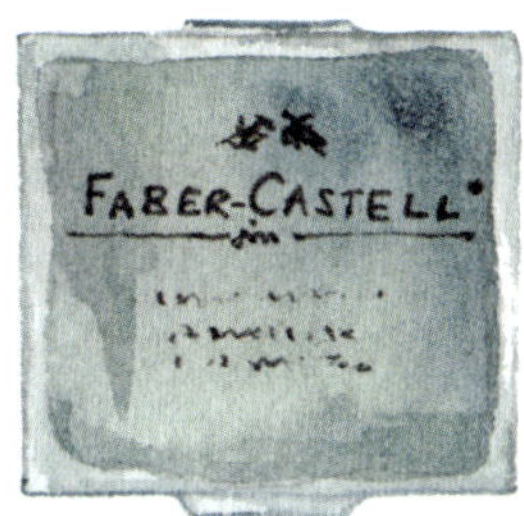

Soft eraser

Paper

All the book's projects are done on cold-pressed (also called NOT) watercolour paper. It's hard to improve your painting when using cheap, thin paper as the results are often disappointing. If you were to invest a little bit more in either paints, brushes or paper, I'd say spend the extra on paper and don't be afraid to use it! Look for 300gsm thickness and cotton content. My favourite affordable brands are Frisk and Daler-Rowney's The Langton Prestige.

Water jar

Any lowball glass (short tumbler), mug or Tupperware will do as long as its sides aren't too high. I prefer a clear vessel so I can see when to replenish the water. Painting with swamp water will inevitably affect the colours on your page. I work with two jars of water: one to clean off the brush and the other to dip the newly clean brush into.

Paper towel

Use this to blot and thoroughly clean your brush.

Pencil and erasers

Equip yourself with an HB pencil for sketching, a soft eraser for fading pencil lines before painting and a hard eraser for removing any remaining visible lines after painting. I have shaped my soft eraser into a cylinder so I can roll it over pencil lines. This is the best way to fade the pencil and leave no residue from the eraser.

Palette

You will also need a palette; a ceramic plate will be just fine. If you are working with plenty of wet colour, it is wise to buy a palette with wells that compartmentalize the paint. You can buy plastic, ceramic and enamel metal palettes. Ceramic is best for mixing watercolours (hence why I often end up using a plate).

The Loxley folding plastic palette is the best-sized palette I've found for holding plenty of colours with lots of space for mixing. If I could get an equivalent in ceramic, that would be the ultimate palette! To prep the plastic I scrubbed it with wire wool to rough up the surfaces.

How Much Water?

Water is the vehicle for the colour; how much or how little we use makes all the difference to your painting. You should aim for a smooth, seamless finish when it comes to watercolour washes and blended colours. However, 'mistakes' with water can lead to quirky effects like dry brushing and 'blooms' – it's worth remembering them for later on in the book alongside all the 'good' techniques!

HOW TO PAINT WITH THE RIGHT AMOUNT OF WATER

Always work with a wet brush
Wet bristles allow the paint to flow like a felt-tip pen. Even when painting concentrated colours and tiny dry details you will want your brush to be damp at least. Before painting, swirl your brush around in your jar of water and pull it up against the rim to squeeze out the excess water. This helps you avoid unexpected drops of water racing down the bristles and blooming out into the paint.

Prepare your colours first
Make space in your palette and pre-mix your colours to the desired consistency. The paint consistency chart on page 15 is a great way to get a feel for how your paint will behave.

Control
A pool of watery paint in your palette doesn't mean you have to create puddles on the page. It's all about how much liquid you load onto the brush in the palette. A simple way to control this, once you've swept the brush back and forth in the palette liquid, is to hold it aloft, bristles down, and see if a water droplet forms at the tip. If it does, lightly dab it off on the edge of the palette and you'll have a more manageable amount of liquid to paint with.

Timing
Your wet page will slowly start to dry, so the blend will be dependent on how long you leave it before adding your second colour. With all colours ready prepared in the palette, you can be in charge of the pace of the painting. (Extremely hot and dry or cold and wet climates will affect the paint drying speed.)

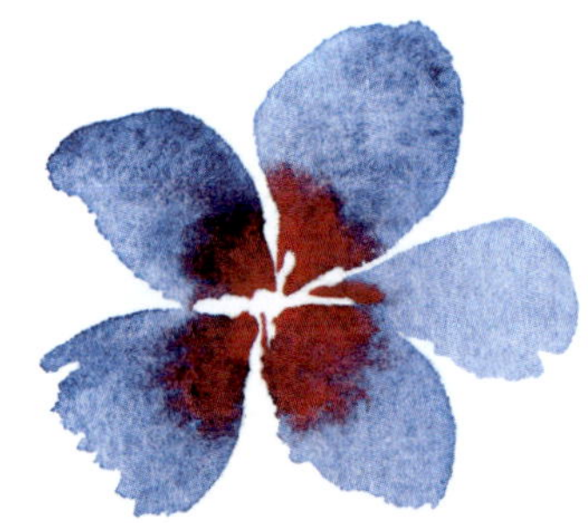

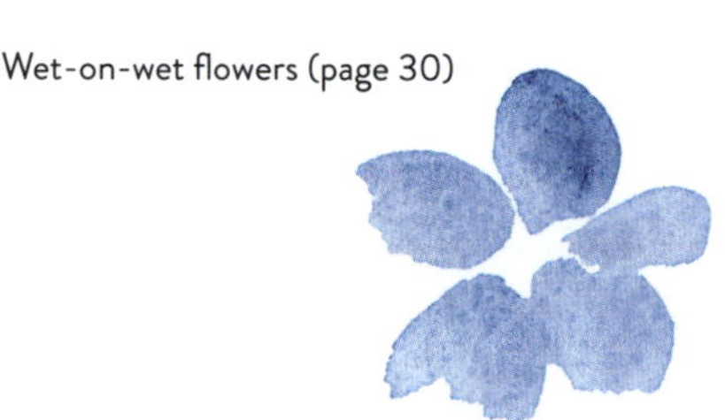

Wet-on-wet flowers (page 30)

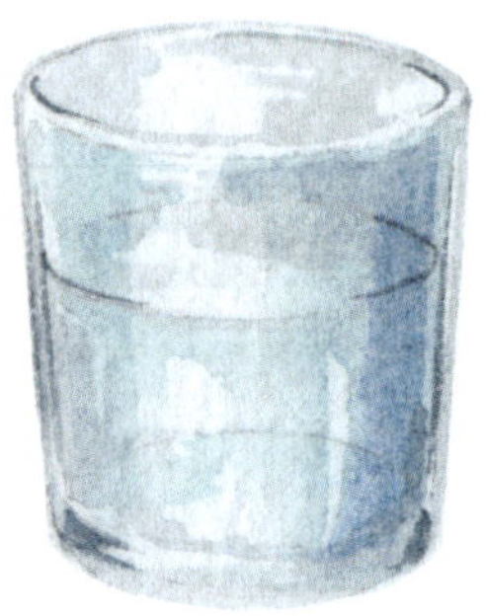

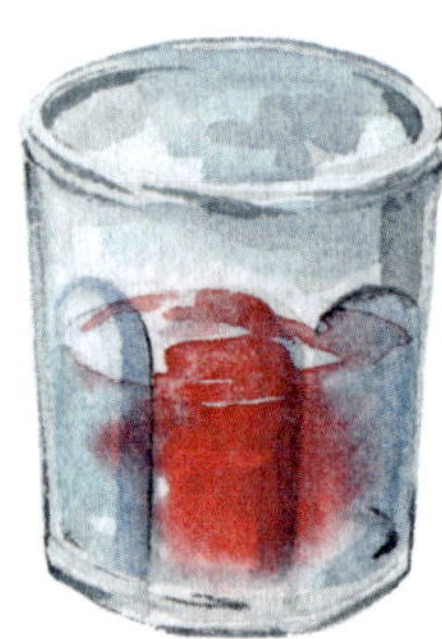

Water jars

Two clusters of circles

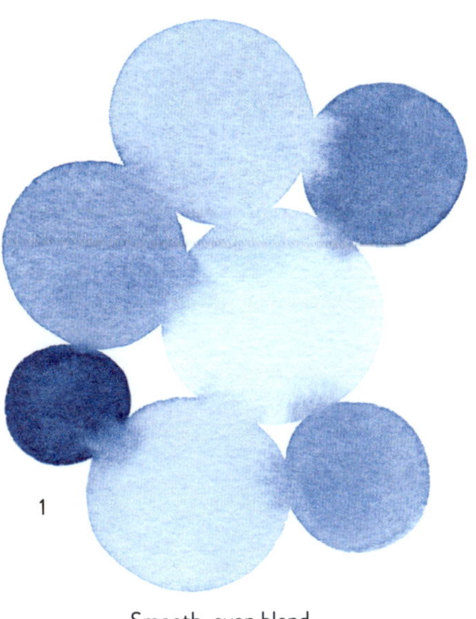

1

Smooth, even blend

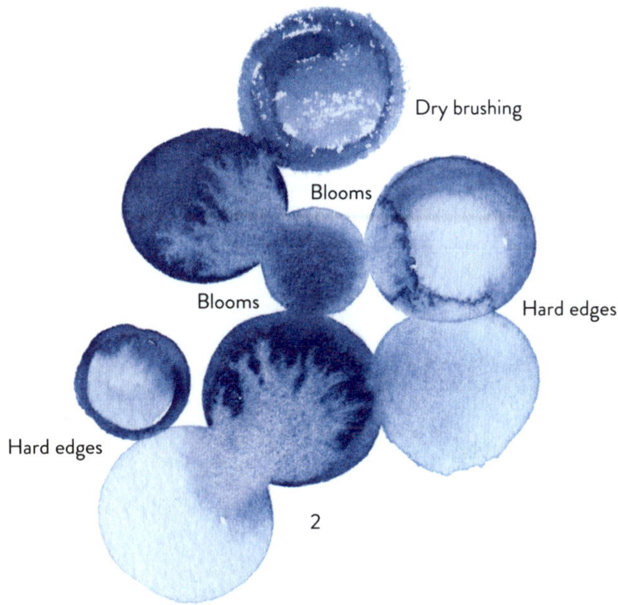

The first cluster above shows a smooth, even blend between the shapes regardless of the paint consistency.

Wet on wet
When introducing more paint into a wet painting, the smoothest results are achieved by matching the wetness on the paper to the wetness you're about to add with your next brushstroke.

This second cluster of circles above shows the following:

Blooms: Instead of matching the wetness of the already painted circle, too much water was added, so that it rushed into the painted circle and disrupted the colour.

Dry brushing: There was not enough water on the brush or in the paint mix to create a smooth flow.

Hard edges: Too much time had passed between painting the circle outline and filling it in, leaving a hard edge.

NOW TRY
Paint a circle of French Ultramarine with your size 4 brush and quickly fill it in. From there, experiment with adding overlapping circles in different paint consistencies but try to keep the blend even by matching the wetness of liquid each time. Eventually your circles will dry – see how many you can paint and blend before they do. As your confidence builds, so will your speed.

GO WRONG!
Try a cluster of circles with as many mistakes as possible – paint a circle with no water; paint one with way too much water; go fast and slow… You'll soon start to find your happy medium.

How Much Paint?

Watercolour paint looks dark and intense in the palette; it needs to be woken up with water to release the vibrant colour. I often compare watercolour paint to food colouring – you need only the tiniest amount of this deeply concentrated pigment. The water is the vehicle for it to transform in the palette and on the page.

Watercolourist Joseph Zbukvic compares paint consistency to familiar liquids like tea and milk. I have a lot of milk in my hot beverages so I've tweaked his comparisons a little to herbal tea and black coffee. I've given a ratio of paint to water (e.g. 90/10), though it's more of a guide to give you a 'feel' when mixing in your palette.

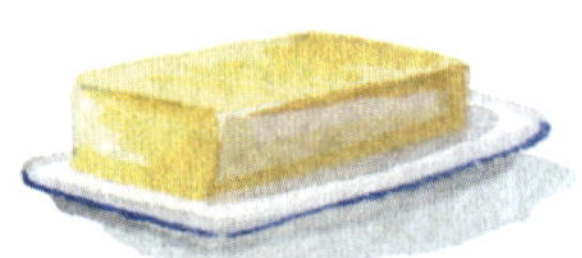

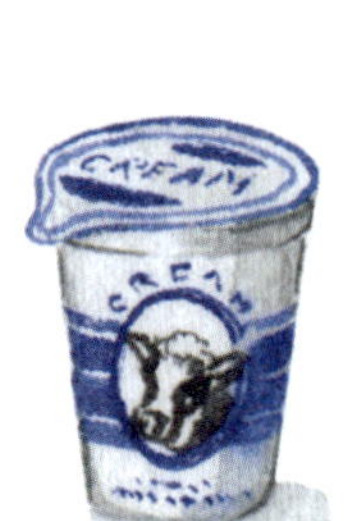

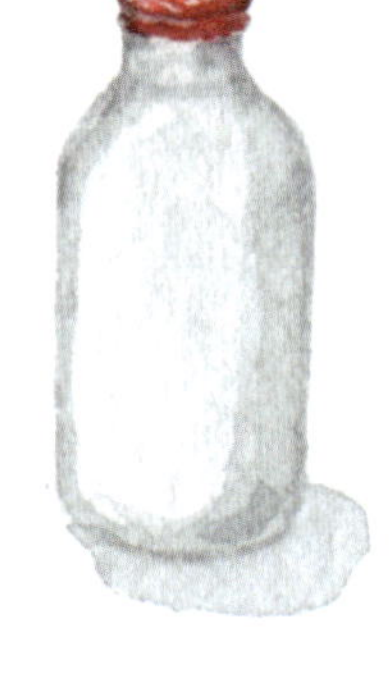

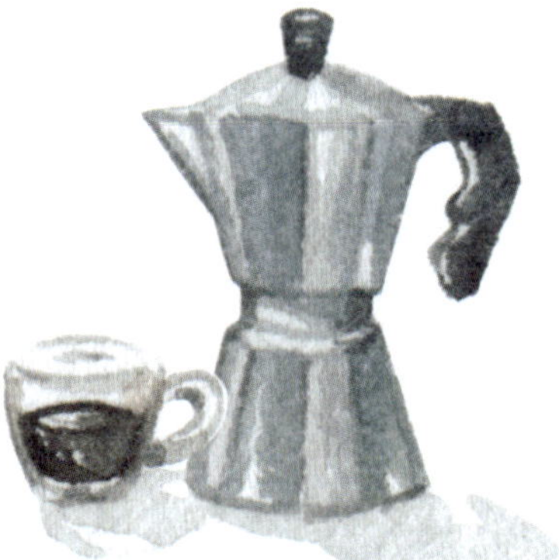

NOW TRY
Wake up Alizarin Crimson in your palette and have a go at mixing these consistencies. (If you're using tubes of paint you will be able to paint 'butter' without any water.) You've already seen in 'How Much Water?' (page 12) how to transfer only what you need onto your page. First paint the swatches on a dry page.

Prompt
The paint consistency also determines how it behaves and travels on a wet page. Thoroughly clean your size 8 brush and wet a section of the page. Now try these colours again on the wet page. We will revisit painting onto wet paper with more nuance throughout the book.

Throughout the book I describe paint in tea and coffee terms but I will also use words like 'dilute', 'transparent' and 'wash' which are akin to the tea end of the scale and words like 'concentrated', 'dark' and 'detail' that require cream- and butter-like consistencies.

DRY	CONSISTENCY	WET
	Butter: Thick with no movement, good for dry brushing and heavy accents (90/10, or no water at all if using tubes!)	
	Cream: A thicker consistency and slow movement, ideal for detailed layers (70/30)	
	Milk: The midpoint of paint and water, moving more slowly in your palette and cleanly off the brush (50/50)	
	Black coffee: A little more paint, making for a heartier colour, still with good fluidity (30/70)	
	Herbal tea: The most dilute tone, perfect for glazes and washes (10/90)	

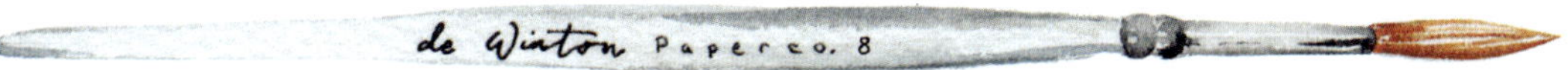

How to Paint

This is your chance to paint freely with no end goal other than to fill every corner of the page! This is the warm-up where we will come across some basic techniques and see what these pointed round brushes can do.

Don't forget to keep your brush damp at all times and refresh your water jar regularly. Choose either red or blue (yellow is not as easily visible) and let's go.

I recommend you try every exercise with all three of your brushes; I will demonstrate with a size 4 brush.

Have a look at the pointed round brush. It has a fine tip (even the largest sizes can paint beautiful fine lines) and a belly (the bulk of the bristles). If your brushes are brand new, they may have a crispy coating on them that can be worked out easily by massaging them with your fingers.

Load the brush with paint and sweep across the page. How does it look? Dried out, near transparent or somewhere in the middle? You're looking for a milky consistency when doing drills like these. Check out the paint consistency chart on page 15 to get your mix just right.

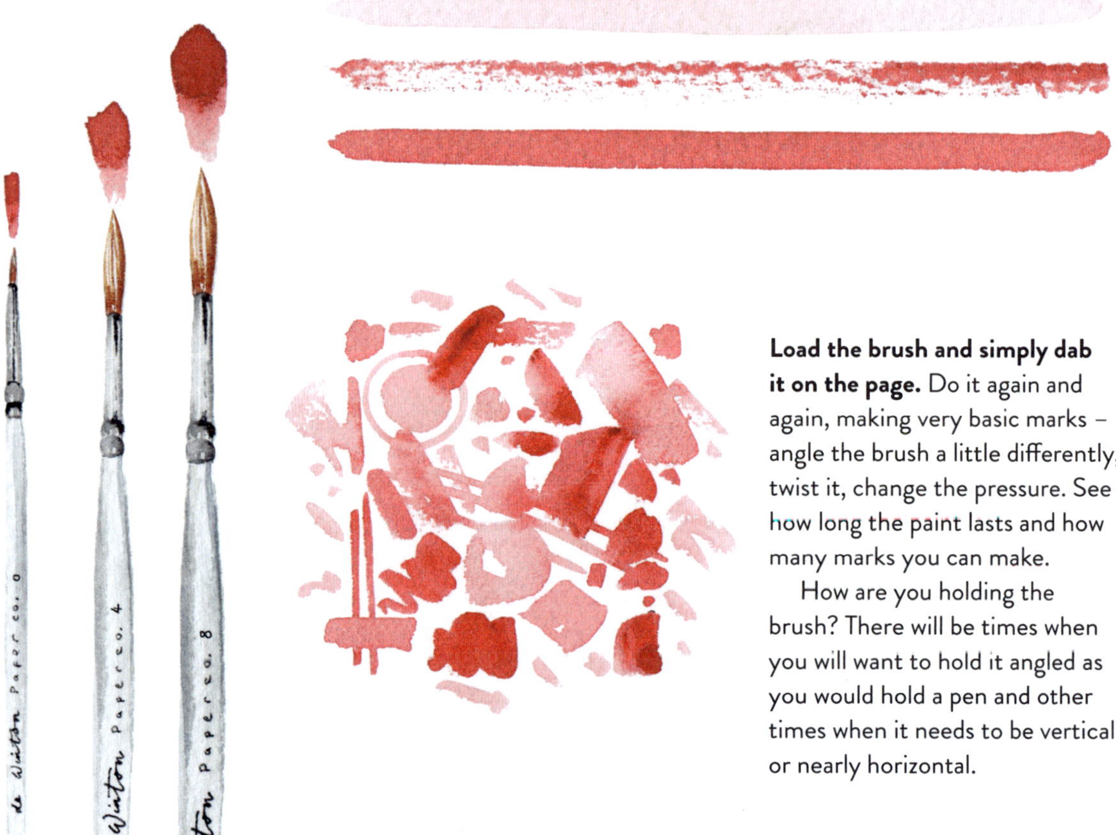

Load the brush and simply dab it on the page. Do it again and again, making very basic marks – angle the brush a little differently, twist it, change the pressure. See how long the paint lasts and how many marks you can make.

How are you holding the brush? There will be times when you will want to hold it angled as you would hold a pen and other times when it needs to be vertical or nearly horizontal.

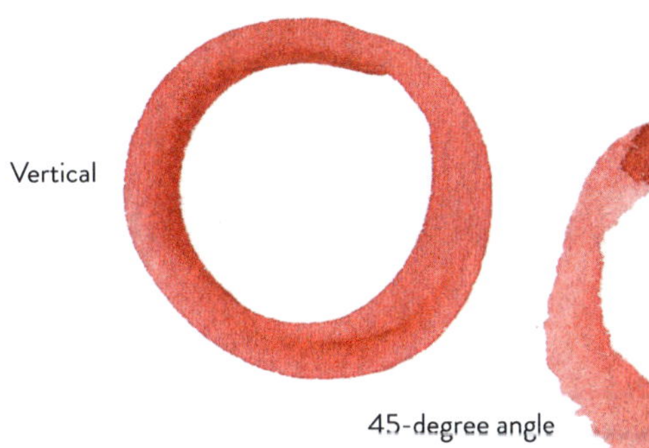

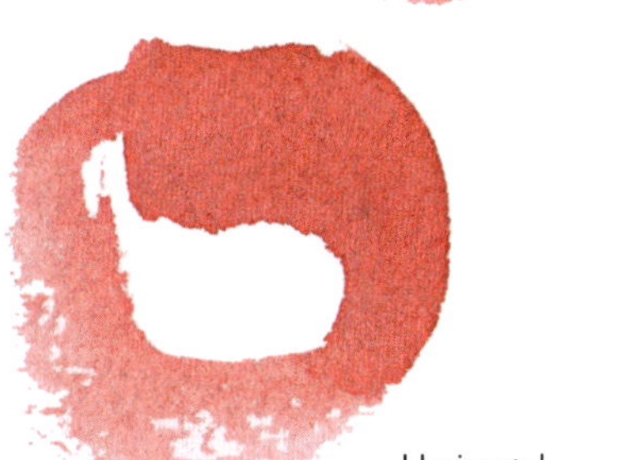

Paint a circle. First keep the brush vertical, then at a 45-degree angle and finally near horizontal. You'll soon see the effect the angle will have on your brushstrokes.

Load your brush and paint the thinnest line you can. Use just the tip of the brush. (Check for a water drop on the tip after loading. Dab and twist the tip on the palette to get a perfect fine point ready for painting.)

Draw another and another – see if you can get the line progressively thinner while keeping it as even as possible. (I find that a vertical brush gives the best results. Is that the same for you?)

Thin, thinner, thinnest!

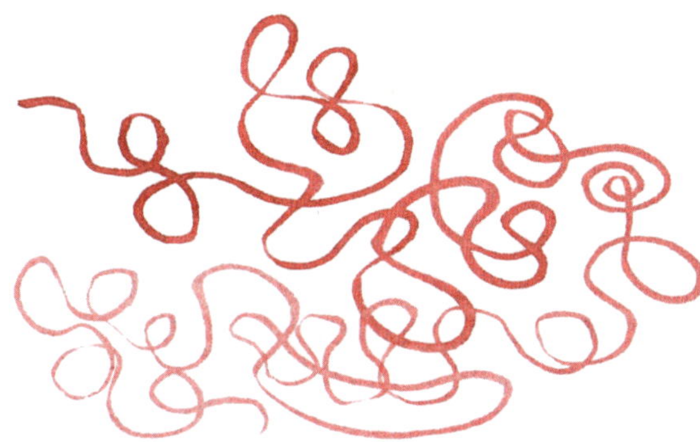

What happens if your thin straight line goes wiggly? Are you holding the brush differently now?

Next paint the thickest line you can. Load the brush and drag the full length of the bristles across the page with the brush angled low. However much liquid there is on your brush, it's likely to run out quite fast. Simply dip the brush in your water jar and use the clean wet bristles to smooth the stroke and extend the paint along the page. (When it comes to painting large areas later on in the book, there will be better-suited brushes.)

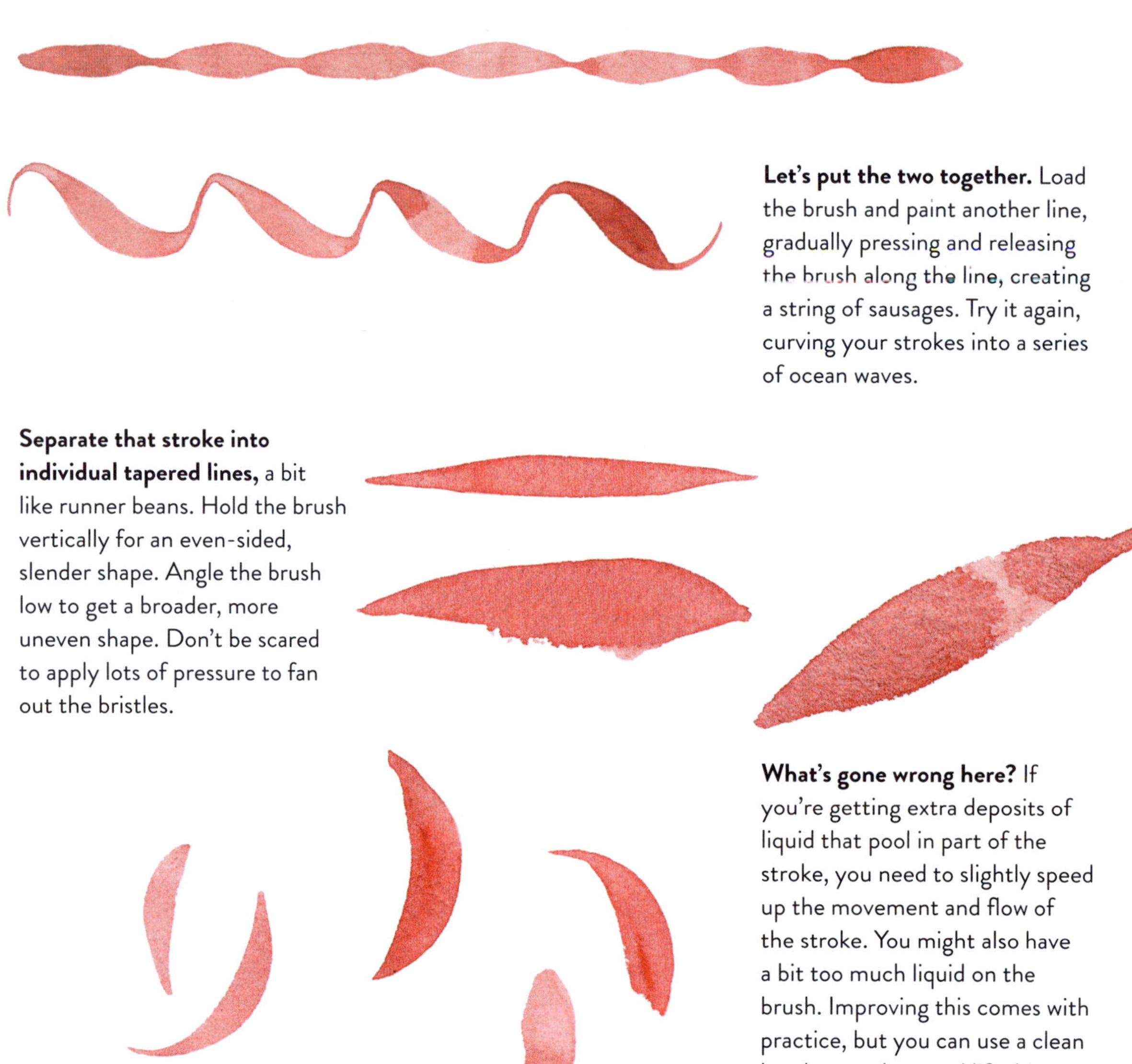

Let's put the two together. Load the brush and paint another line, gradually pressing and releasing the brush along the line, creating a string of sausages. Try it again, curving your strokes into a series of ocean waves.

Separate that stroke into individual tapered lines, a bit like runner beans. Hold the brush vertically for an even-sided, slender shape. Angle the brush low to get a broader, more uneven shape. Don't be scared to apply lots of pressure to fan out the bristles.

What's gone wrong here? If you're getting extra deposits of liquid that pool in part of the stroke, you need to slightly speed up the movement and flow of the stroke. You might also have a bit too much liquid on the brush. Improving this comes with practice, but you can use a clean brush to soak up and lift this extra liquid off after painting the stroke.

Curl the tapered line and make a C-curve and an S-curve. These strokes are starting to resemble leaves and petals. (Painting objects in abstract colours like these allows you to focus simply on mastering the shapes and strokes.)

SIMPLE LEAVES

1 Draw a pencil curve which will act as the central line of your leaf. Starting with the tip of the brush at one end of the pencil line, paint a fine line. Move the brush along one side of the pencil line, pressing down so the full thickness of the bristles creates a gradually thickening line. Keep going, smoothly lifting the brush back to just the tip and touching the page at the other end of the pencil line. Your leaf should have a finer tip and rounded bottom.

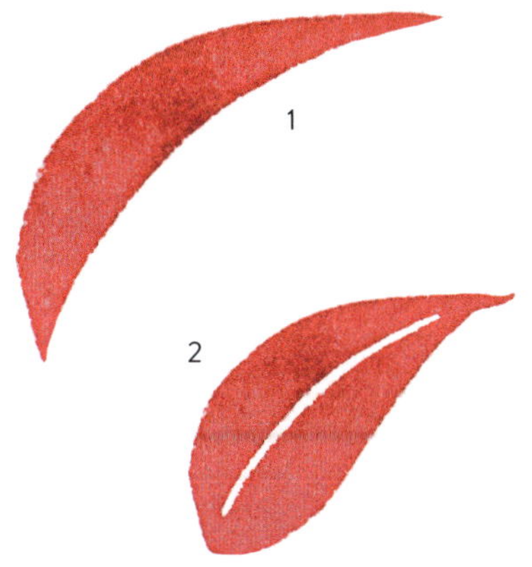

2 Load up your brush again and start from the same point with a mirrored stroke, leaving a tiny sliver of unpainted space down the middle. If your pencil line is curved, your second paint stroke will have to accommodate this curve. Play around with leaves bending in all different directions until you feel confident enough to paint them onto a stem.

3 For many people these leaves don't make much sense until they're on a stem. Draw a faint curved stem and numerous curves branching off. These aren't branches; they are central leaf lines. Paint the stem with the fine point of the size 4 brush and then proceed to paint in each leaf with the same brush.

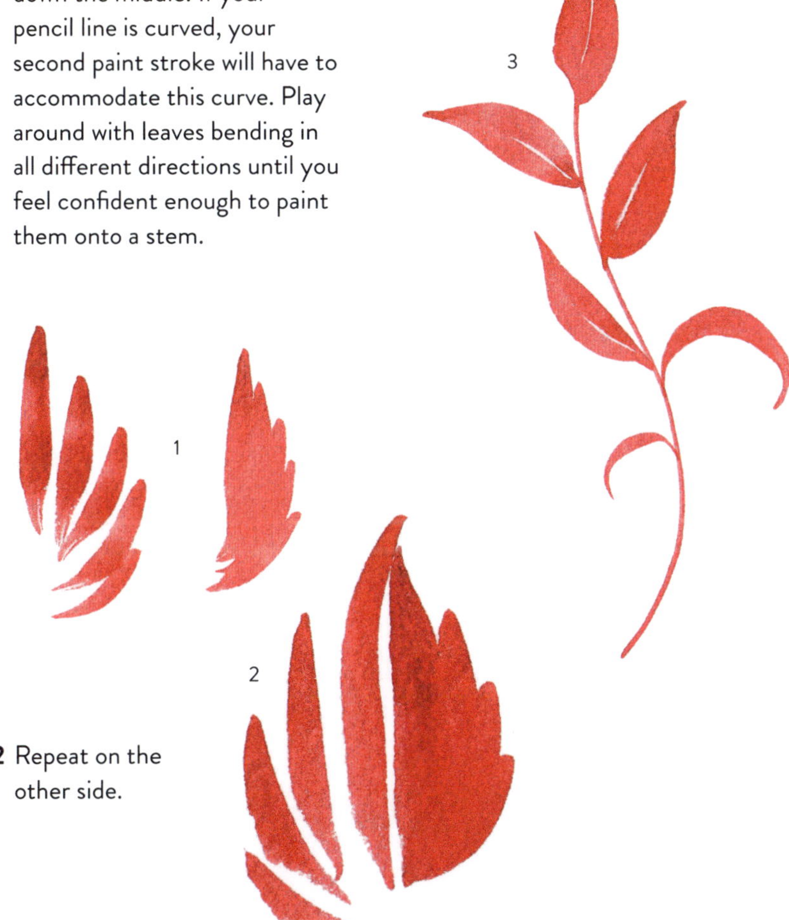

SERRATED-EDGE LEAVES

1 Paint a tapered line. Paint another, slightly shorter line by its side with the tip curving out but coming down into the central base point. Add another slightly shorter line and repeat until you've created one half of a serrated leaf. The illustration shows you the lines more spaced out and then painted together to create one side of the leaf.

2 Repeat on the other side.

PETALS

The C-curves and S-curves already closely resemble petals. You can build them up with repeated strokes to get the shape you need.

You've now got all the strokes to paint your first little flower!

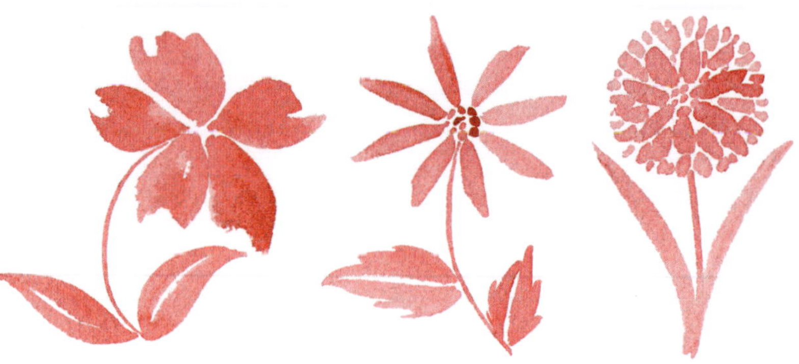

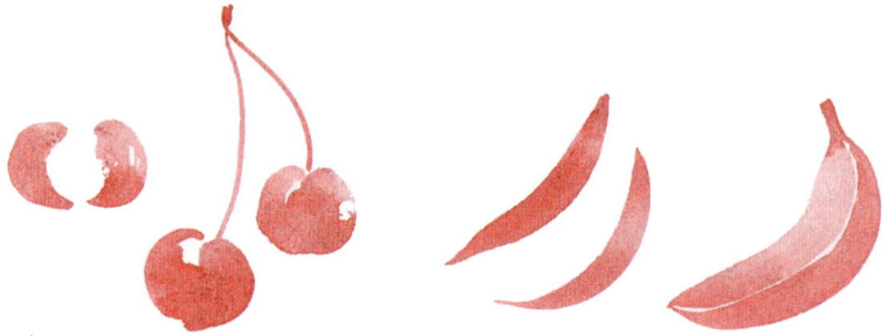

SIMPLE SHAPES

By rounding off the points you can start to transform those strokes into simple shapes and objects.

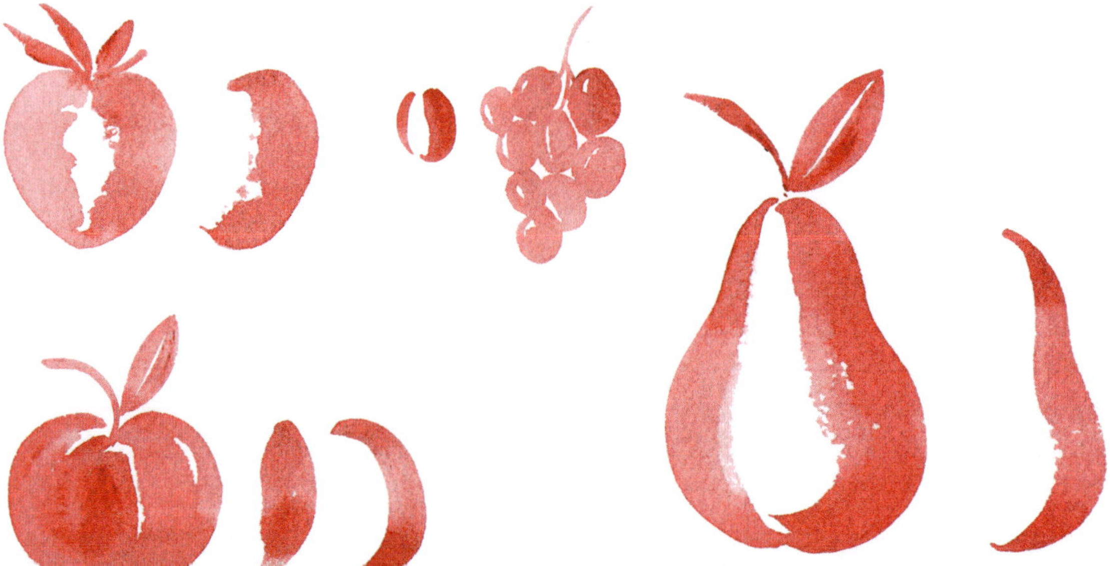

GLAZING

Glazes are transparent watercolour layers. They act like filters to add luminosity to a painting, warming it up or cooling it down. Try glazing on top of your simple fruit and flowers. Even yellow will have a slight impact.

For the grapes, I painted each one and let it dry before painting its neighbour. Look how the crisp edge of each glaze resembles a fine outline.

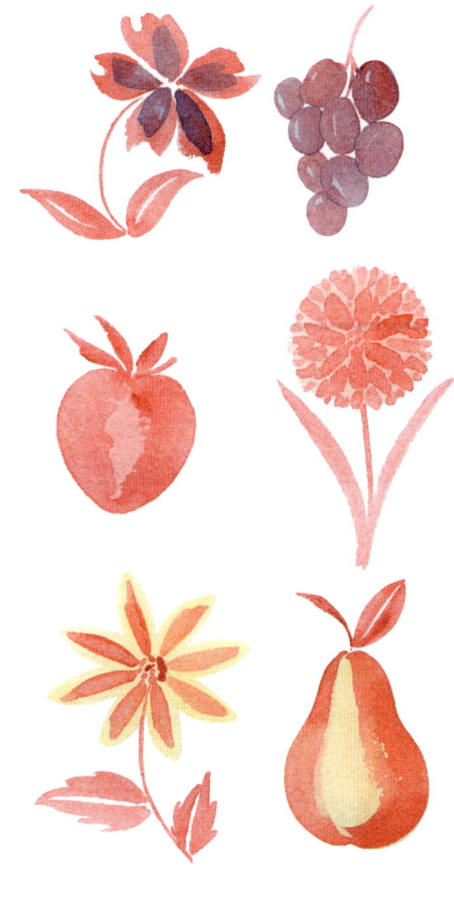

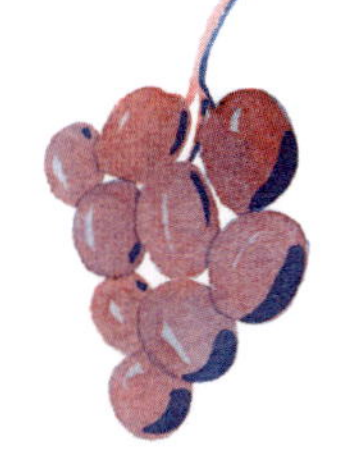

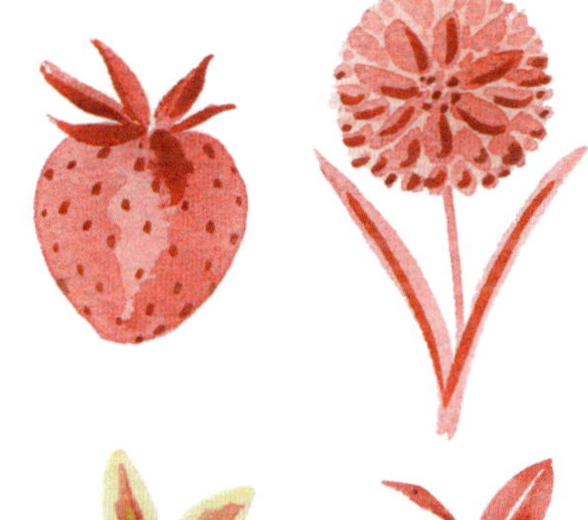

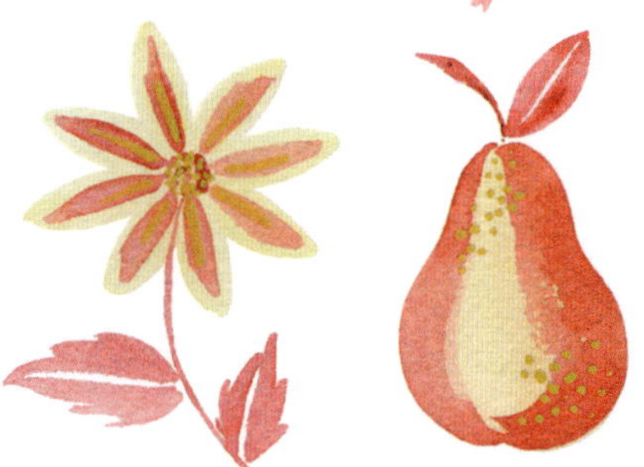

LAYERING

With these concentrated layers of paint, it is far easier to add a darker/concentrated colour layer to a lighter/dilute one than the other way around. In the projects I will always start with a light wash and build it up in intensity, layer by layer.

Try layering on top of some of your simple fruit and flowers. Yellow will struggle, but Blue and Red are strong enough to show up easily. Once a layer of paint is completely dry, you can add further layers of colour and detail with no fear of their bleeding into each other.

Terminology

You will see these words and phrases repeatedly throughout the book.
Here's a helpful definition of each.

Analogous: Colours next to each other on the colour wheel

Background: The area of a painting farthest from the viewer, characterized by low detail and cool colours

Belly: The main body of the bristles on a brush

Blend/bleed: Two wet colours merging seamlessly

Bloom: A burst of water in standing paint

Blot: To remove paint from a wet painting using paper towel

Clear water wash: Painting clear water onto the page with no paint

Complementary: Colours on opposite sides of the colour wheel

Consistency: Thinness or thickness of paint

Contrast: The variation of light and colour found in a painting

Dry brush: A paint-loaded brush from which as much water as possible has been removed with the aim of creating a painted finish with lots of unpainted space showing through

Dry on dry: Painting a concentrate-consistency paint onto a dry surface

Foreground: The area of a painting closest to the viewer, usually characterized by high detail, vibrancy and warmth

Glaze: Diluted colour, painted over the top of something you've already painted (and which has dried), to add a new dimension to the painting

Hard edge: Created when you don't blend your colours

Highlights: The lightest parts of a painting, sometimes unpainted

Hue: A colour in its pure form

Intensity: Brightness or dullness

Layer: To build up opaque layers of paint to give depth and detail to a piece

Lift: To remove colour from a wet page, usually with a clean wet brush – good for creating highlights

Line and wash: Layering loose watercolour with fine line ink drawings to create energetic artworks.

Load: To get paint on the brush in the palette

Lowlights – also Accents: The most concentrated layer of paint, usually added last to heighten contrast

Mask: To place down masking fluid or masking tape before painting, to keep an area unpainted

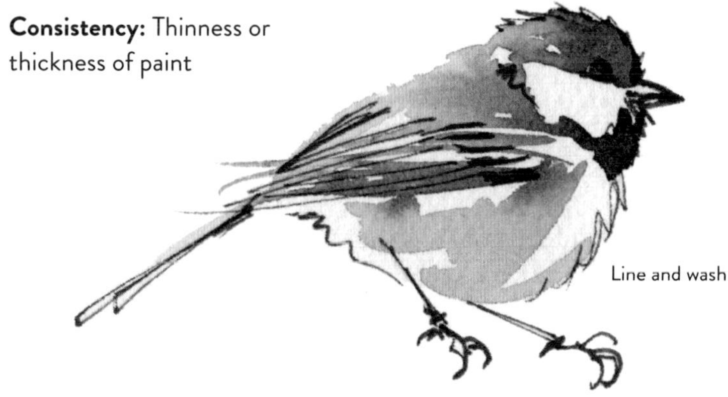

Line and wash

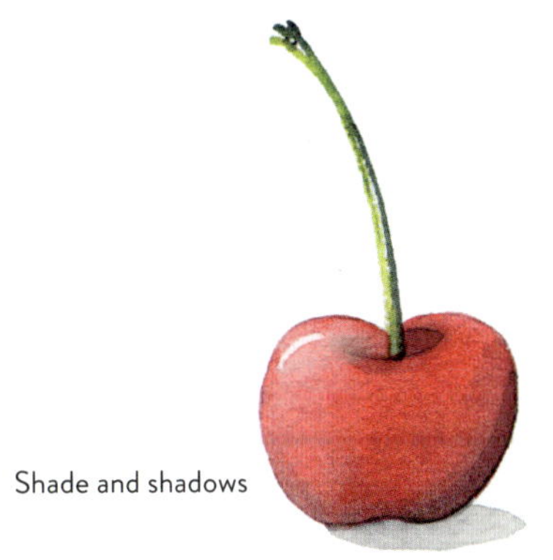
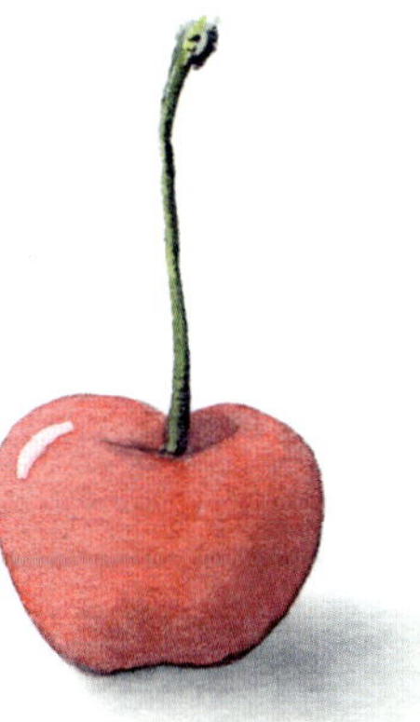
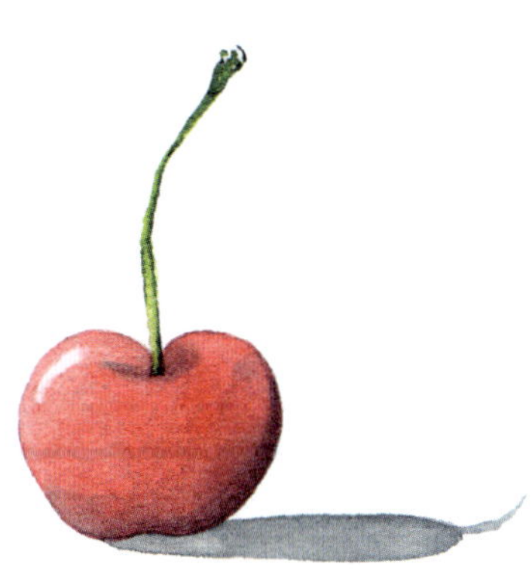

Shade and shadows

Mid-ground: The area between the foreground and background

Muddy: Term used to describe where the watercolour has lost its transparency and freshness, caused by overworking the area with the brush

Overworked: Term used to describe a painting that lacks spontaneity and freshness, because the watercolour has been over-manipulated, resulting in dull, muddy colours

Blotting

Shade: The shadow on an object

Shadow: The shadow cast by an object

Texture: Using the brushstrokes to create visual texture on the subject

Tip: The end of the bristles on a brush where they make a fine point

Underpainting: The base layer of watercolour

Unpainted space – also Negative space: Areas left unpainted to give the effect of reflected light, snow, etc.

Value: Dark to light scale of colour

Wake up: To add water to the concentrated dry pans or blobs of paint in the palette to get them ready to use

Wash: To put paint mixed with water onto the paper (you will come across flat wash, gradient wash and variegated wash in this book)

Wet on dry: Painting a dilute consistency paint onto a dry surface

Wet on wet: Painting on a wet surface

The Big Three Techniques of Watercolour

This book will show you all sorts of ways to apply paint to paper, but everything comes back to the three fundamentals of watercolour painting.

DRY ON DRY

By watercolour's standards, 'dry' means a minimal amount of water and a fairly sluggish movement in the paint (cream or butter consistency). The paint is concentrated and the colour heavy. When it is painted onto a dry page (either unpainted or a dried layer), it stays where it's put.

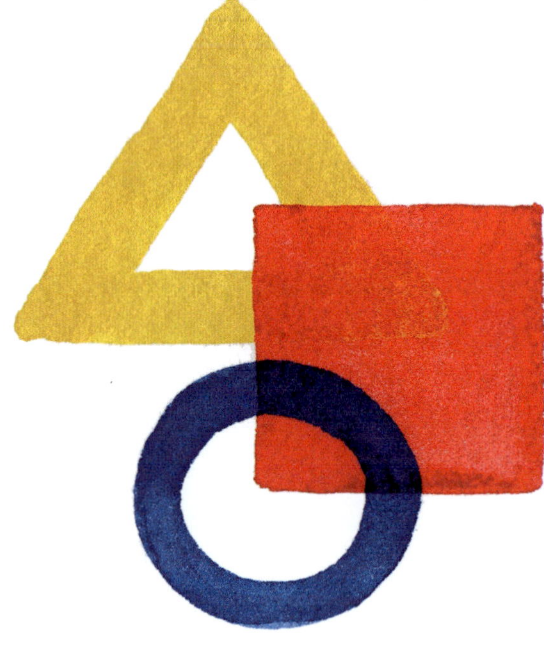

WET ON DRY

With more water in the mix, the colours perk up and the paint moves with more fluidity (milk, coffee or tea consistency). Painted onto a dry page, it stays where it's put but the increased amount of water means we can see through to the layers below. These transparent layers are called glazes.

WET ON WET

This is possibly the most exciting watercolour technique. The blends, bleeds and blooms will depend on the consistency of your paint and the amount of water. Wet on wet can either refer to painting onto a fully wetted surface or how two wet-painted areas interact on an otherwise dry page.

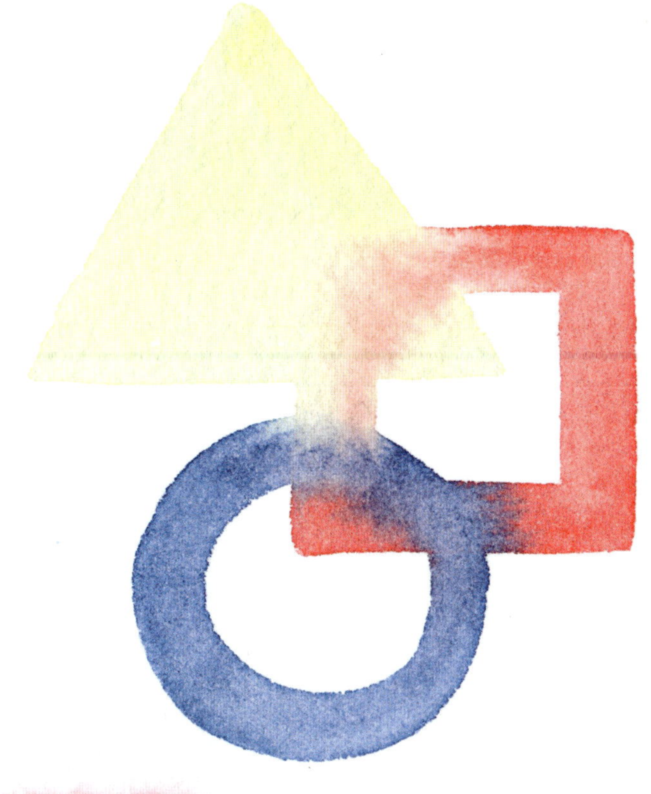

Primary shapes

Using your three primary colours, try painting triangles, squares and circles in these three styles.

Colours
Alizarin Crimson (Red)
Cadmium-Free Yellow (Yellow)
French Ultramarine (Blue)

Brushes
Pointed round size 8

Value, Scale and Painting with One Colour

Water is the key to achieving light and dark shades in watercolour, otherwise known as value. One colour can create a huge range of values simply by adding water.

You may have come across white watercolour paint, but it's not used to lighten colour. Instead, it acts as a thickener to create an opaque, creamy paint that makes it easier to layer light watercolours on dark backgrounds. For delicate, pale colours, just add water!

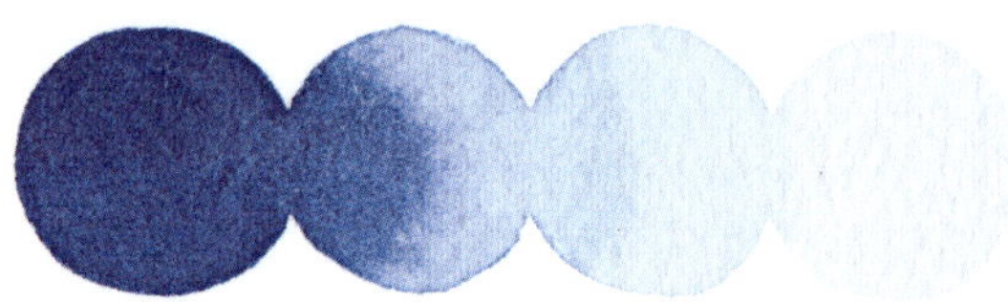

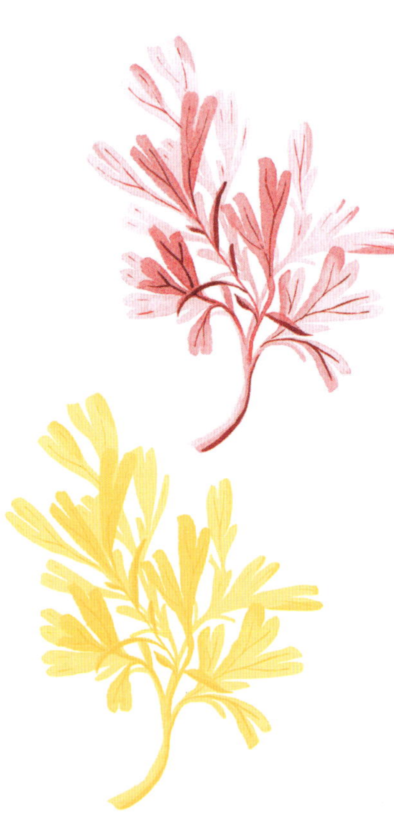

NOW TRY

Paint a milk consistency circle of French Ultramarine with a size 4 brush. Quickly clean off the brush in your water jar but leave it wet enough to paint a circle of clear water, just overlapping the first circle. Wash off your brush and repeat the step, over and over until no more colour can flood into the newest circle. You've created a continuous colour value chart!

Circles that look clear when wet will form the most delicate crisp edge of colour as they dry – what's left of the pigment races to the edge of the watery barrier. This technique makes for beautiful petals and translucent shapes.

With such a broad value range, you can paint a whole piece with a single hue.

Prompt
Paint seaweed in the other two primary colours. Are the changes in value as easy to see as the blue?

Level
Beginner

Brushes
Pointed round sizes 4, 0

Colours
French Ultramarine (Blue)

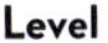

1 Paint a tea-consistency curving stem with branches with your size 4 brush. Extend each branch by pressing down on the bristles to thicken the line. Paint tapered lines fanned out in pairs to create the seaweed leaves. Allow to dry.

2 Paint milk-consistency additional stems and branches repeating the techniques of step 1. Add a sweep of paint to the outer edge of the main stem and some leaves on the first layer. Allow to dry.

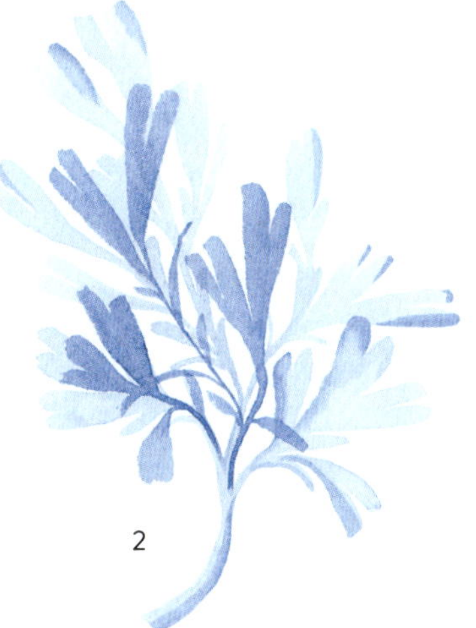

3 Use your size 0 brush to paint cream consistency fine lines that travel and fork up the paired leaves on all layers. Add a sweep of paint to the outer edge of the main stem and some smaller leaves. Allow to dry.

How to Mix Colours

There is no better starting point for colour mixing than the three primary colours. As explained on page 10, I have chosen to use Alizarin Crimson, French Ultramarine and Cadmium-Free Yellow. Here I refer to them simply as Red, Blue and Yellow.

MIXING NOTES

When mixing two colours together, one will often pack more punch than the other. Sometimes it's obvious: Blue dominating Yellow. At other times it's a lot closer: Blue vs Red might require some experimentation.

HOW TO MIX:
Blue and yellow

With your size 8 brush, deposit some yellow in a space in your palette and add water to get it to a milk consistency. Thoroughly clean off your brush and do the same in a separate (but not too faraway) area for Blue.

For an even mix it's vitally important that both colours have a matching consistency.

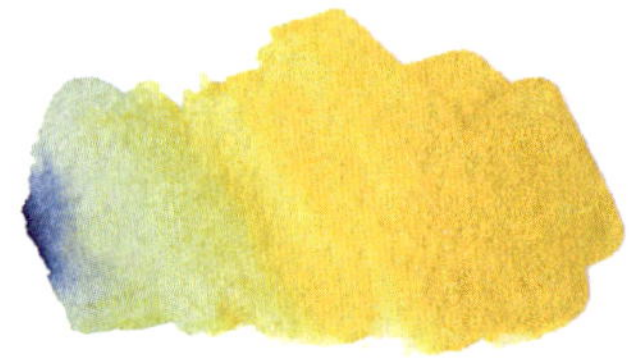

Clean off your brush and introduce a tiny amount of the stronger colour (in this case, blue) over to the large pool of yellow.

Let it touch the edge of the yellow paint and carefully start mixing it in.

Even a tiny amount of the stronger colour will impact the yellow and soon you will have a lime green. (It's worth trying this the other way round to see how difficult it is for a small amount of yellow to have any impact on the blue.)

Introduce more blue to change the colour further.

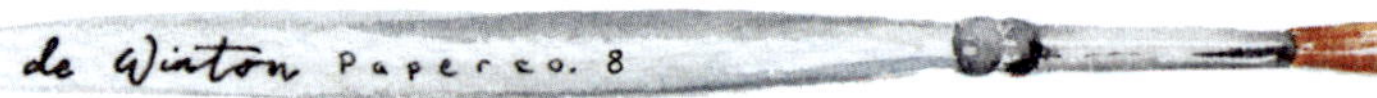

GOLDEN RULES OF COLOUR MIXING

Use a large brush to mix paint – it will speed things up and give you larger paint-mix quantities. Have a few jars of clean water and a paper towel to clean brushes between colours.

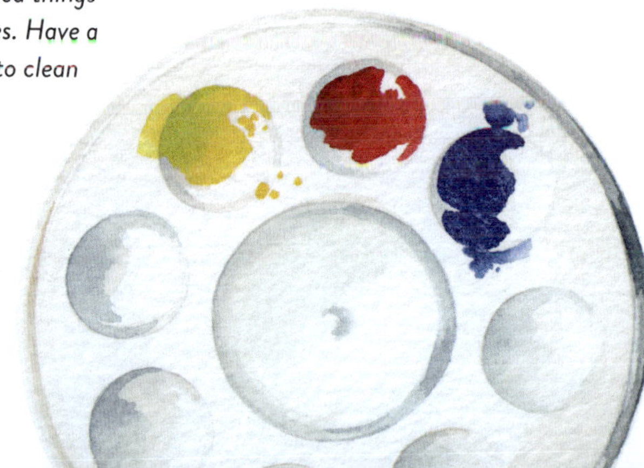

COLOUR MIX SWATCH CHART

There are so many mixable shades from three colours, it's a great idea to create a swatch chart as a handy reminder of them all.

You can either do this freehand or draw a pencil grid with **three** columns and five rows resulting in fifteen squares. 12mm (½ inch) is a good size for each colour square.

Paint a saturated swatch (I always start with my weaker colour, in this case yellow) in the top left square. Dilute your colour and paint a swatch in the next column, dilute it further and paint a swatch in the final column, showing a row of gradually diluted yellow. Repeat the process with your stronger colour (blue) in the bottom row.

Then mix the colours to swatch the gradual change of yellow to blue including the more diluted versions. Try all three mix variations with the primary colours.

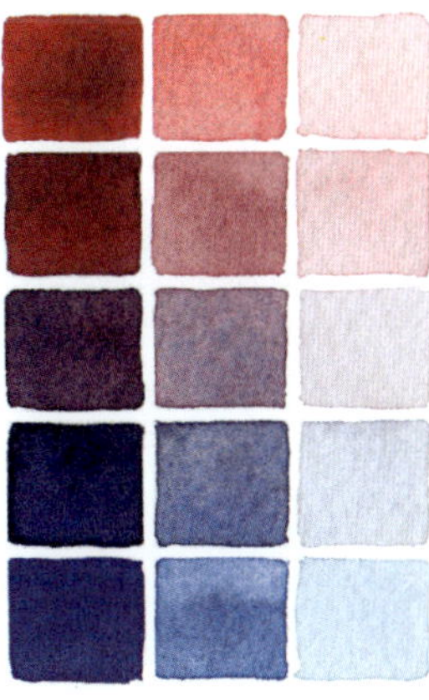
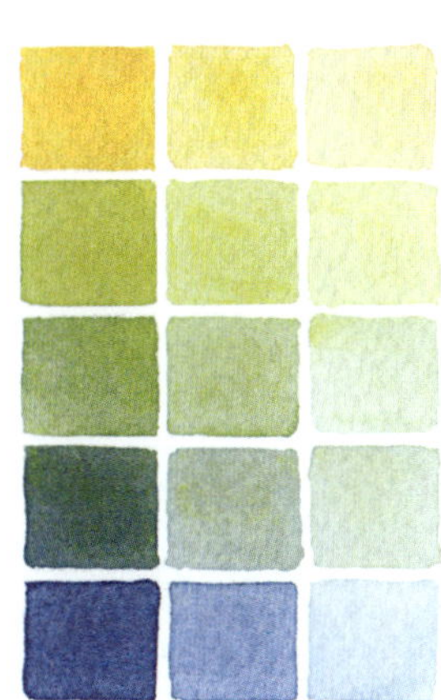
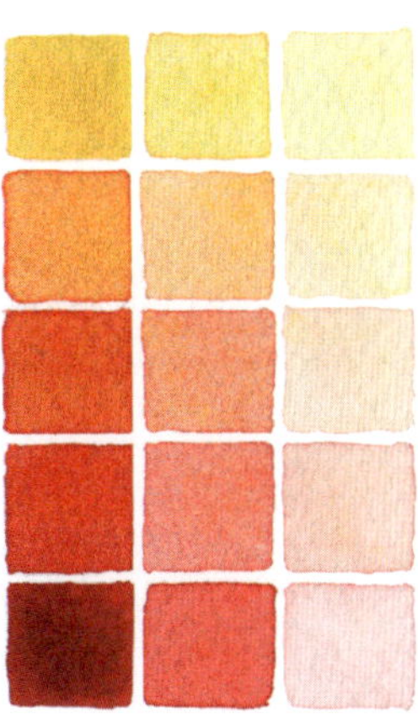

COLOUR WHEEL

The colour wheel is another fantastic visual display of how these three colours work together. Draw a pencil circle 10cm (4in) in diameter and a smaller one inside it. Paint concentrated swatches of Red, Blue and Yellow at three even points around the circle. There is room between the primary colours for the three shades you mixed in the colour swatch chart.

The beauty of this full circle is you can now see each shade's complementary colour directly across the wheel.

Yellow – Purple
Blue – Orange
Red – Green

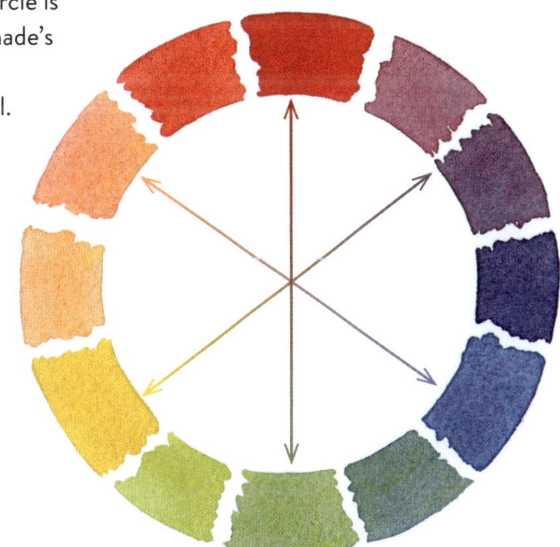

Wet-on-Wet Flowers

Of the big three, wet-on-wet is the most exciting and unruly technique. The results you get will depend on a number of varying factors: the paint consistency, the dampness of the page and the timing of dropping in a new colour. The good news is it's fun to practise this technique!

Level
Beginner

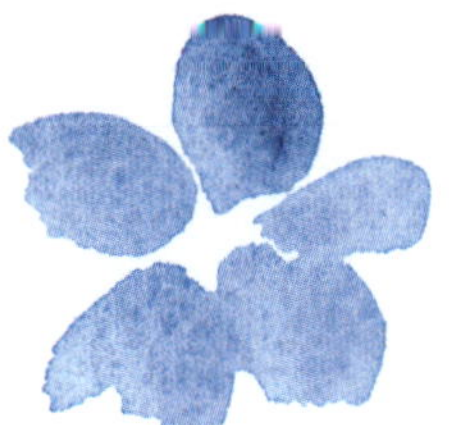

Using the simple petals and leaves from the basic brushstrokes shown on pages 18–21, mix up a range of colours from your three primaries and use your size 8 brush to fill a page with colour-blend flowers.

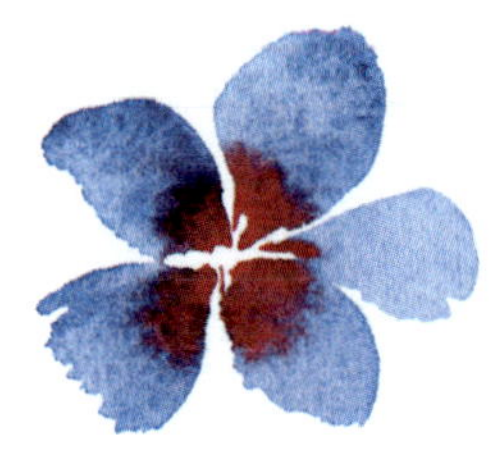

Overlap them, drop colours onto the petals, and observe what works and what doesn't as you progress across the page. You can see the seamless wet-on-wet blends as well as the blooms and imperfect bleeds on this piece.

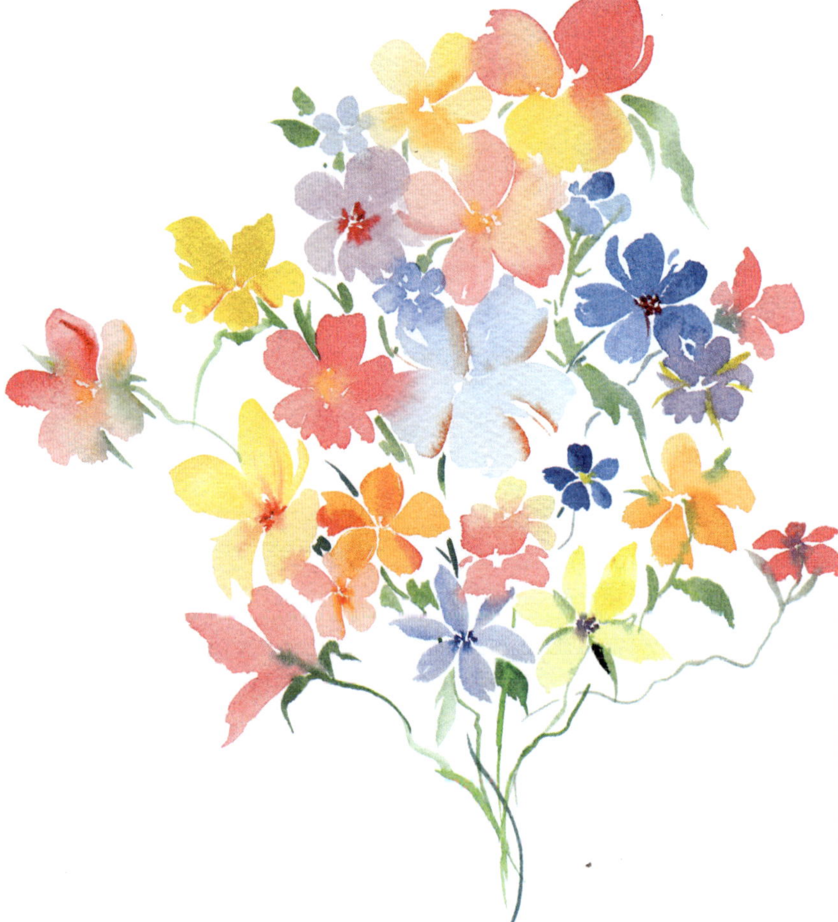

Prompt
Paint wet-on-wet flowers in a bouquet arrangement. Place them on a page with stems and leaves in between while maintaining the wet-on-wet technique.

Hue, Intensity, Value

Hue is the colour in its pure form.
Intensity is its brightness or dullness.
Value is how light or dark it is.

A great way to dull a colour's intensity is to mix in some of its complementary colour. Did you know you can mix two primary colours to make the third's complementary colour?

Blue's complement is orange.

Yellow's complement is purple.

Red's complement is green.

We can use hue, value and intensity to create a rounded and textured bumblebee, still just using the primary colours.

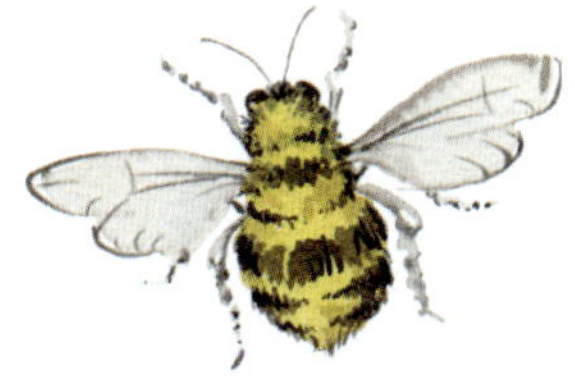

For the bee tutorial, see pages 32–3

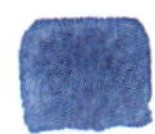 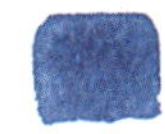 

Hue   Value dark to light

The complementary colour to Blue is orange – made from Red and Yellow

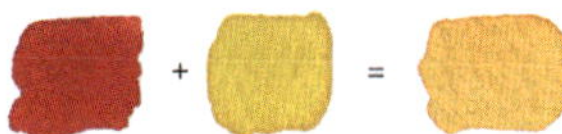

Intensity is dulled by adding the complementary colour

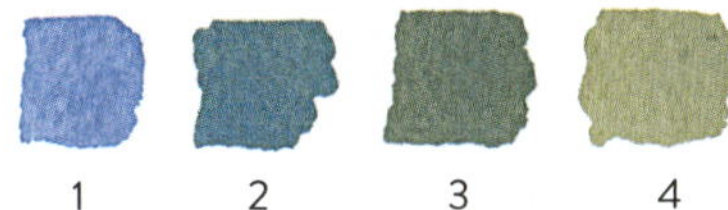

1 2 3 4

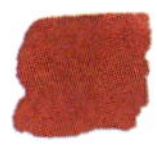 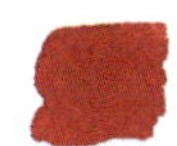 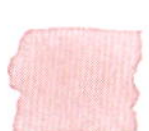

Hue   Value dark to light

The complementary colour to Red is green – made from Blue and Yellow

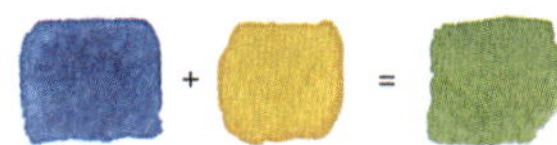

Intensity is dulled by adding the complementary colour

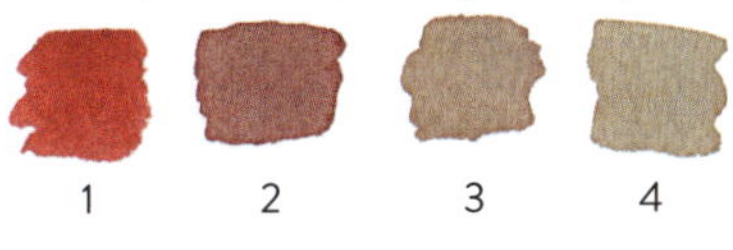 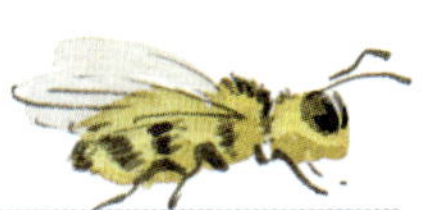

1 2 3 4

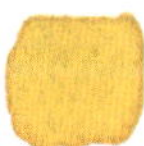 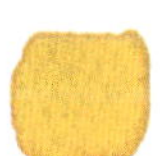 

Hue   Value dark to light

The complementary colour to Yellow is purple – made from Blue and Red

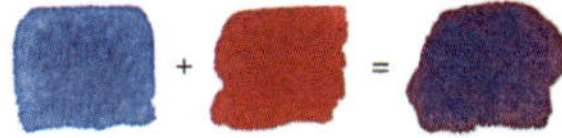

Intensity is dulled by adding the complementary colour

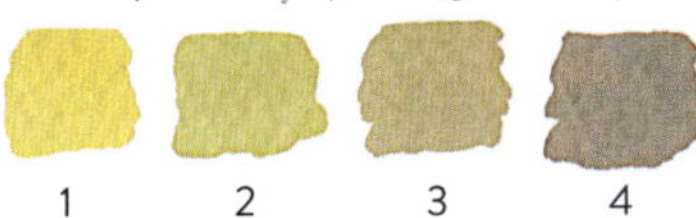

1 2 3 4

TUTORIAL: Bee

Level
Beginner

Colours
Alizarin Crimson (Red)
Cadmium-Free Yellow (Yellow)
French Ultramarine (Blue)

Brushes
Pointed round sizes 4, 0

You will also need
HB pencil, soft and hard erasers

Mixes
Stripes mix: Alizarin Crimson,
Cadmium-Free Yellow, French
Ultramarine
Wings Mix: Use the stripes mix and
dilute to 10%

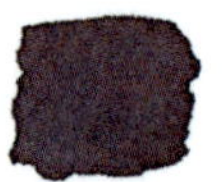

Stripes

Wings

MIXING NOTES

Create a purple from Alizarin
Crimson (50%) and French
Ultramarine (50%). Mix into
Cadmium-Free Yellow to make an
intensity scale of yellow tones.

When mixing all three primary
colours to make a deep grey, I find
it takes a few rounds of adding the
three colours to get the right mix.
When concentrated, this colour
resembles a dark slate grey for the
black bee stripes; when diluted it's
perfect for transparent bee wings.

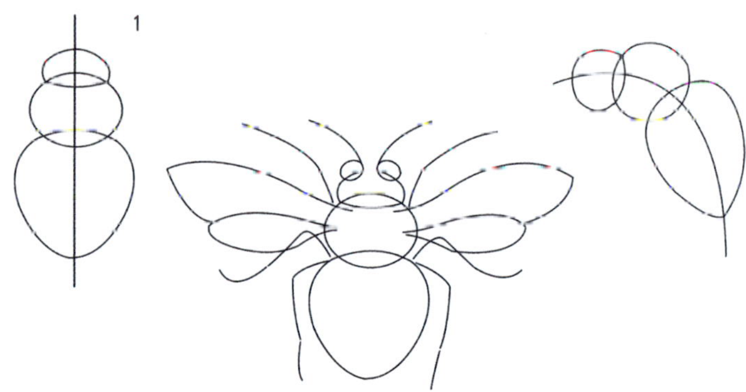

1 Draw a vertical pencil line.
Along that line draw a slightly
stocky oval shape for the
thorax. Below that overlap it
with an upside-down egg shape
for the abdomen, and above
it overlap it with a squashed
oval head.

Add simple outlines for wings,
eyes, legs and antennae. You
can draw different positions and
angles by starting with a curved
central line and building your
shapes along its curve.

Roll with a soft eraser to
lighten the pencil to a faint
sketch.

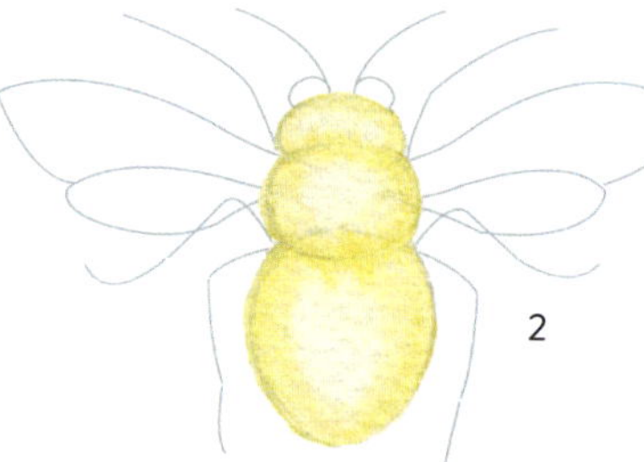
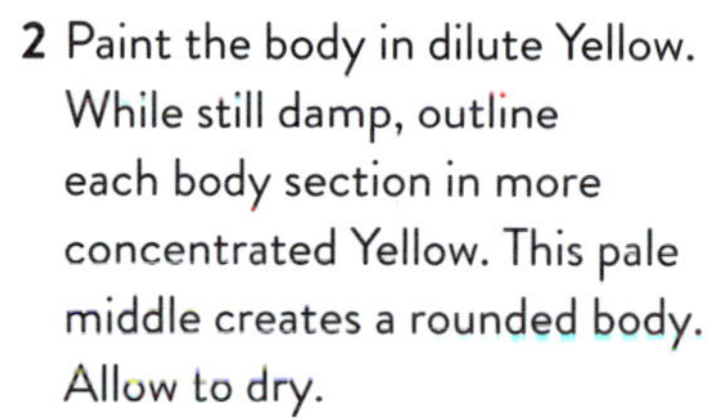

2 Paint the body in dilute Yellow.
While still damp, outline
each body section in more
concentrated Yellow. This pale
middle creates a rounded body.
Allow to dry.

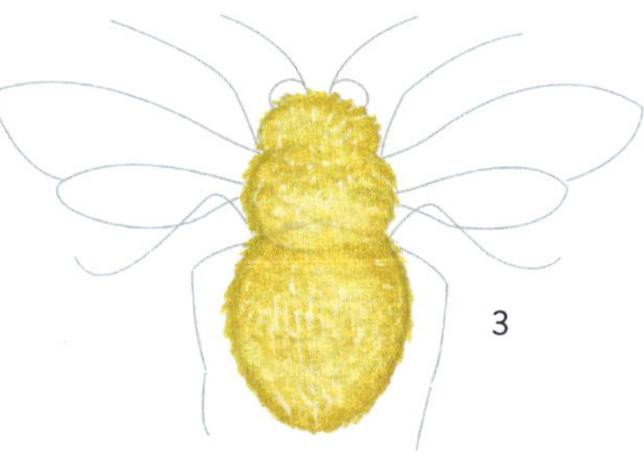

3 Using your 'intensity scale 2
yellow', (page 31) paint textured
hairs all over the body with your
size 0 brush. Start at the edges
and work your way inwards as
the paint starts to run out on
your brush. Allow to dry.

4 Using your 'intensity scale 3 yellow', paint another layer of textured hairs, leaving the centre of each section. Paint a dilute sweep of this colour along the leg joints. Allow to dry.

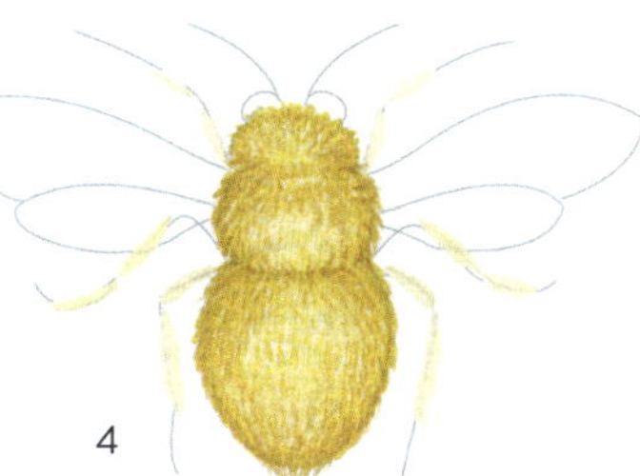

5 Paint the wings with your wings mix. Add further structure to the legs and eyes with your stripes mix, using your size 0 brush. Allow to dry.

6 Use your concentrated stripes mix to paint the bee stripes in textured hairs with your size 0 brush. Add fine lines for antennae and wing detail. If you're struggling to get an intensely dark colour, use your brush to scoop up concentrated paint to mix and you will get a nice little amount of really dark mix. Add a second layer for lowlights on the edges of the bee body and eyes.

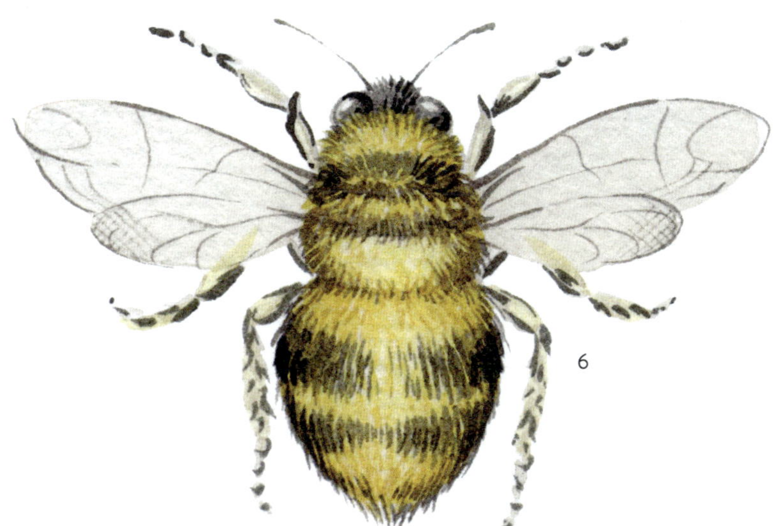

NOW TRY
Loosened-up bees

1 Draw your shapes with the brush and add your yellow texture, all while the paint is still wet. This gives a lively energy to your bee paintings.

2 Paint your dark mix wings and leave to only dry partially before scribbling concentrated dark mix hairs, legs and wing details. Finish with a few accents of 'intensity scale 3 yellow' on the bee bodies to act as shadow.

Prompt
Now you have the basic drawing structure for many insects. Experiment with different colour mixes to paint all sorts of bugs!

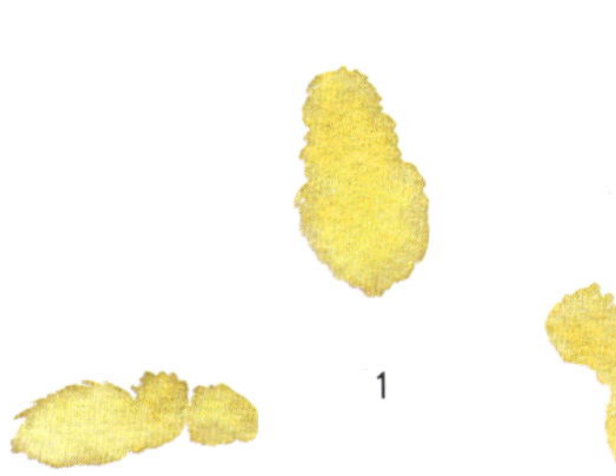

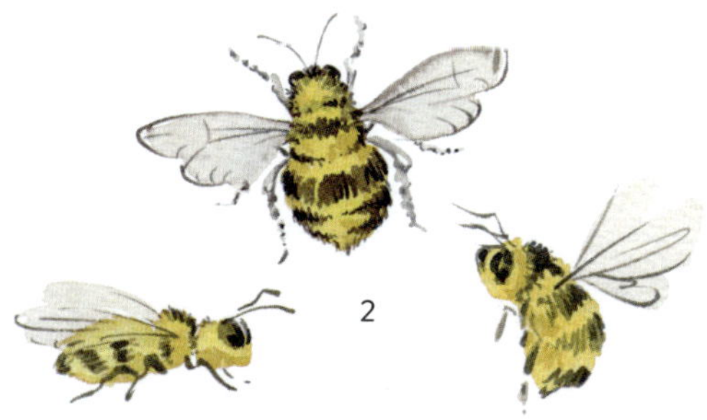

Washes

Washes are expanses of dilute watercolour on unpainted paper. You can add colours and gradients to make skies, sunsets and seascapes. Later on in the book you'll come across 'glazes'; also diluted colour, glazes go over the top of something you've already painted (and that has dried) to add a new dimension to the painting.

Colours
Alizarin Crimson (Red)
Cadmium-Free Yellow (Yellow)
French Ultramarine (Blue)

Brushes
Pointed round size 8

Alizarin
Crimson

Cadmium-
Free Yellow

French
Ultramarine

Flat

Gradient

Gradient slip-up

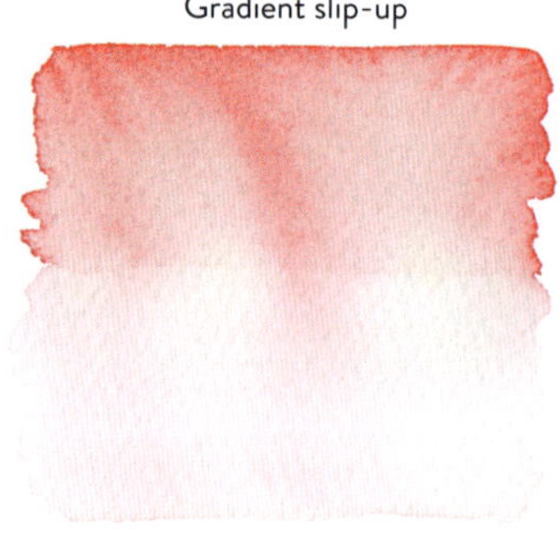

FLAT WASH
One colour in a consistent value:
Mix a large amount of tea-consistency paint. Load your brush with paint by soaking the full length of its bristles in the paint. At the top corner of the paper, paint a horizontal stroke. Start another stroke that overlaps underneath the first. Continue, adding more watery paint mix when your brush starts to dry.

GRADIENT
Fading one colour out to transparency:
Start in the same way as a flat wash. When you want to start fading out your colour, exchange more paint mix for clear water.

POSSIBLE SLIP-UPS:
Loading more water on your brush than needed for the area you are painting can lead to 'blooms' – bursts of water in the standing paint. (There are times when blooms can be intentional, adding wonderful and irregular texture and character to a painting.) If your page looks like this, be sure to dab excess water off your brush on the rim of your water jar before painting. Keep an eye on the sheen of the paper to judge its wetness; if it starts to lose its glossiness, be careful to add more water or paint.

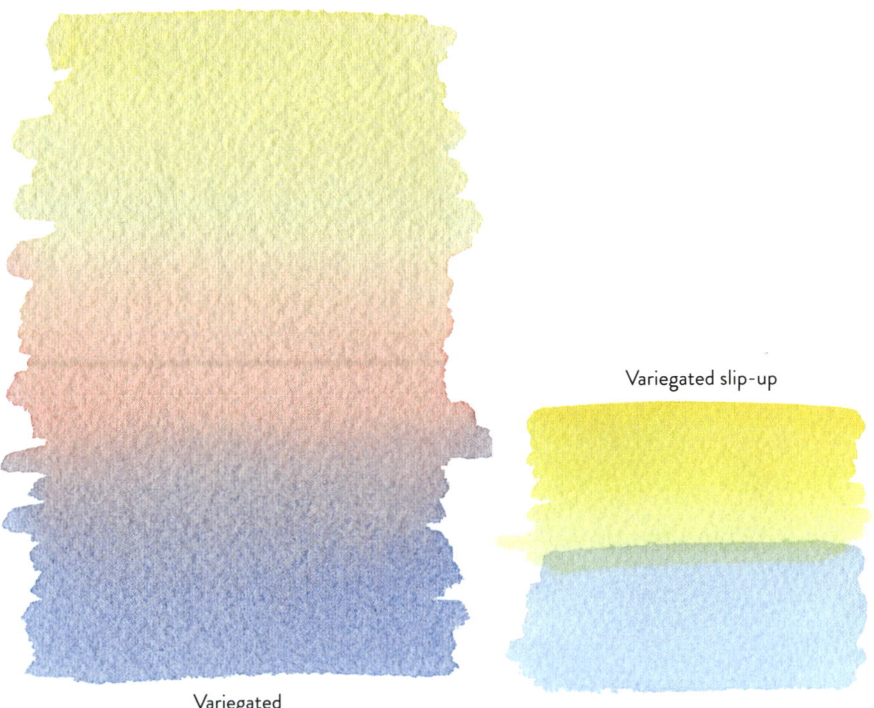

Variegated slip-up

Variegated

VARIEGATED

Transition from one colour to another: Mix equal tea consistencies of each colour in separate areas. Load your brush with the first colour. Start in the same manner as the flat wash and introduce the new colour as you work your way down. Clean off your brush between colours but try to keep the paint consistency even for all colours.

POSSIBLE SLIP-UPS:

Leaving too much drying time between adding new colours can lead to hard edges. Prepare all your colours in advance to avoid this.

Wet on wet

WET ON WET

Dropping colour into a wash: Create your background wash, then clean off your brush and pick up a new colour that's the same consistency as the wash paint mix. Lightly dab or stroke the new colour on the wash – the fewer brushstrokes the better. The dampness of the paper will determine how far the dropped-in colour will spread.

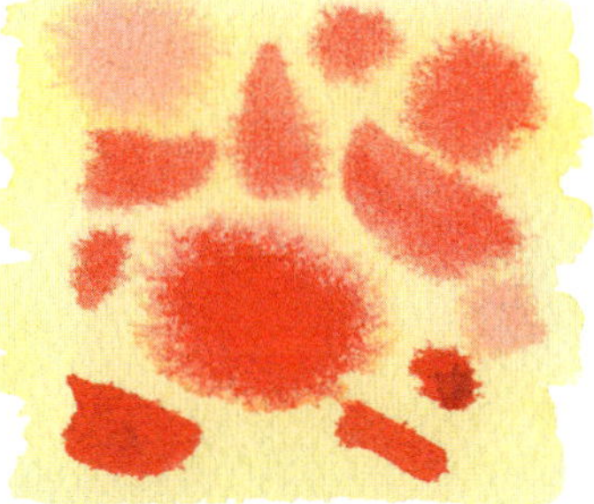

Wet-on-wet slip-up

POSSIBLE SLIP-UPS:

If your page looks like this, have you left your wash drying for too long before introducing new colours? Is your new colour a different consistency to the wash?

Watercolour-wash ice lollies

Once you've got the hang of the different washes, you can shape your washes into fun objects. Ice lollies are a perfect subject to play with this technique.

TIMING AND WETTING THE PAPER

Different levels of paper wetness play a vital role in determining the type of piece we want to create. On pages 24–5 we looked at the big three: dry on dry, wet on dry, and wet on wet. Now we can add more nuance with our paint consistencies and paper wetness.

The more you practise the easier it will be to pick a paint consistency and paper wetness and to predict the effect.

Dry, damp, moist and wet: A dry page could be an unpainted page or a completely dry painted page. Wet turns to damp and then moist as the page slowly dries, so timing is everything!

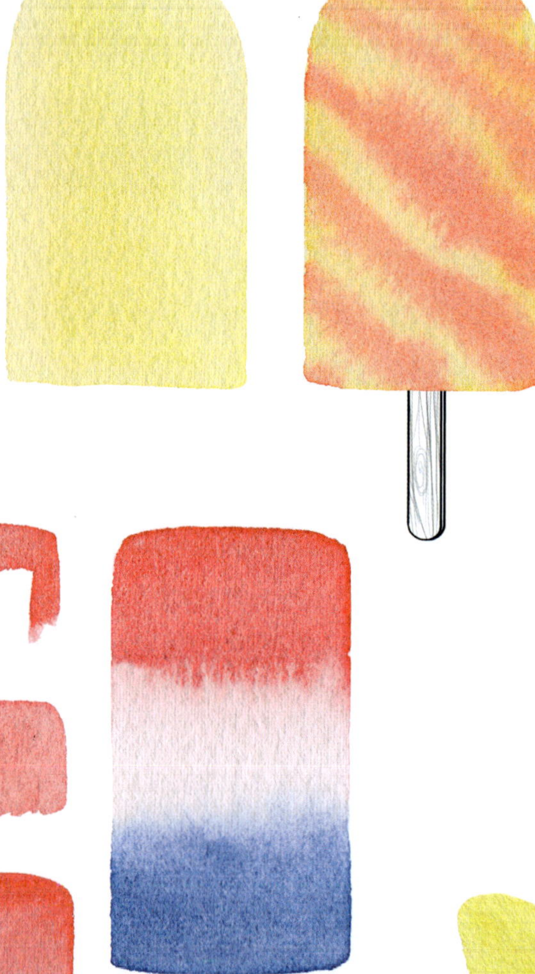

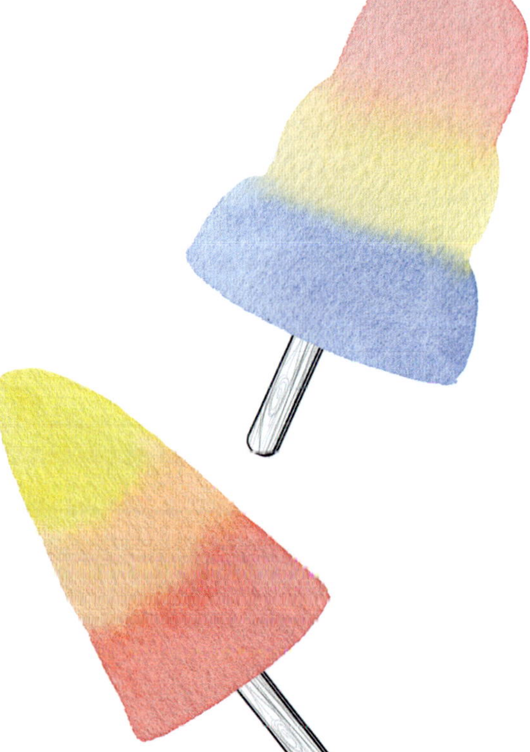

PAINT-AND-PAGE COMBINATIONS

Here are some paint-and-page combinations that I love to use.

DRY

Butter on dry: Dry brushing, heavy, thick application of precise detail

Tea on dry: Glazing a luminous colour over a dried painted layer or simply starting a painting with the lightest colour first

DAMP

Tea on damp: Washes of skies with blotted-out clouds

MOIST

Milk on moist: Dropping colours into petals and watching them feather out

WET

Coffee on wet: Soft-focus distant trees around a misty lake

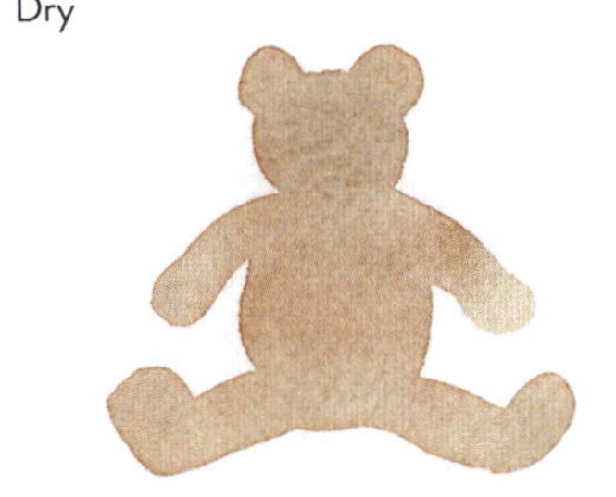

Dry

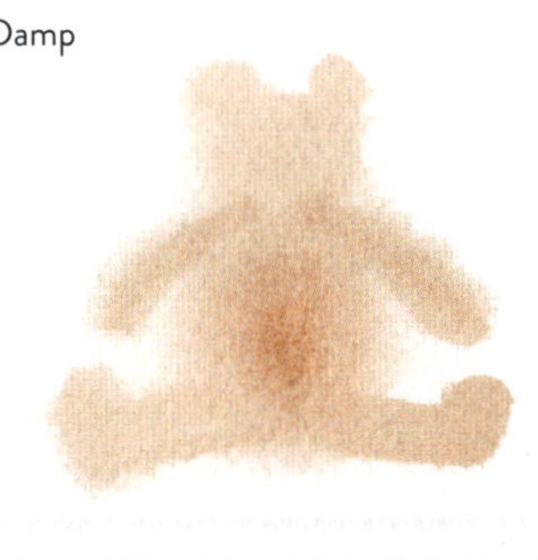

Damp

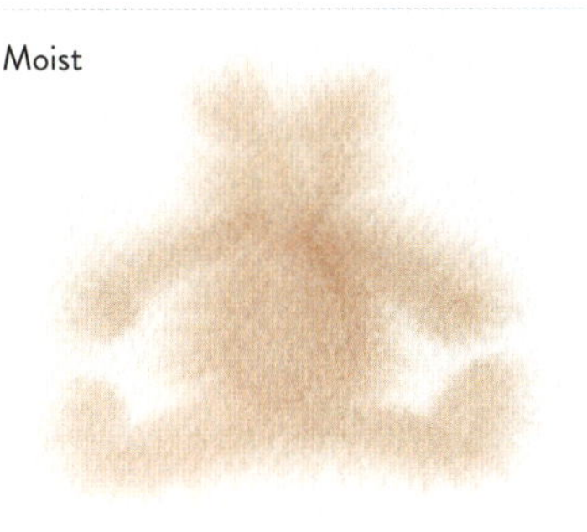

Moist

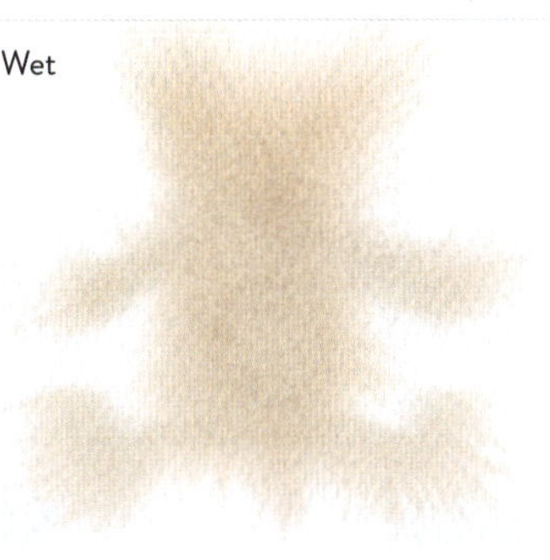

Wet

NOW TRY
Dry, damp, moist and wet teddy bears

Some subjects benefit from a fuzzy edge – try painting this teddy bear on different page wetnesses:

• Section off four areas of your page with either a pencil line or washi tape.

• Mix Yellow, Blue and Red together to make a brown in a coffee consistency. In one section, paint a simple teddy bear with your size 4 brush: use an oval for the body, circles for the head and ears, curved strokes from either side of the neck for arms, and one curved line across the base of the body with blobs for feet.

• Use your size 8 brush to wet the other three sections: make sure your brush and the water are clean. Soak the brush in the water and paint an even coverage of water, moving swiftly. Avoid leaving puddles of water. Hold the page up to the light, the reflection will show you if you have missed a bit.

• Start a timer for about six minutes (tweak the timings according to your environment). Immediately paint the bear on one section; this section is 'wet'. Once three minutes have passed, paint the bear on another section; this is 'moist'. Once the timer is finished, paint the bear in the remaining 'damp' section.

Harmonious Colour Palettes

The natural world shows us endless examples of harmonious colour palettes. Just look outside in any season; the trees, greenery, flowers, light and shadows work together because they coexist.

The colour wheel holds a similar symbiosis where each colour is the product of those next to it and the complement of the one directly opposite.

Analogous colours
These offer a straightforward way to find a harmonious palette as they sit next to each other on the colour wheel. They work well together because they share similar pigments.

NOW TRY
Analogous coloured leaves
Prepare analogous colours Yellow, orange and green to a tea consistency and fill a page with simple leaf shapes using the basic brushstrokes on pages 18–19, changing your colours as you build the leaf with your brush.

Analogous colours

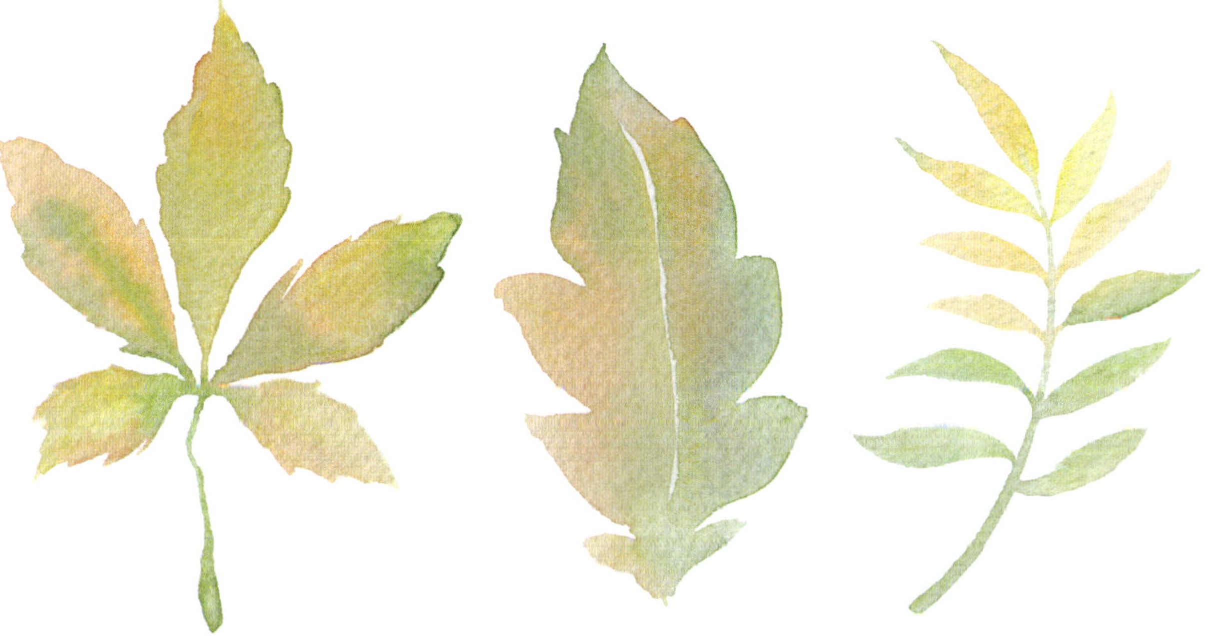

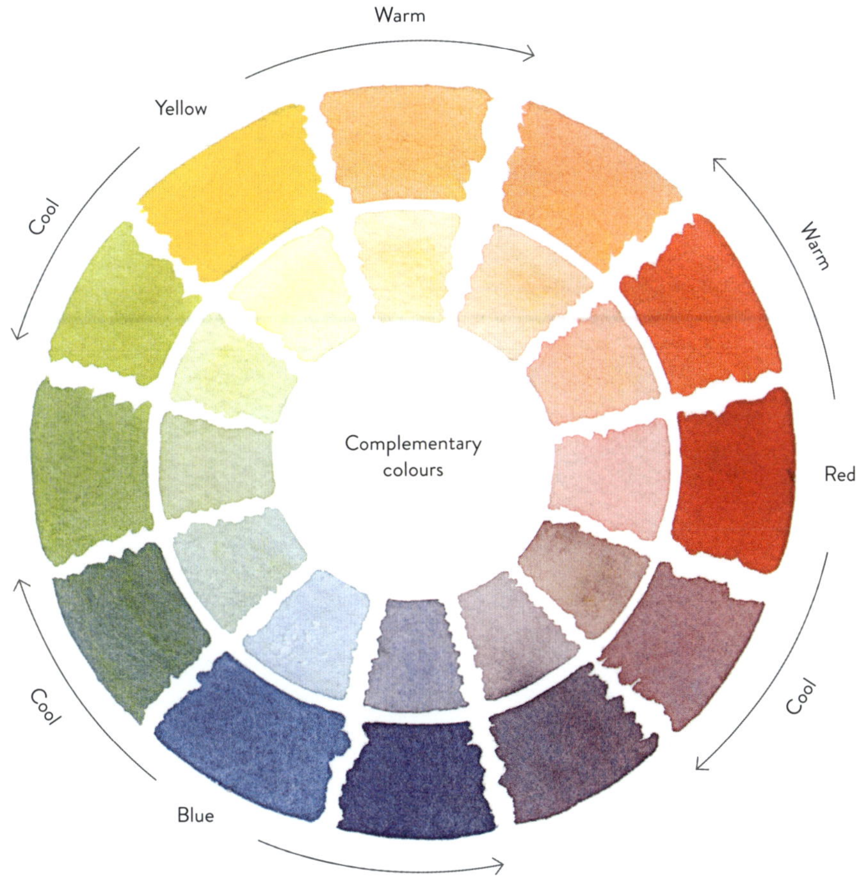

Complementary colours

These look loud and discordant when side by side in full concentration, but their pairing is my starting point for a well-balanced colour palette.

This colour wheel shows a fully saturated circle of colours as well as a diluted one. If you take into account each colour's value scale, you can pair these complementary colours much better, such as a pale pink with a deep green. Go one step further and consider the cool and warm shades either side of these colours on the colour wheel.

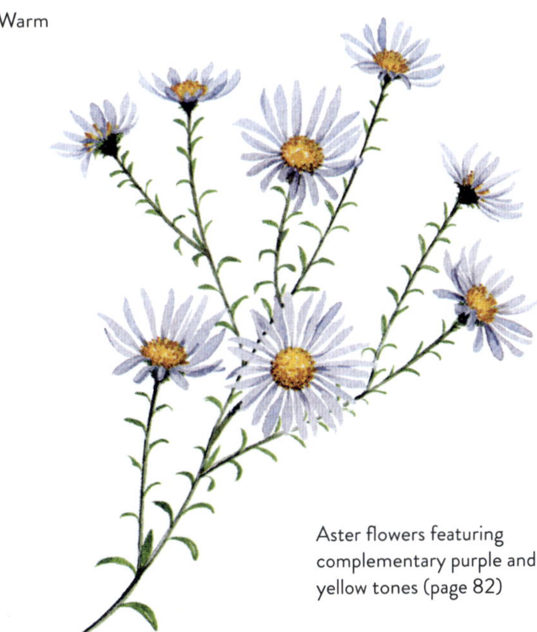

Aster flowers featuring complementary purple and yellow tones (page 82)

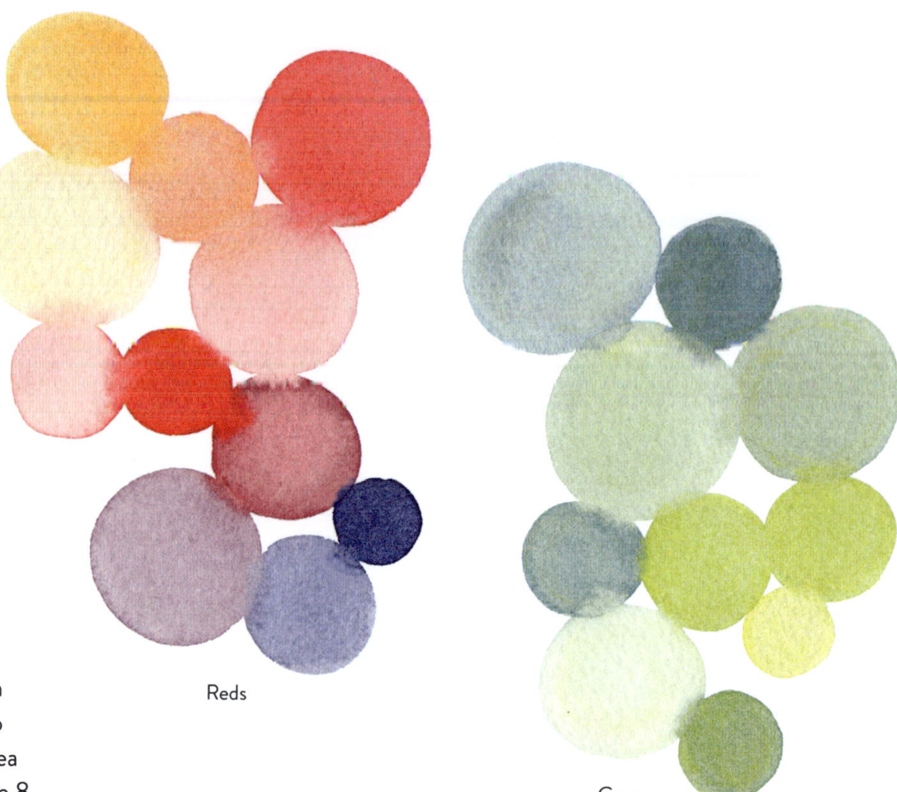

Reds

Red and green

Have your red and its warm and cool shades ready to go in the palette (coffee and tea consistency). With your size 8 brush, paint a circle of pure Red. Clean off the brush and begin to experiment with different shades (peach, blush, orange; purple, mauve, burgundy, etc.) with overlapping wet circles of paint. Also experiment with the value scale, painting diluted circles and heavily concentrated ones.

Clean off your brush and repeat the process with green in a separate cluster.

A few colours from both clusters will jump out as seeming more harmonious than the others. Swatch those colours and aim for five or six tones to get a palette of well-tuned colours, perfect for any illustration.

Greens

Choosing colours to match a reference

The more you play with the colours and mixes in the palette, the more confident you will become in matching colours to reference photos. Swatching colours from mixes and writing notes on how you got each colour is a great idea. It's also important to note that watercolour dries approximately 30% lighter so these swatches will be invaluable. Practice and play give you an extensive knowledge about your colours and paints.

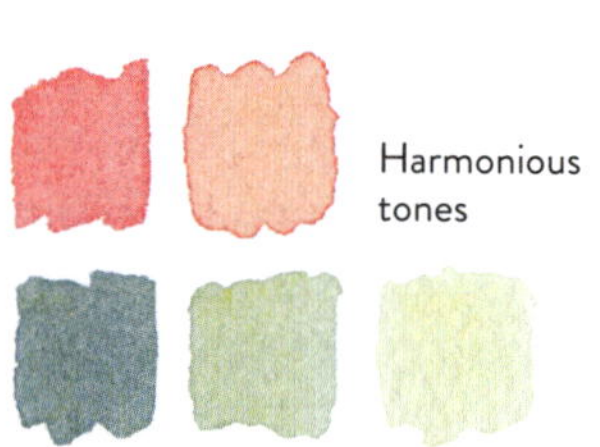

Harmonious tones

NOW TRY
Swatch-inspired painting

Once you have your swatches, what do they remind you of? For me it's peaches, blossom and spring branches. Fill a page with simple shapes using the basic brushstrokes on pages 16–18.

Peaches and
blossom

Round vs Flat

Without contrast, paintings are flat and lifeless. Here's a perfect place to start: creating roundness with a single colour.

Draw two circles, then wake up Alizarin Crimson with your size 8 brush. Paint the first circle with consistent colour. This looks flat and two-dimensional.

Paint the same consistent colour around the inner edge of half of the circle. Clean off your brush and use the wet bristles to draw the pigment across the circle, resulting in a circle with a paler middle and darker edge.

 # A Round Tomato

Some of us need a visual guide to help us see this roundness in a two-dimensional shape, so why not draw the curves in a grid over the shape? Soon you'll start to visualize roundness without marking out the grid each time. Then you can paint in curving strokes that follow the swell of the shape.

Level
Intermediate

Colours
Alizarin Crimson (Red)
Cadmium-Free Yellow (Yellow)
French Ultramarine (Blue)

Brushes
Pointed round sizes 4, 0

You will also need
Ruler, HB pencil, soft and hard erasers

Cadmium-Free Yellow mixed with Alizarin Crimson

   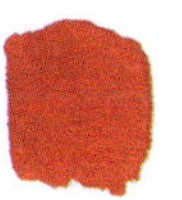

Cadmium-Free Yellow mixed with French Ultramarine

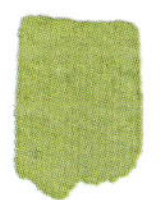 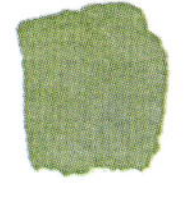 

Shadow mixes:

 Alizarin Crimson with green from the above mix

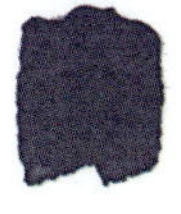 Alizarin Crimson, French Ultramarine and Cadmium-Free Yellow

DRAWING

1 Draw a round tomato shape and use a ruler to draw a straight-lined grid across it. Draw a second tomato shape and imagine that shape inflating and the grid expanding; the straight lines will start to curve. That is the shape to paint.

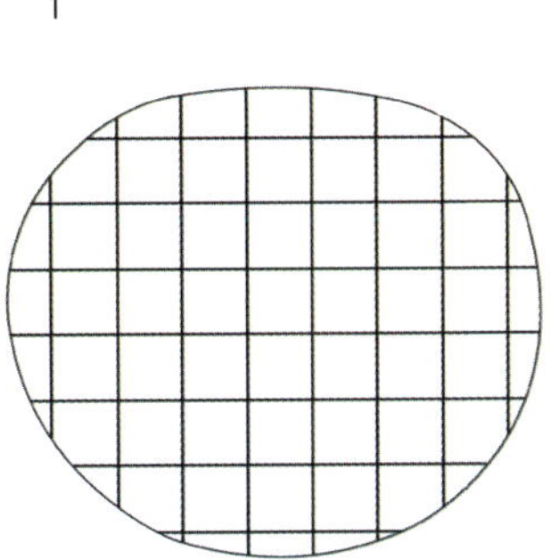

MIXING NOTES
Mix a little Red into Yellow and see how many orange-to-red tones you can create. You will also need to mix a range of greens by adding a little Blue to Yellow. Once you have a green, mix it into some Red to get a deep burgundy.

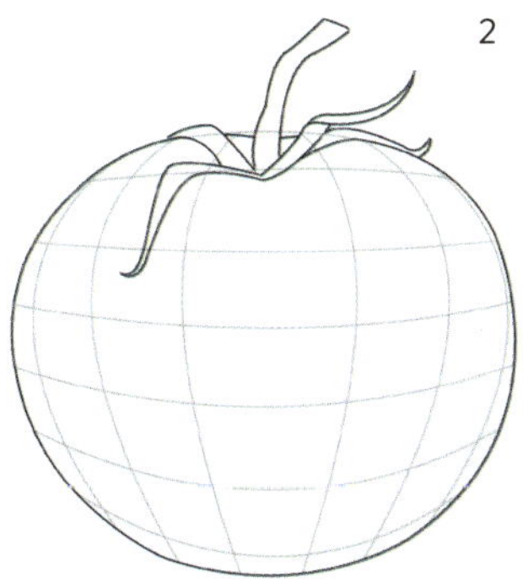

2 Fade the curved grid with a soft eraser, and draw in a tomato stalk.

PAINTING

1 With a clean size 4 brush, wet the inside of the tomato, avoiding the stalk. When it is damp, paint a coffee-consistency wash of your most yellowy orange, starting around the outer edge and following the curves inwards (don't get any more colour on the brush) until your paint runs out and leaves you with an unpainted patch on the top corner.

2 While still wet, paint a wash of a slightly more red tone using the same technique as step 1.

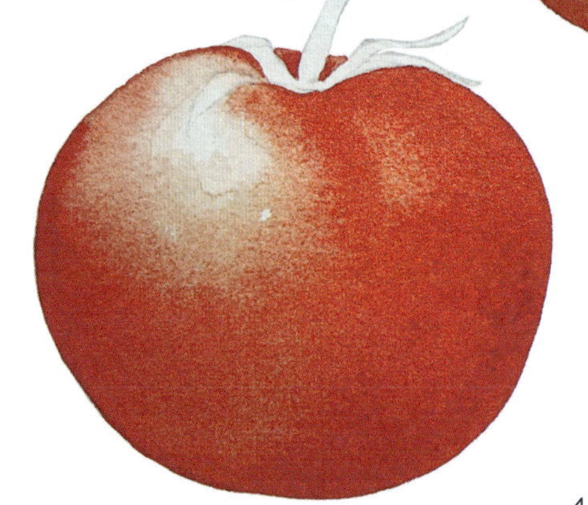

3 While still wet, paint a wash of a slightly redder tone using the same technique as steps 1 and 2.

4 While still wet, paint a curving sweep of the burgundy in the bottom corner across from the unpainted highlight. Allow to dry fully.

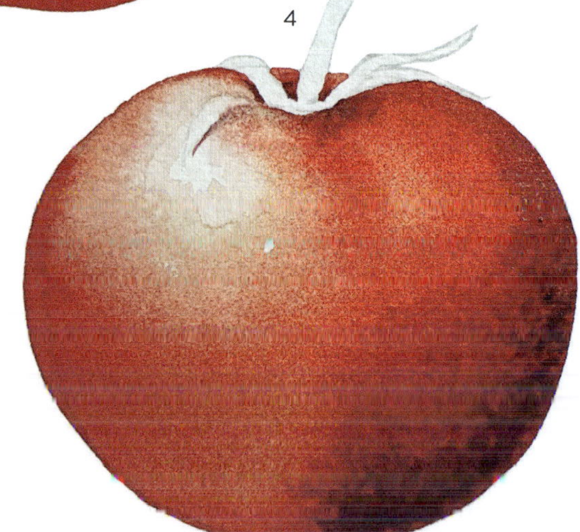

5 Fill in the stalk and leaves with a coffee-consistency wash of your most yellowy green with your size 0 brush. Once dry, this is a good time to rub out any visible pencil.

6 Increase the blue in your green mix and paint a sweep of colour along the shadowy side of the stalk and leaves with your size 0 brush while still damp. Allow to dry.

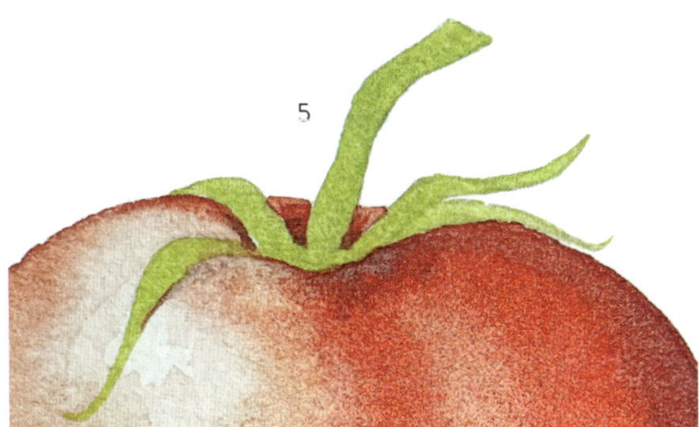

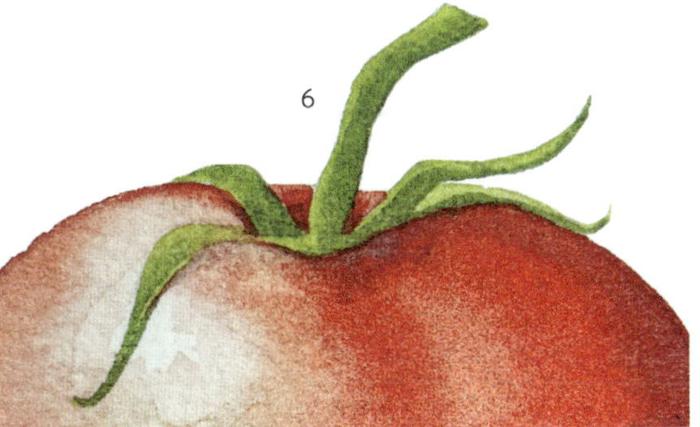

7 Mix a cream-consistency yellow and blue to make a dark green. Layer lowlights along the shadowy side of the stalk and leaves with your size 0 brush.

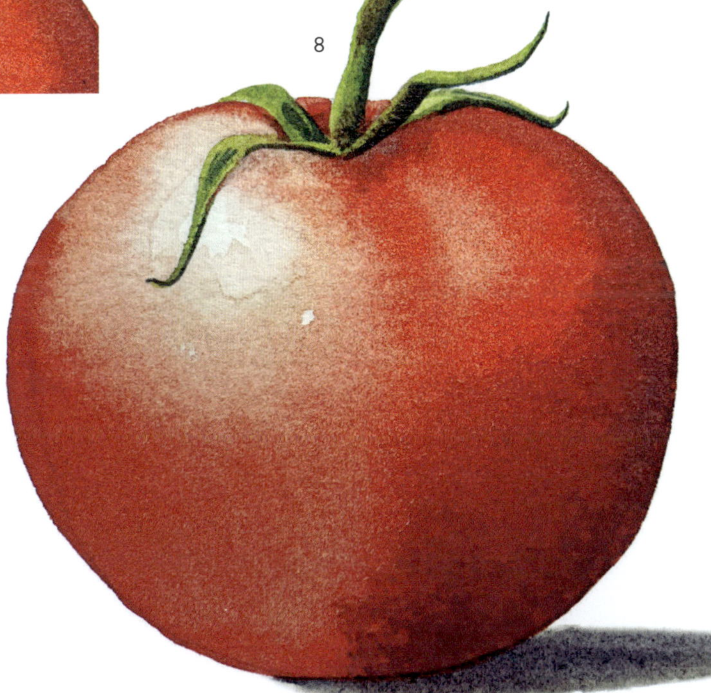

8 Mixing all three primary colours together results in a brown tone. Add a little more blue and you start to get an inky grey. Paint a tea-consistency oval along the ground. If it's too pale, increase the consistency a little and add some more right underneath the tomato. With your size 0 brush, paint a tiny amount along the shadowy side of the stalk and leaves.

Texture

Here are four fruits with distinctive textures: shiny cherry, hairy kiwi, dimpled lemon and velvety fig. Try each one, paying close attention to the way you can use brush, paint and water to achieve these finishes that make each fruit so distinctive.

TUTORIAL: Four Fruits

Level
Intermediate

Colours
All swatches are mixed
from Red, Blue and Yellow

Brushes
Pointed round sizes 8, 4, 0,

You will also need
HB pencil, soft eraser

SHINY CHERRY
The high shine of a cherry is achieved with many layers of glazes, hard edges of unpainted space, and wet-on-wet blends of deep colours.

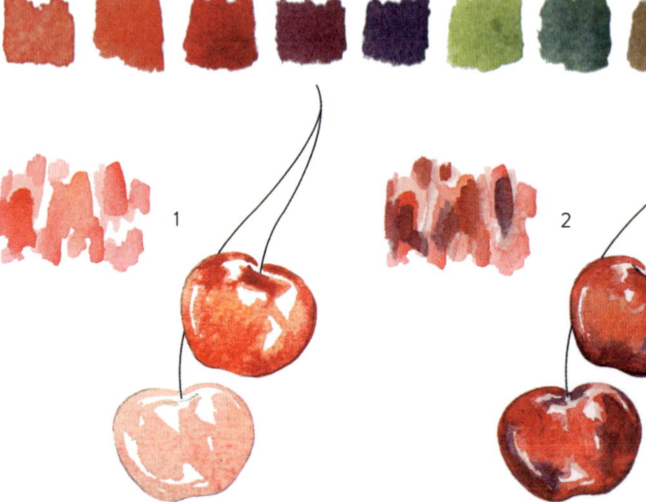

1 Draw round shapes with indents at top and bottom. Add a stalk. Paint tea-consistency washes of warm red tones with your size 4 brush. The lower cherry here shows an initial wash, while the higher cherry shows wet-on-wet additions of stronger consistency red tones. Leave unpainted areas of shine. Allow to dry.

2 Once dry, start to glaze patches of colour (begin to introduce cooler cherry tones by adding blue to red). Drop in deep purple tones around the base while still wet. Allow to dry.

3 Repeat step 2 with deeper red and purple glazes. You could even add some yellow to a purple mix to turn it to burgundy and add to the base of the cherry. Once dry, mix green and brown shades to paint the stalk with your size 0 brush.

HAIRY KIWI

1 Draw a pencil oval. Add a curved tip to the bottom and a stalk base to the top. Roll with a soft eraser to lighten the pencil.

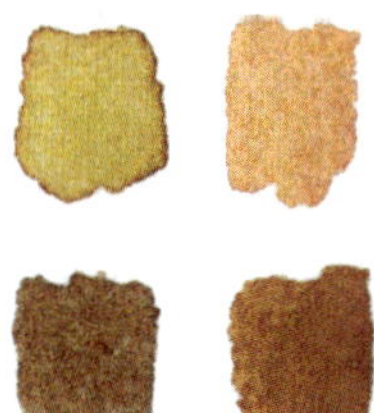

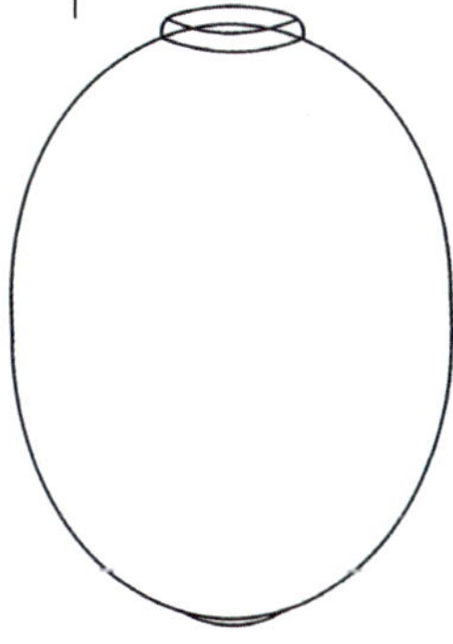

Can you think of other fruit and veg that share these distinctive textures? Why not try painting them with these techniques?

2 First, to create a rounded shape, paint ochre (coffee) around the edge with your size 8 brush, with more coverage towards the bottom of the fruit. With a clean wet brush, draw the diluted colour inwards for a rounded shape. Add some textured strokes to the stalk.

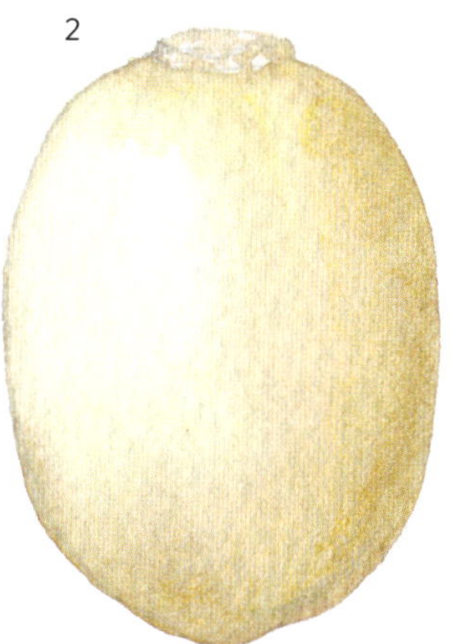

3 Add some more red and blue to your ochre to move into a deeper-brown palette in the same consistency as before. Once you have some colour on your size 4 brush, dab it a few times on the paper towel to remove excess liquid and dry brush (see page 50) in a circular scrubbing motion over the fruit, starting at the edges and working your way inwards as the paint runs out.

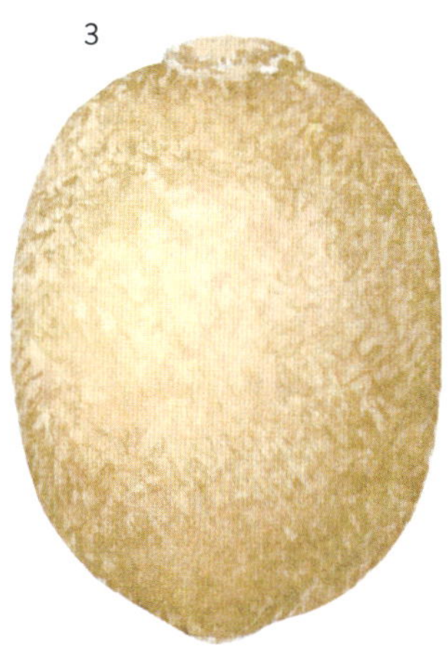

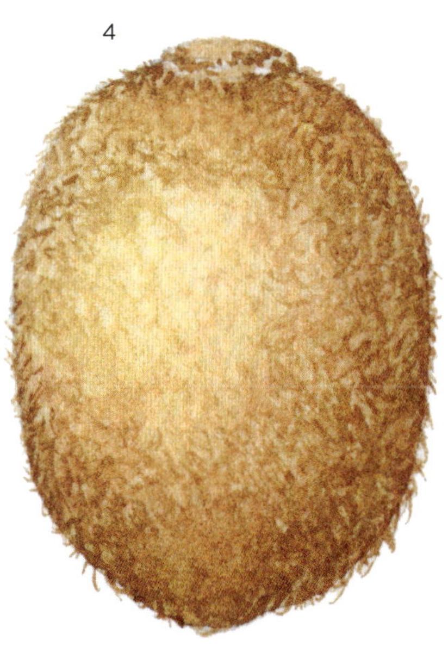

4 With your deepest brown (milk), paint a hairy edge all the way around with your size 0 brush. Move these little strokes inwards onto the body of the fruit, working your way inwards as the paint runs out.

DIMPLED LEMON

1 Draw a pencil oval. Add a curved tip to the bottom and top as well as a stalk and leaf. Roll with a soft eraser to lighten the pencil.

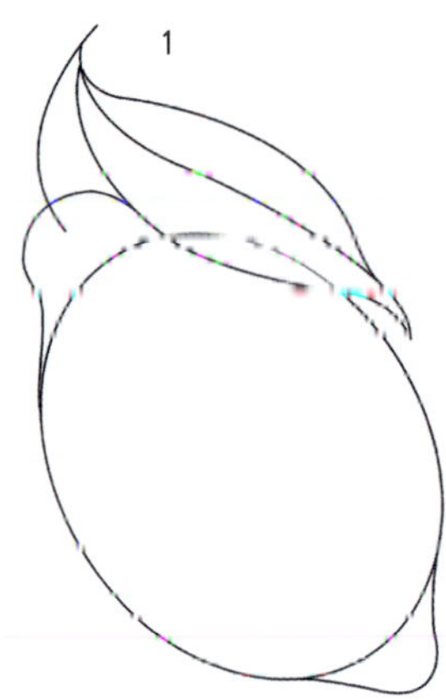

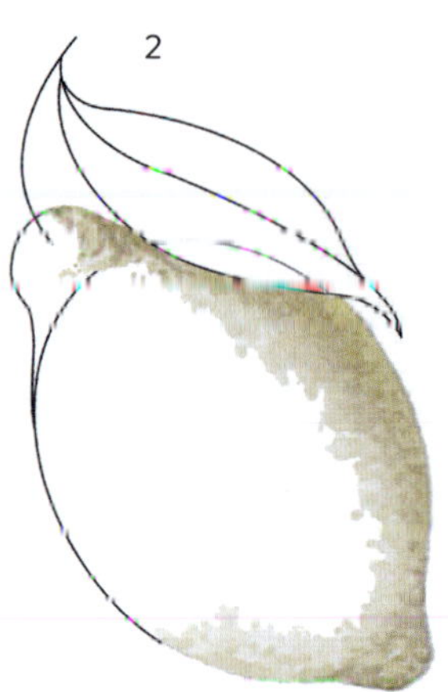

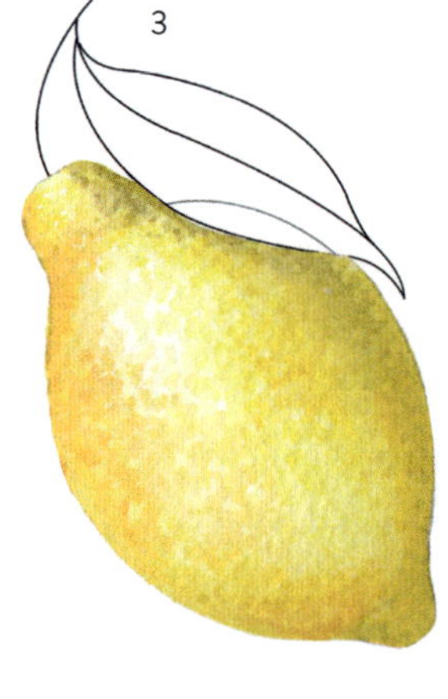

3 Once fully dry, use a wash of Yellow around the edge of the whole fruit and draw the colour in with some clean wet strokes and dabs of Yellow. Add dabs of orange to the lighter side of the fruit.

2 Using a complementary mix of Yellow and purple, paint a wash along one side with your size 4 brush and dab the colour into the middle of the fruit. Allow to dry.

4 Once dry, add more concentrated texture with tiny C-curves of Yellow, orange and a complementary mix with your size 0 brush. Paint the leaf and stalk in dilute yellow–green, using a stronger green to pick up the curves and undulations of the surface.

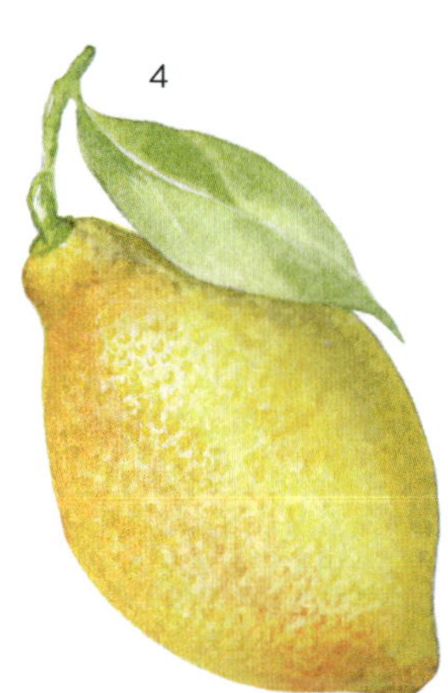

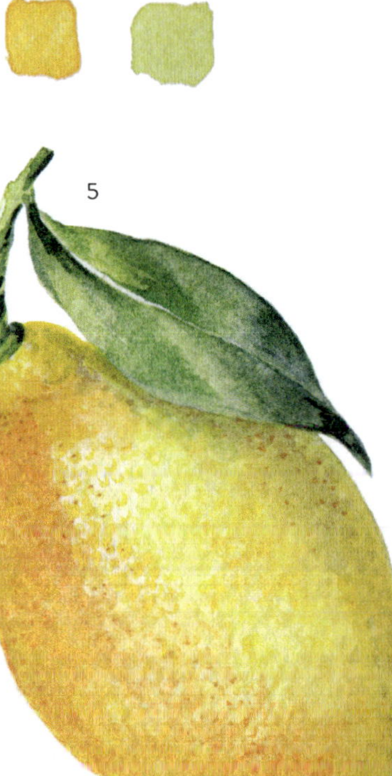

5 Once dry, use your size 0 brush to dot up and down the dimples in concentrated versions of the colours beneath. Add a more concentrated lowlight to shadowy parts of the leaf.

VELVETY FIG

It's hard to articulate the finish of a fig – its surface absorbs light with a myriad of softly blended luxurious colours. 'Velvety' seems fitting.

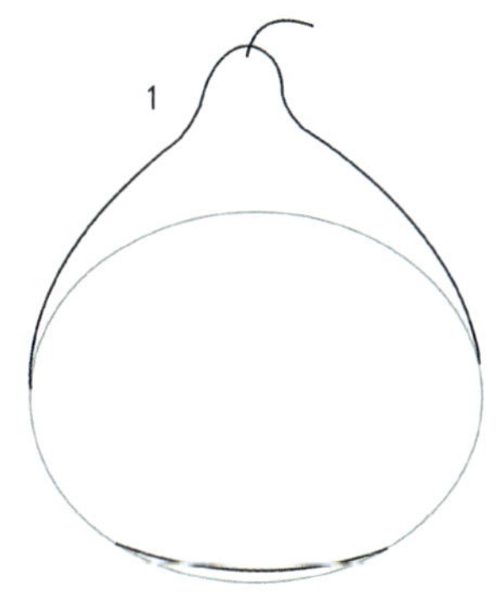

1 Use a pencil to draw an oval shape much like a sideways balloon. Add a curved tip and a stalk to the top. Roll with a soft eraser to lighten the pencil lines.

2 To achieve this blended finish you need to have all your colours ready-mixed so you can work quickly. With your size 4 brush, paint alternate streaks of gold and blush with streaks of dilute purple to the base.

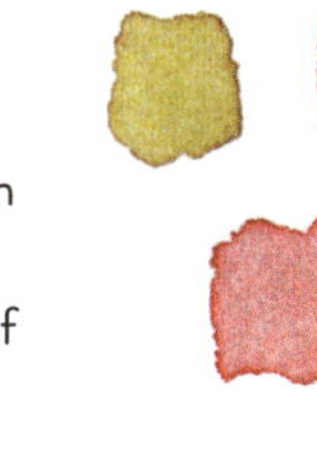

3 Layer up streaks of purple and burgundy while still damp, leaving small gaps of the golden layer underneath.

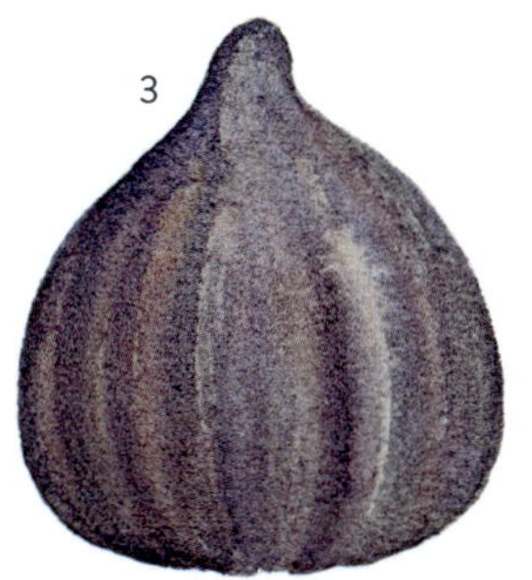

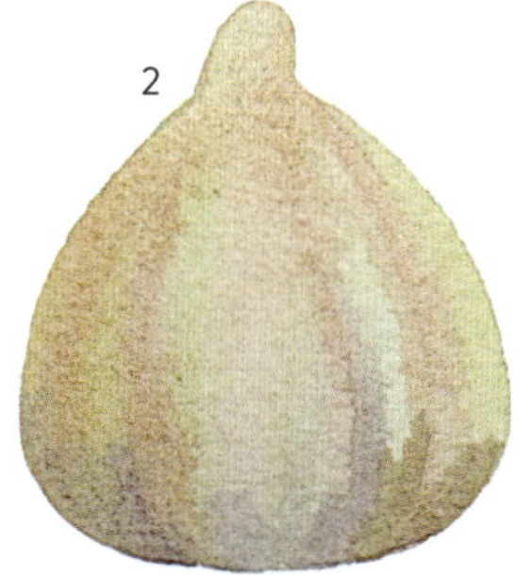

4 While still damp, increase the concentration of your purple tones and focus on darkening the edges to create a rounded appearance.

5 While your painting is still damp, clean your brush and paint a few streaks, lifting some of the colour away. Finish with a few vibrant streaks of pinks and purples. With your size 0 brush, paint in a yellow–green stalk with burgundy lowlights.

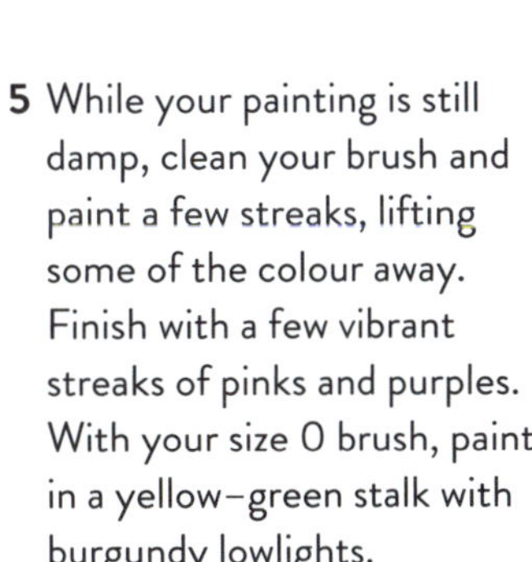

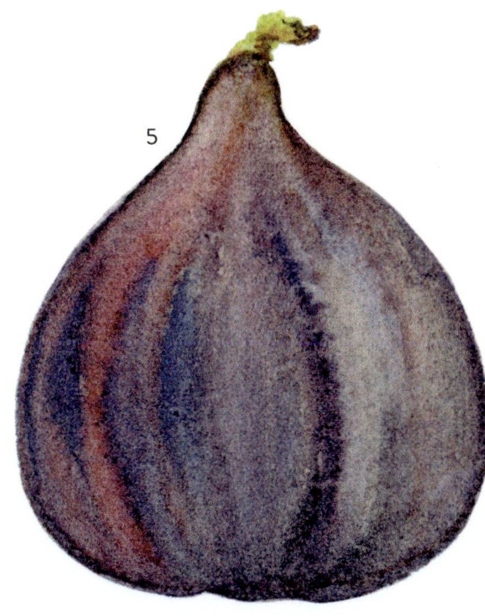

Dry Brushing, Lifting and Blotting

It's easy to forget that what you don't paint can be just as important as what you do paint. Dry brushing, lifting and blotting are three useful techniques that celebrate the absence of paint.

Dry brushing

Blotting

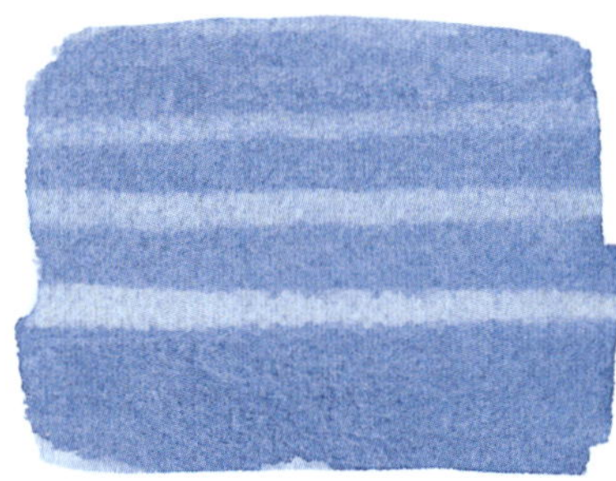

Lifting

DRY BRUSHING

With your Blue paint in a milk consistency, load the brush and gently blot off excess liquid on your paper towel. The paint breaks up as the brush sweeps over the texture of watercolour paper. Perfect for sparkling light on water, textured items, and minute detail.

LIFTING

Lifting is the act of removing paint from a damp surface with a clean, damp brush to create soft highlights. Your painted surface needs to be wet to lift. Of all the techniques, this is the one I've found hardest to master, but remember that the results will become all the clearer once the paint has dried. You can buy brushes specifically for the purpose of lifting. Paint a wash and experiment with different brushes.

BLOTTING

Blotting uses a sponge or scrunched-up paper towel to remove the paint, most notably to make fluffy clouds on a blue-wash sky.

Use different sizes of paper towel and other items like cotton buds and cotton wool. Scrunched-up paper will provide fluffy clouds; laying down larger creased pieces makes amazing snowy landscapes; and small folded corners of paper towel give great control when blotting out more definite shapes.

We can put all three techniques into practice in this basic landscape, using just Red, Yellow and Blue.

Divide a rectangle into three sections, as shown below; the top is the sky. Paint a gradient blue wash with your size 8 brush, getting paler towards the bottom (this helps give the impression of distance). Blot clouds with a scrunched-up tissue. (Make them larger at the top of the painting to again help with perspective.)

Once dry, use your size 8 brush to paint the next section, then paint a gradient wash of yellowy-green to orange for a field. Lift diagonal lines of colour to show perspective on the ploughed field with your size 4 brush. Allow to dry.

For the bottom section, dry brush lines of blue to create a sparkling river at the foot of the field. You could use your size 8 or 4 brush for this.

Prompt
Can you think of other uses for dry brushing? Tree foliage? A rough terracotta pot? Experiment with a page of swatches and see how dry you can get your brush.

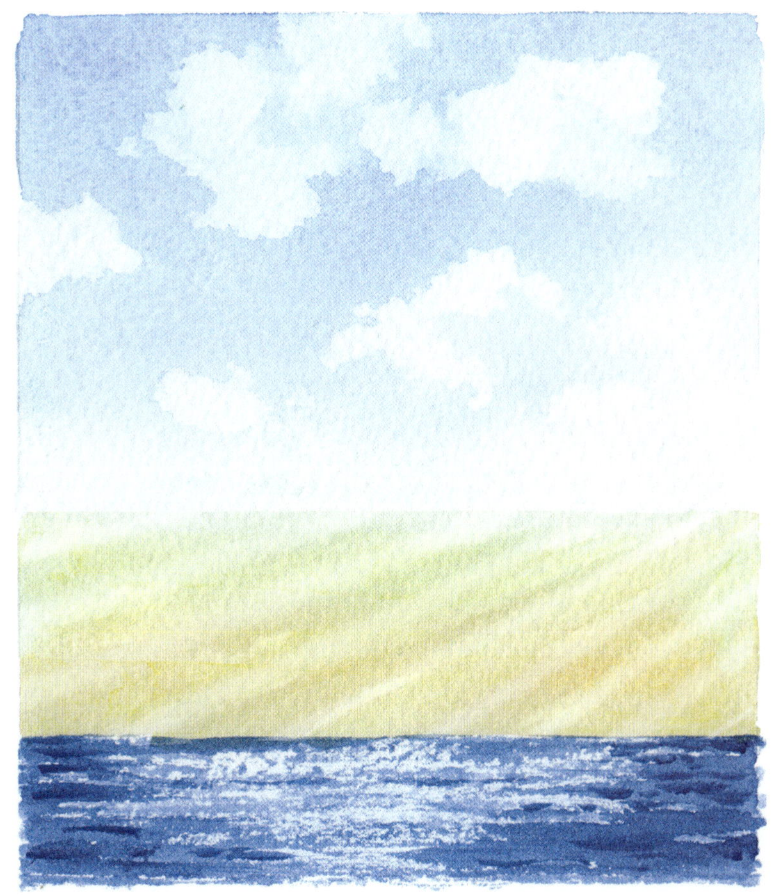

Complementary Colours

Colours on opposite sides of the colour wheel are complementary colours. This means they can be used to great effect in compositions, working in harmony together. They can also be used to desaturate one another and create really effective shadows.

TUTORIAL: Oranges on a Branch

We can mix so many colours from our primary three. This bunch of oranges on a branch is a perfect project to try.

Level
Intermediate

Colours
Alizarin Crimson (Red)
Cadmium-Free Yellow (Yellow)
French Ultramarine (Blue)

Brushes
Pointed round sizes 8, 4, 0

You will also need
HB pencil, soft and hard erasers

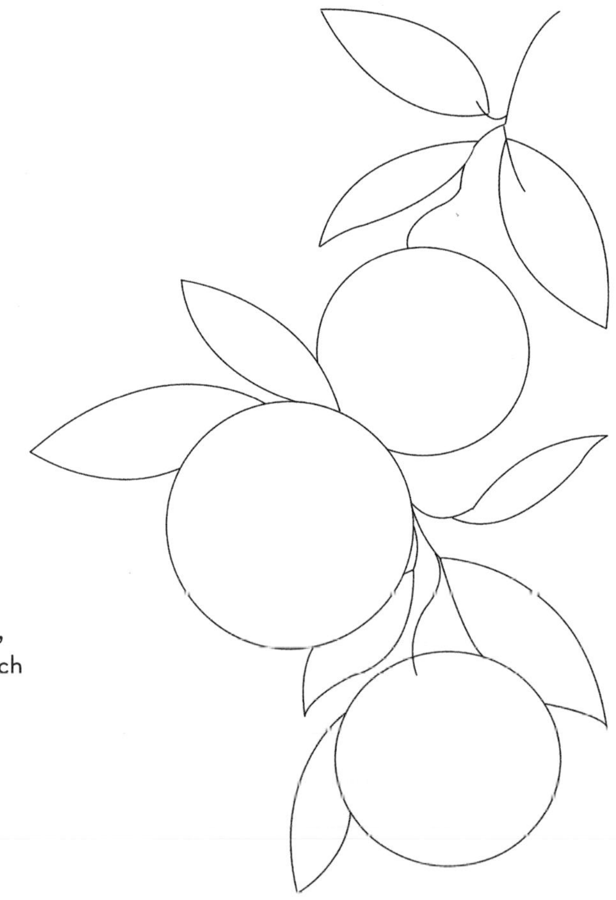

DRAWING

1 Draw circles for your oranges, then link them up with a branch and leaves.

Cadmium-Free Yellow mixed with French Ultramarine (tea)

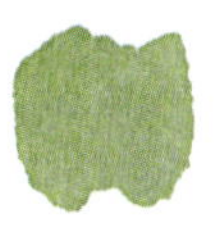

Cadmium-Free Yellow mixed with French Ultramarine (cream)

French Ultramarine (tea)

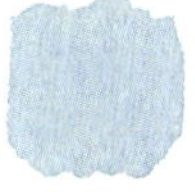

Cadmium-Free Yellow mixed with Alizarin Crimson (coffee)

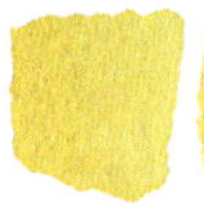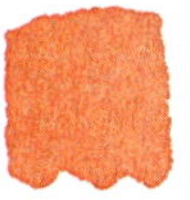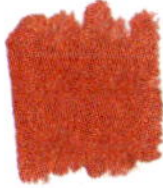

Complementary colours mixed

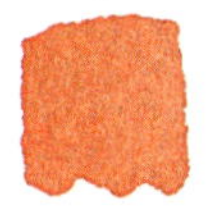 + 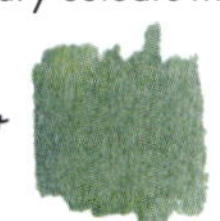 = 

MIXING NOTES

Mix a little Red into Yellow and see how many orange-to-red tones you can create. You will also need to create a range of greens from mixing a little Blue into Yellow. Once you have a green, mix it into some Red to get a deep, shady burgundy.

PAINTING

1 With a clean size 8 brush, wet the whole page. Paint a yellowy green (coffee) with your size 8 brush around the oranges, along the branch and in the leaves. It will feather out across the lines. Immediately add a greener tone to the curve of the oranges and on the leaves. Use your size 8 brush to paint dashes of wet-on-wet French Ultramarine (tea) around the edge of the green. Allow to dry.

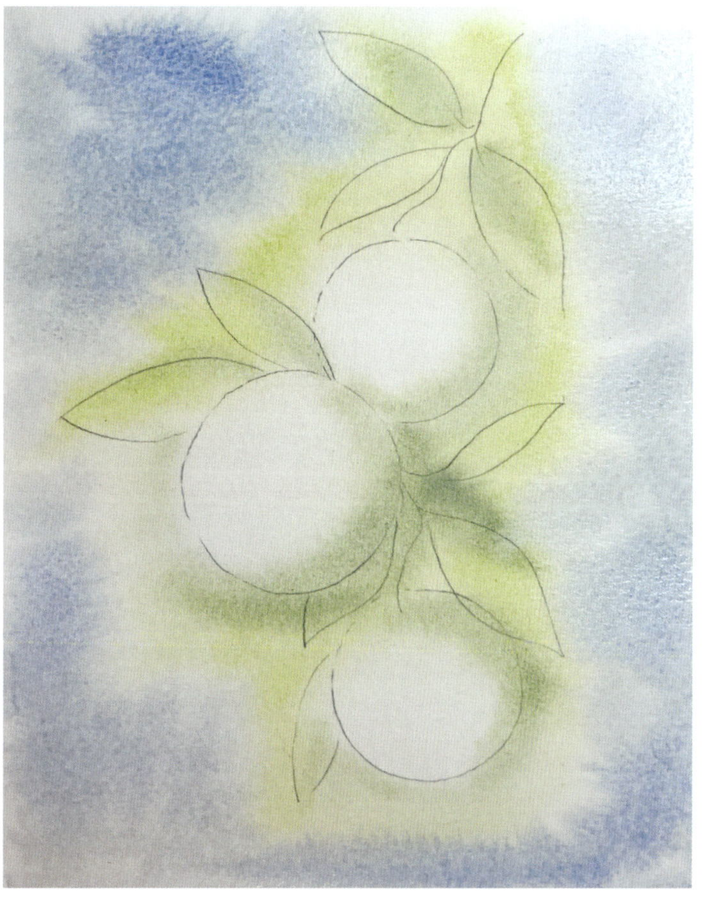

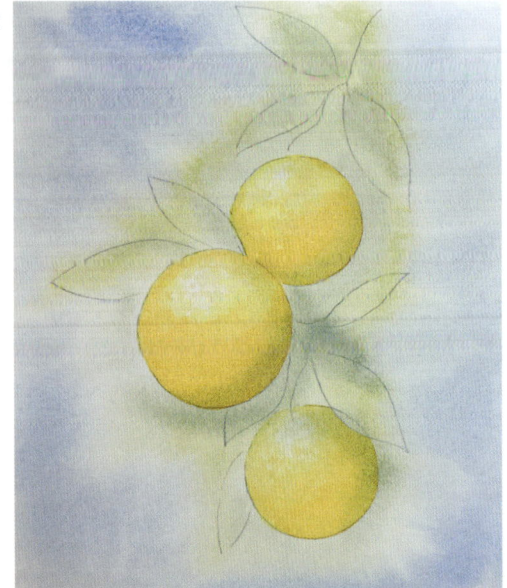

2

2 Paint a coffee-consistency wash of your most yellowy orange with your size 4 brush, starting around the outer edge and following the curves inwards (don't get any more colour on the brush) until your paint runs out and leaves you with an unpainted shine on the top corner. Clean the brush off and blot it on paper towel. Dab the wet colour inwards to the unpainted area to create a mottled texture. While still damp, paint a wash of a slightly more orange tone using the same technique.

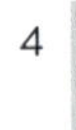

3 While still wet, paint a wash of a slightly more red tone using the same technique as steps 1 and 2. Paint green leaves (coffee) in the pencil lines with your size 8 brush. While wet, blend in blue–green tones to add depth. Add more leaves to create a full branch.

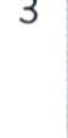

3

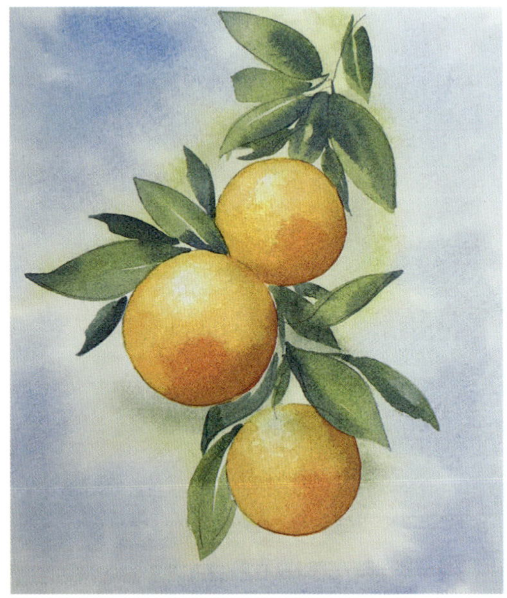

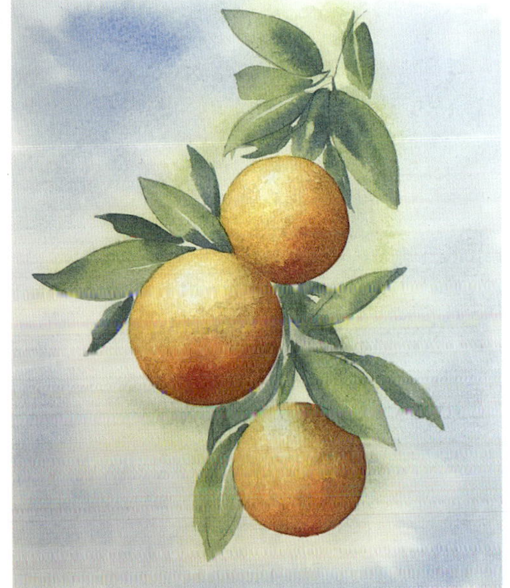

4

4 The oranges will have dried, paint a curving glaze of the complementary brown colour (tea) along the shadowy edge. Clean and blot your brush and dab the colour up into the body of the orange. Dab some Red at the base of each fruit.

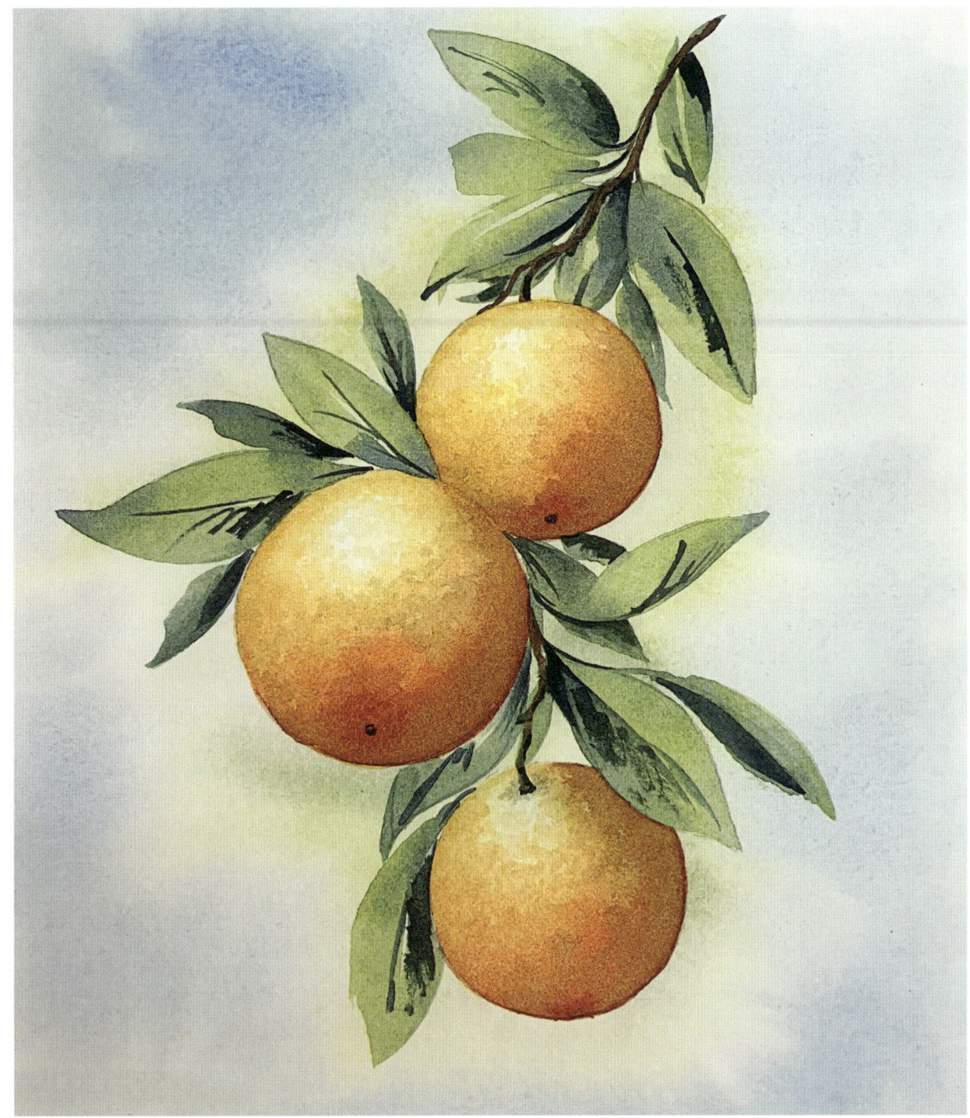

5 Mixing all three primary colours together results in a brown tone. Paint this along the branch where visible in a milk consistency. Mix a cream-consistency Yellow and Blue to make a dark green. Paint lowlights along the shadowy side of the branch and leaves with your size 0 brush. Paint a mark at the base of the oranges where visible. Once dry, rub out any visible pencil with the hard eraser.

Prompt
If you changed the fruit to red apples, how would that affect the complementary tones of the green leaves?

Glazing and Layering

Watercolour paintings are made up of many layers. We start with light washes and colours that can be easily built upon with increasingly concentrated, dark layers. You can either work fast with the wet-on-wet technique or patiently wait for paint to dry and apply layers and glazes.

All watercolour paints can be diluted to transparency, but each colour has a different pigment make-up. You can see if a watercolour is transparent, semi-transparent or opaque by studying the paint tube. (Each brand has its own way of displaying this information.) The more transparent a colour, the better it is for glazing.

Glazing: Transparent layers act like filters to add luminosity to a painting, whether warming it up or cooling it down.

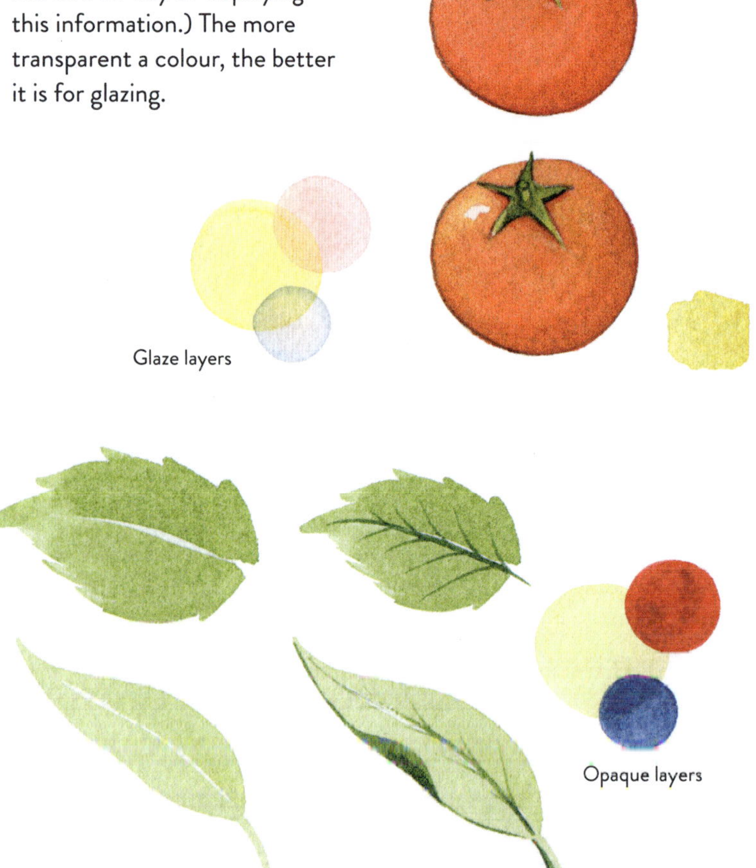

Glaze layers

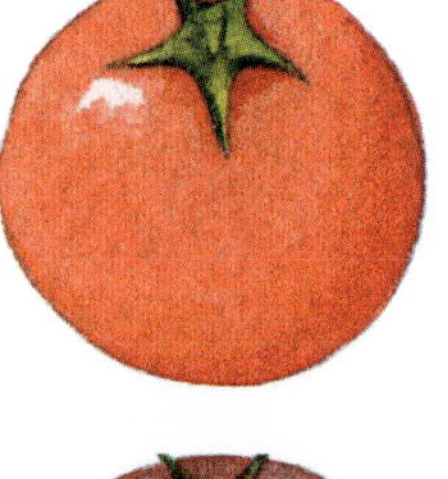

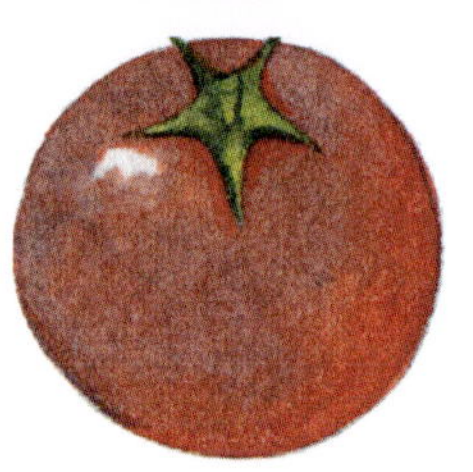

Opaque layers

Layering: Opaque layers give depth and detail to a piece.

These techniques make use of a colour's full spectrum of value, which expands the potential of a limited palette.

TUTORIAL: Seashells

Shells are the perfect subject to play with glazes and layers, as they come in all kind of shapes and gnarly, pearlescent and patterned textures.

Level
Beginner

Colours
Alizarin Crimson (Red)
Cadmium-Free Yellow (Yellow)
French Ultramarine (Blue)

Brushes
Point round sizes 4, 0

You will also need
HB pencil, soft and hard erasers

MIXING NOTES

Play with the colours in your palette to create a range of dilute tones for your seashells. Don't forget to also mix some concentrated counterparts for the layering stage.

CLAM SHELL

DRAWING

1 Draw an uneven rounded shape, a bit like a potato. On one side, draw two S-curves into a pinched point. Roll with a soft eraser to lighten the pencil to a faint sketch.

PAINTING

2 Paint dilute C-curves of your chosen colours with your size 4 brush (I used Blue and a green mixed from Yellow and Blue) to fill the clam shell surface. Leave slivers of unpainted space and keep your colours light. Allow to dry fully.

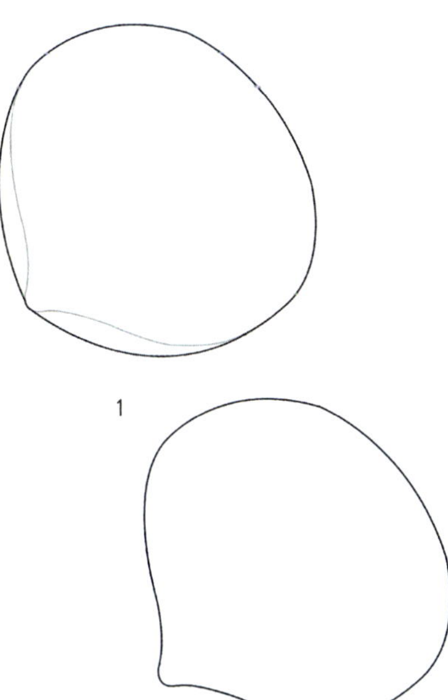

3 You can paint the same colour or slightly adjust the blue or green mixes. You just need to make sure the paint is transparent for it to be a glaze. Paint short sweeps of colour along one side of the shell. Try not to labour the brushstrokes; even when fully dry, repeated heavy brushstrokes on top can disturb the lower layers. Try glazing different sections of the shell for added texture. Allow to dry.

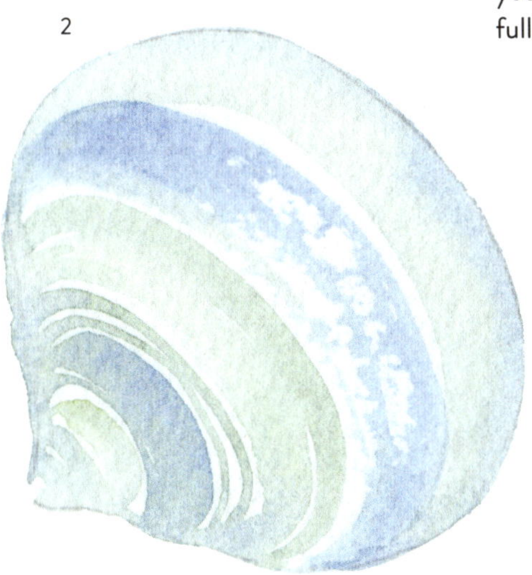

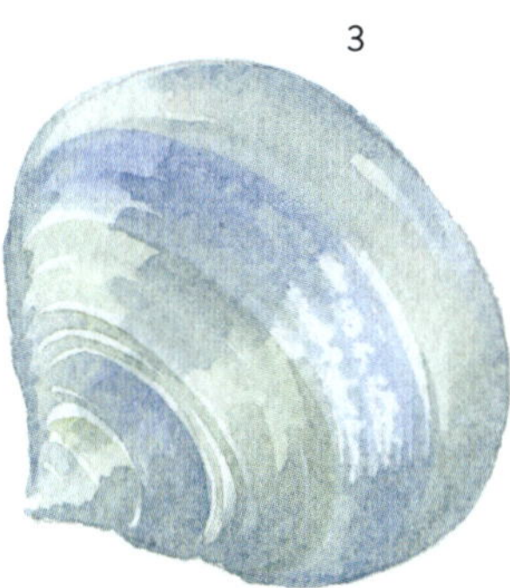

4 Increase the concentration of the colour a tiny bit, and glaze further accents on top. Allow to dry. At this stage the shell looks good; the glazes have added texture and roundness in a soft, glassy way. You could finish here.

5 Mix a highly concentrated version of your green and Blue colours, in a cream consistency. This thick paint will be a layer not a glaze. With your size 0 brush, paint fine lines that follow the curve of the original clam shell texture. Layer additional lines on the shadowy side of the clam shell.

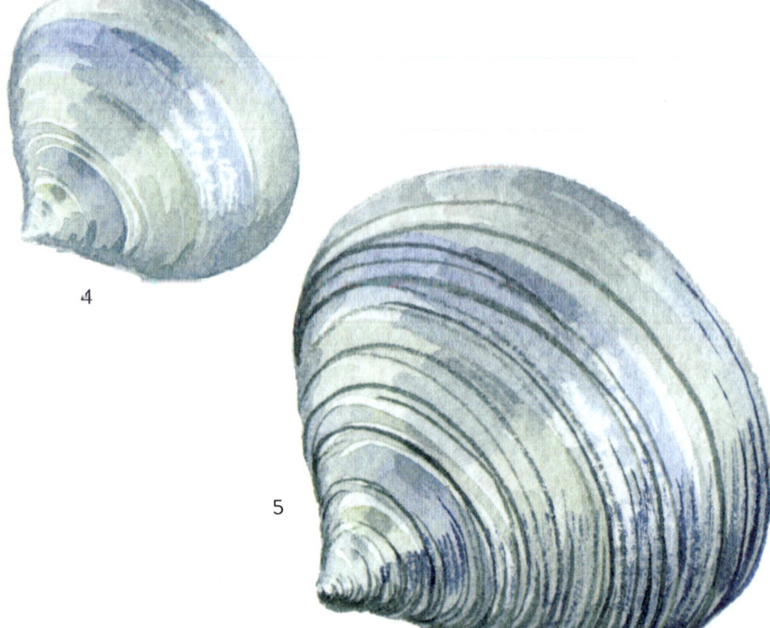

LUMINOUS GLAZE SCALLOP SHELL AND SPOTTY COILED SHELL

1 Draw the basic shell shapes in pencil. Roll with a soft eraser to lighten the pencil to a faint sketch.

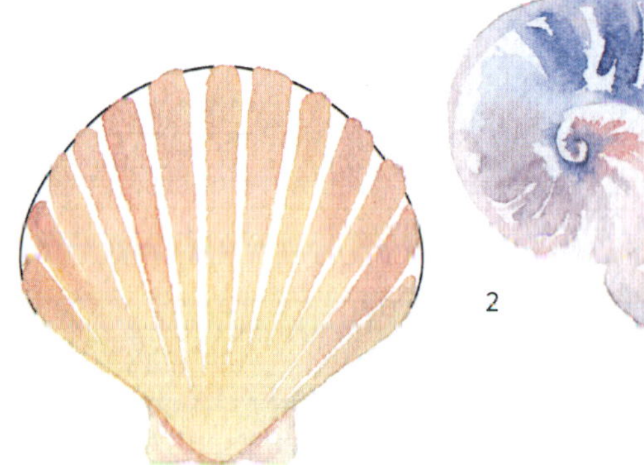

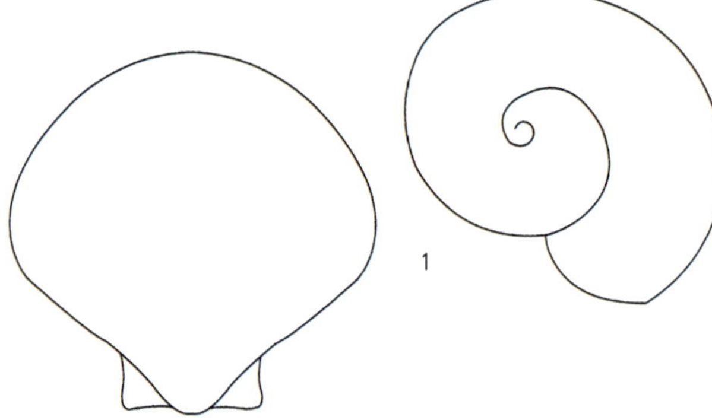

2 The scallop shell uses Red and Yellow, the coil Red and Blue. Play around with mixing the two hues in your palette to create dilute tones. For the scallop, paint peachy-yellow lines fanning from the centre. While the watercolour is still wet, drop in some Red at the tips. For the coil shell, work your way around the coil scribbling multicoloured strokes (leaving some unpainted space). Allow to dry.

3 To create the raised ridges of the scallop shell, start at the outer edge, glazing the top section of the painted lines with Yellow. Then paint Yellow in the unpainted gaps, coming a few millimetres lower. This gives the appearance of a strip of colour over the undulating ridges. Repeat this technique down the shell. For the coil shell, repeat the previous step with additional lumps and bumps to the edge of the shell to build up the vibrance and texture. Allow to dry.

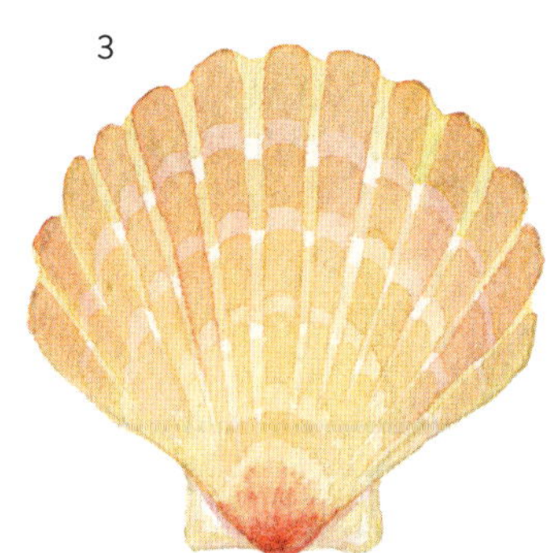

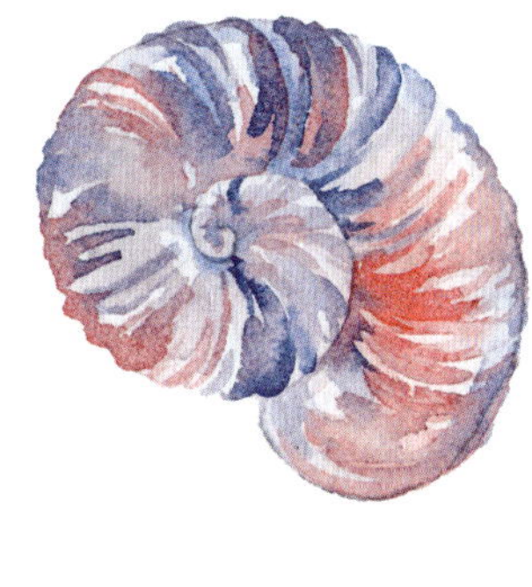

4 Glaze a strip of Red down the side of each fanned line on the scallop shell. Glaze dilute coloured spots to the coiled shell.

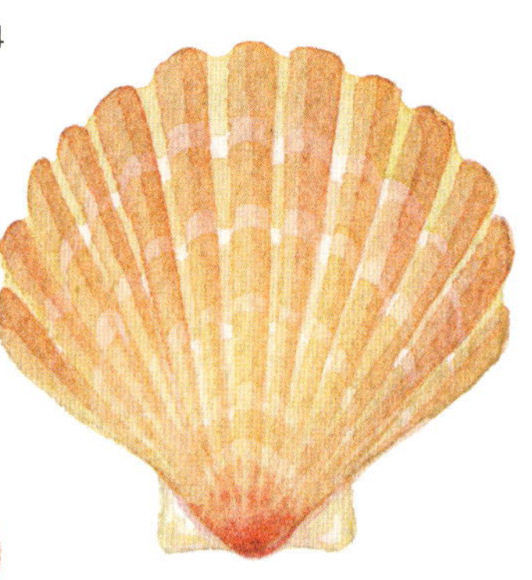

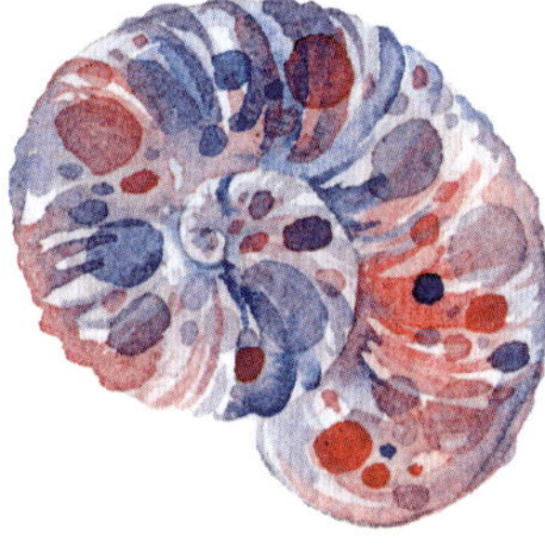

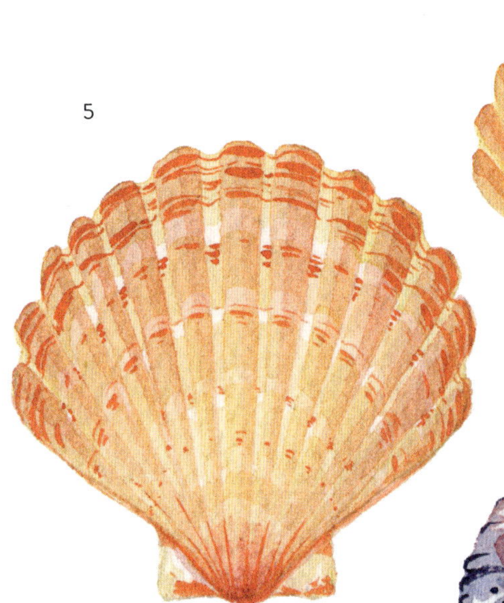

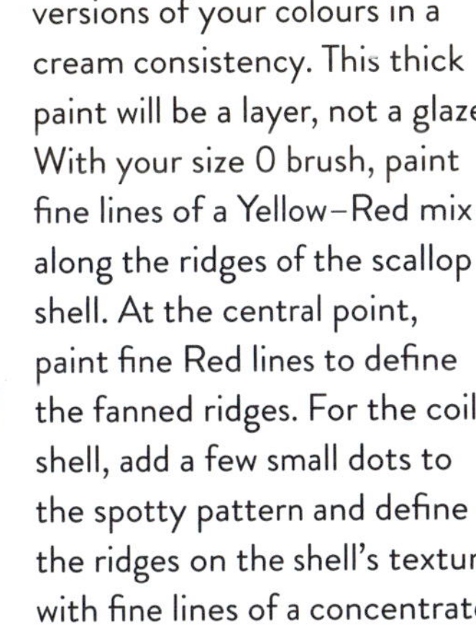

5 Mix highly concentrated versions of your colours in a cream consistency. This thick paint will be a layer, not a glaze. With your size 0 brush, paint fine lines of a Yellow–Red mix along the ridges of the scallop shell. At the central point, paint fine Red lines to define the fanned ridges. For the coil shell, add a few small dots to the spotty pattern and define the ridges on the shell's texture with fine lines of a concentrated Red–Blue mix.

> **Prompt**
> *Scour the shore for more seashell shapes, and play around with the glazing and layering techniques.*

How to Start and Stop a Painting

Warm up the brain, brush and body: Abstract scribbles and strokes are a great way to switch your brain into a creative mode while also activating the muscles, which need to feel relaxed in order to paint freely.

Prep your paints: First plan your harmonious colour palette. Wake up those colours and mix them with water to your required consistencies. I like to have a piece of scrap watercolour paper to swatch colours before they go onto my painting to prevent unwanted surprises. Don't forget the key to a light and luminous watercolour piece is to limit the number of colours you're using.

Start with the simplest thing: A pencil line drawing can be a great way to help you start, but keep it minimal and simple. It should be no more than the basic scaffolding of your scene: a horizon line for a landscape, ovals and lines for an animal's body, or a curving line for the stem of a plant.

Have a plan: The more you try to correct a watercolour painting the worse it looks. That's why it's a good idea to make a plan before you start. That might be a reference photo or a little sketch. I like to think through my process and write a list of tasks in order.

Get comfortable: If it's not possible to allocate a dedicated space for your watercolour painting, at least make sure you have a consistent source of light and access to clean water to refresh your water jars. Ensure, too, that you're sitting comfortably.

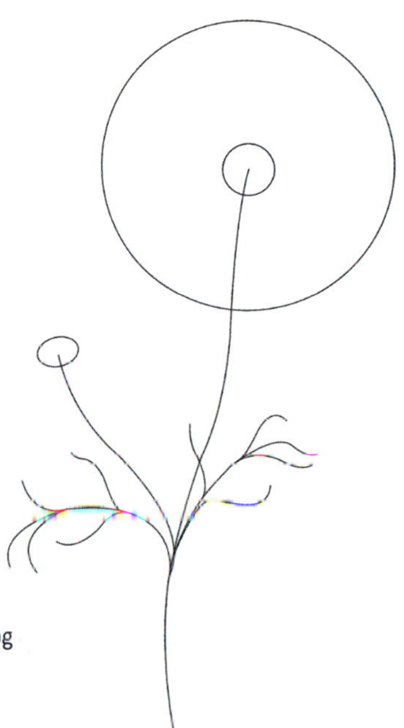

Basic scaffolding

STOPPING

Knowing when to stop: Identify the moment where your watercolour could go from being light and luminous to heavy and laboured. The tips below will help you know the moment to stop before you've gone too far.

Keep it light: Even with lowlights and final details, don't let your paint layers go on too thickly – use light washes of colour. You can always add more but it's tricky to take away.

Paint confidently: Leave the paint alone to do its thing. Don't dab over and over. And don't use brushes that are too small.

Keep it varied: With the same level of detail across the board, every inch of your painting will be fighting for attention. Instead choose where you want the viewer's eye to go and then focus on that.

Walk away; If it's not working, walk away and come back to it later. In the heat of the moment it's hard to find solutions. The passing of time allows you to see the good in it and maybe you won't need to make any changes. But if you do, it's fully dried by this point and will happily take a last layer of paint.

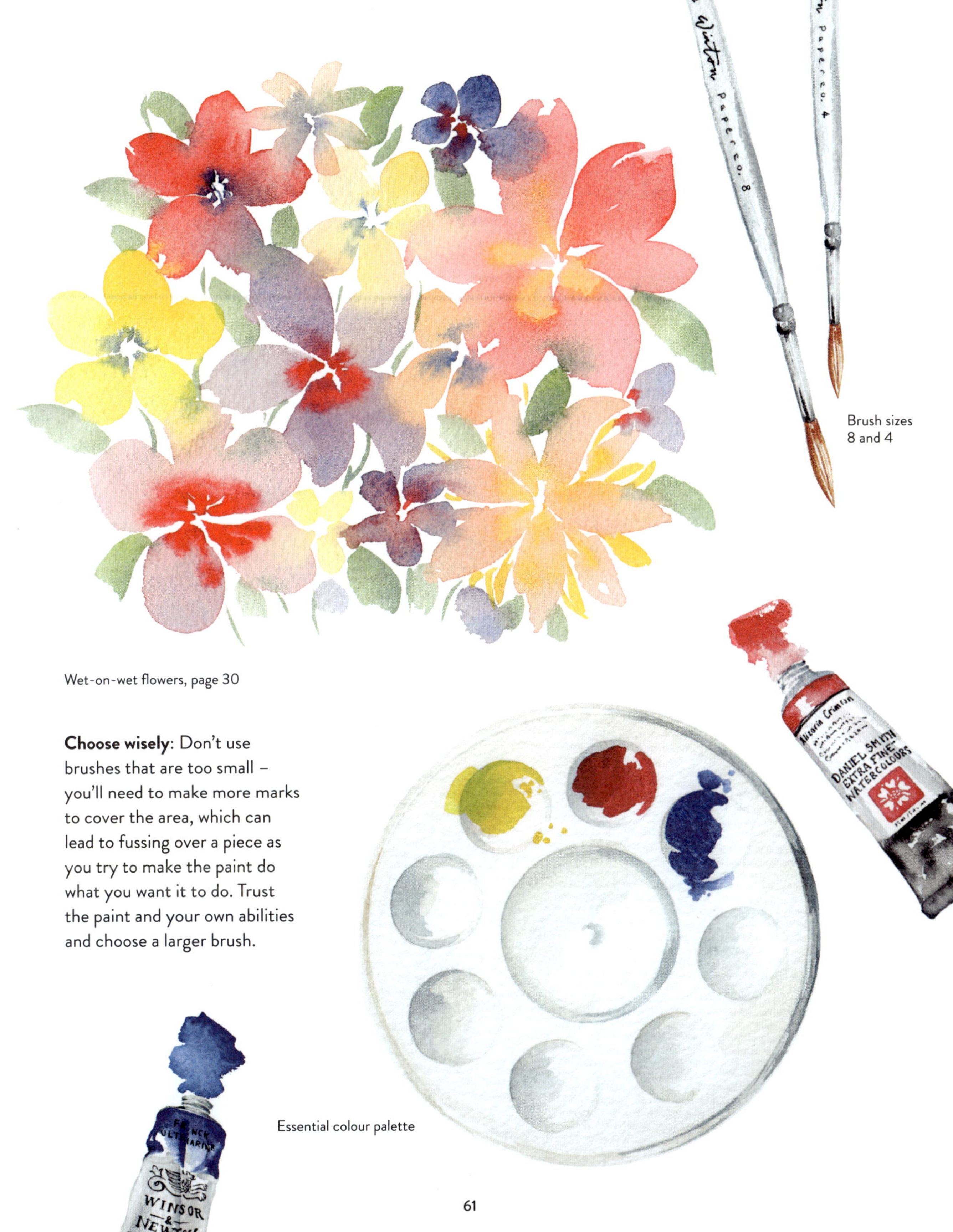

Brush sizes
8 and 4

Wet-on-wet flowers, page 30

Choose wisely: Don't use
brushes that are too small –
you'll need to make more marks
to cover the area, which can
lead to fussing over a piece as
you try to make the paint do
what you want it to do. Trust
the paint and your own abilities
and choose a larger brush.

Essential colour palette

Taking Your Painting Further

'I want to get better at painting' is something we've all said.

BUT WHAT IS 'BETTER'?
How to get better at painting is a huge question, and the list of answers is even bigger: Get better at colour mixing, brush control, texture, water control, composition, technical accuracy, expressive fluidity, mastering different materials...

In a one-hour session, you won't tick off every 'better' goal on your list. One hour isn't long enough to tell the story of your creativity; it is one tiny – but vital – step on a meandering journey which will have plenty of scenic routes and diversions. I'm not sure if we're ever meant to cross the finish line – I certainly haven't. I still make a point of trying to learn something new in my artistic practice every day.

Can you focus on one thing in that hour? Swatching colours on a page, discovering all the marks your brushes can make, line work, shadows, colour mixing? Once you narrow down your focus, the fog of overwhelm will lift and allow you to see a little more clearly.

You're partway through a book full of tutorials and techniques on watercolour. You're doing so well! But don't forget to play. Alongside all the learning, make time for weird and wonky paintings with no plan. Try out, too, the little prompts you'll find accompanying many of these instructions. In doing so you will build your trust of the process and produce paintings beyond belief.

As our materials list broadens, remember the amazing things you have done with just three colours and a few brushes.

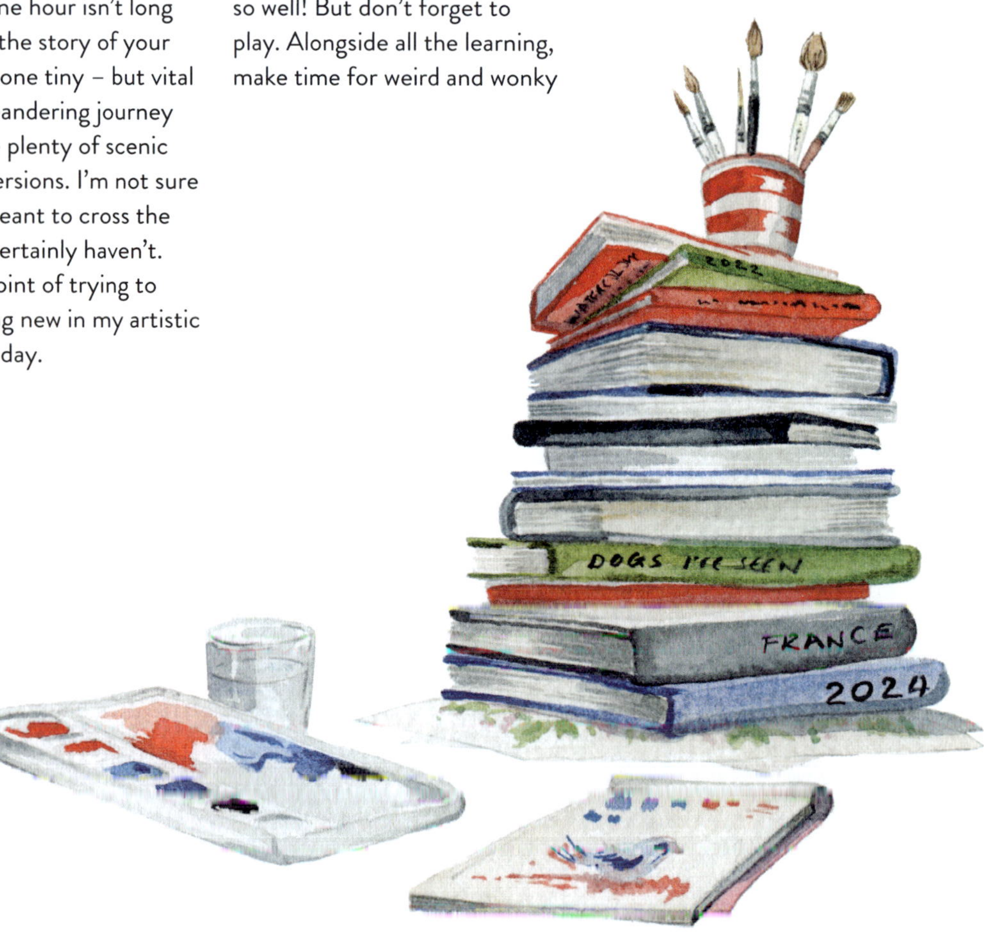

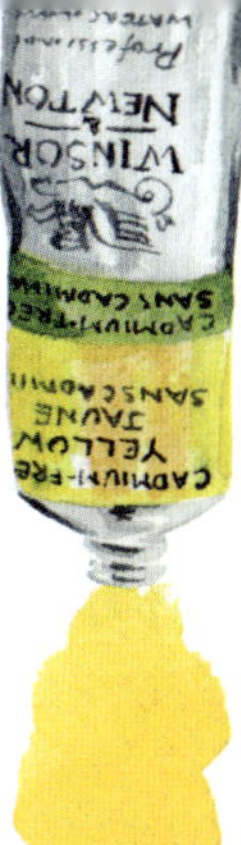

PAINT

Here is my expanded list of colours, grouped into colourful tones, and neutral and earth tones.

If you're looking to assemble a set of colours, there are plenty of ready-made watercolour sets that will offer you a good assortment. Here I'll be continuing with tubes of paint and a Loxley folding palette to house them.

Colourful tones

Opera Rose

Permanent Rose

Alizarin Crimson

Cadmium-Free Red

Pyrrol Orange

Cadmium-Free Orange

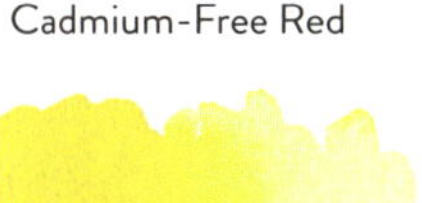

Lemon Yellow

Cadmium-Free Yellow

Green Gold

Sap Green

Prussian Blue

Aqua Green

Winsor Blue

Cerulean Blue

French Ultramarine

Imperial Purple

Neutral and earth tones

Moonglow

Payne's Grey

Ivory Black

Raw Umber

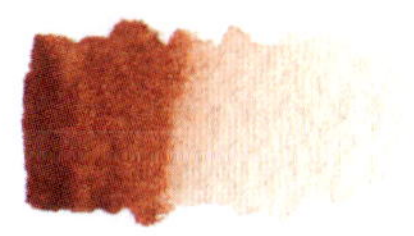

Burnt Sienna

Yellow Ochre

Buff Titanium

BRUSHES

Now we can add in some larger and smaller sizes to the pointed round brushes: 8, 6, 4, 2, 0, 2/0, 4/0.

Rigger brush: Also known as a liner brush, this has long, slender bristles which have revolutionized painting fine stems, leaf detail and animal whiskers.

Mop brush: Large and round, and able to hold plenty of water, it can put down a quick and even wash and is a brilliant addition to any kit when painting landscapes and larger areas of colour. I use a size 6.

Round brush: I use a large size 12 round for large washes with an element of control. Not as pointed as the pointed round but a great brush to have in your kit.

Flat brush: The flat ferrule and squared-off bristles are brilliant for precise corners and edges as well as watercolour washes.

There are many brushes not referenced in the tutorials that you might want to try:

Angled brush: This shape allows for quick transitions between thin and thick lines. Perfect for energetic strokes. If you like to work on an easel, an angled brush allows for greater control when working at an upright surface.

Filbert brush: This curved shape in a flat ferrule combines the characteristics of round and flat tips. It can create some really interesting petal shapes.

Quill brush: These are mop brushes that form a point, making very tiny precise strokes and huge flowing sweeps.

Fan: This is a flat ferrule with a fan of splayed bristles, perfect for texture.

Dagger brush, wedge brush and cat's tongue: These are all brushes with differing lengths of bristle within the brush. They can hold lots of water and make very interesting marks on the paper.

Your brushes will last longer if you clean them thoroughly after use, and never leave them bristles down in a jar of water. The paint will flake off the handle of a brush left in water, making it uncomfortable to hold, not to mention the poor bristles being bent out of shape.

If you're trying out a brand-new brush, head to 'how to paint' on page 16, and put the brush through its paces to find its strengths and weaknesses.

PAPER

The projects in this book continue to be done entirely on cold-pressed (also called NOT) paper. I would also encourage you to invest in a sketchbook or two. I really like the Etchr: Perfect Sketchbook. It's rare to find a sketchbook with cold-pressed 300gsm watercolour paper and it can lie flat on an open page spread. Head to your nearest art store and have a good look at all the journals on offer and find the right one for you.

You can also get smooth hot-pressed paper (great for fine detail work) and rough cold-pressed paper (good for textural, large washes).

Stretching paper: If you work with plenty of water, your paper may buckle. You can prevent this by taping the edges down with masking tape or going one step further and stretching it. To stretch it, soak the paper in clear water. Lay it out on a board and tape it down with gummed brown paper tape. The paper will shrink as it dries, but as it will be held taut by the tape, it will result in a flat surface, ready for watery painting.

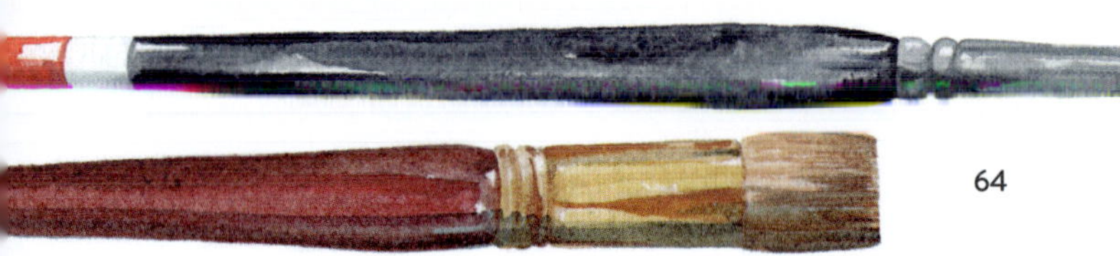

PALETTE

When using more colours, it's
a good idea to find some extra
palette space. I have a few
ceramic plates on hand in addition
to my Loxley folding palette.

To clean or not to clean your palette

If you can bear to leave the mixing
areas of your palette untouched,
you will find lots of wonderful
tones to use in future paintings.
I have one ceramic palette that
I keep clean for fresh mixes and
another (which also houses the
paint) that I keep uncleaned. This
works wonderfully.

WATER JAR

If you've been working with one
jar, try adding a second to see
if you can keep one jar of water
cleaner for longer. Dip the paint-
covered brush in one jar, rinse it
as well as you can and then use
the other jar for a clean dip of the
brush before picking up a
new colour.

PENCILS AND ERASERS

You can buy water-soluble
graphite pencils that dissolve
when wet. I choose to use a
regular HB pencil, working as
lightly as possible, as I like to keep
an eye on the guidelines for as
long as possible. If my drawings
are too heavy, rolling lightly with

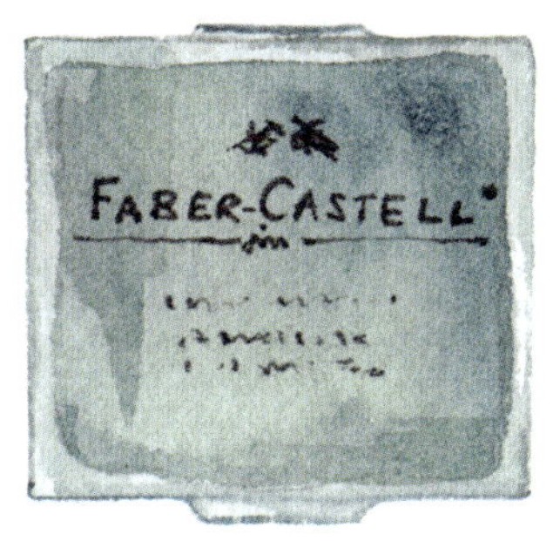

a Faber-Castell Kneadable Art
Eraser (before applying paint)
leaves a faint pencil line. Once
the pencil is painted over, I use a
regular hard Koh-I-Noor eraser
for one last rub-out of any
visible pencil.

PENS

On occasion I've enjoyed
scribbling a pen sketch and adding
a loose wash of watercolour
to quickly document a subject
matter's colours and movement.
I love to use the water-resistant
Daler-Rowney fineliner pens.

MASKING FLUID

Art masking fluid is a yellow-
tinted latex mix which can be
painted on paper and over dry
washes of watercolour to preserve
layers which can be revealed
later. I use Winsor & Newton Art
Masking Fluid. You will want to
allocate a brush just for applying
masking fluid as it won't be fit for
purpose afterwards. Alternatively
you can buy masking fluid
applicators.

COMPASS

This is a very useful addition for
smooth curves and circles.

RULER AND SET SQUARE

Every now and then we need
to draw a horizon line for a
landscape or a right angle.

WASHI TAPE

This is used either to mark out
a crisp area for painting or to
keep a piece of paper anchored
to the desk.

PAPER TOWEL

In the studio I always place my
palette on the edge of a piece of
paper towel to stop it from sliding
about and also to blot my brush
dry. When blotting a brush like
this, you will find hidden paint
lingering in the seemingly clean
bristles, warranting another swish
in the jar of water.

YOUR WORKSPACE

When painting at home, seat
yourself at a table in a space with
as much natural light as possible. I
am lucky enough to have a studio
with a rural view that constantly
revitalizes me. Feeling good in
your environment both mentally
and physically is so important.

Colour Blending

Now that you have a broader range of colours to choose from it's a great idea to get to know these new hues in your palette. Use the mixing guides on page 28 to swatch colours and see how they contrast from concentrated to diluted.

Colour-blend fruit

In the same way that we painted simple fruit shapes in 'How to paint' on page 20, fill a page with wet-on-wet fruit shapes. It's easier to muddy and overwork colours when you're incorporating dark and earthy tones, so keep your brush clean and refresh your jars of water more regularly.

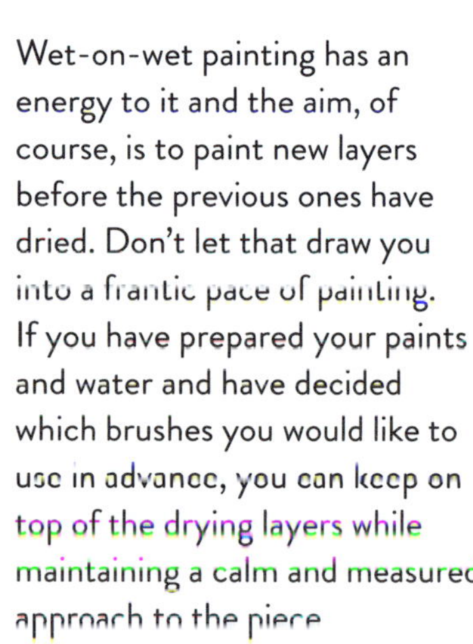

Wet-on-wet painting has an energy to it and the aim, of course, is to paint new layers before the previous ones have dried. Don't let that draw you into a frantic pace of painting. If you have prepared your paints and water and have decided which brushes you would like to use in advance, you can keep on top of the drying layers while maintaining a calm and measured approach to the piece.

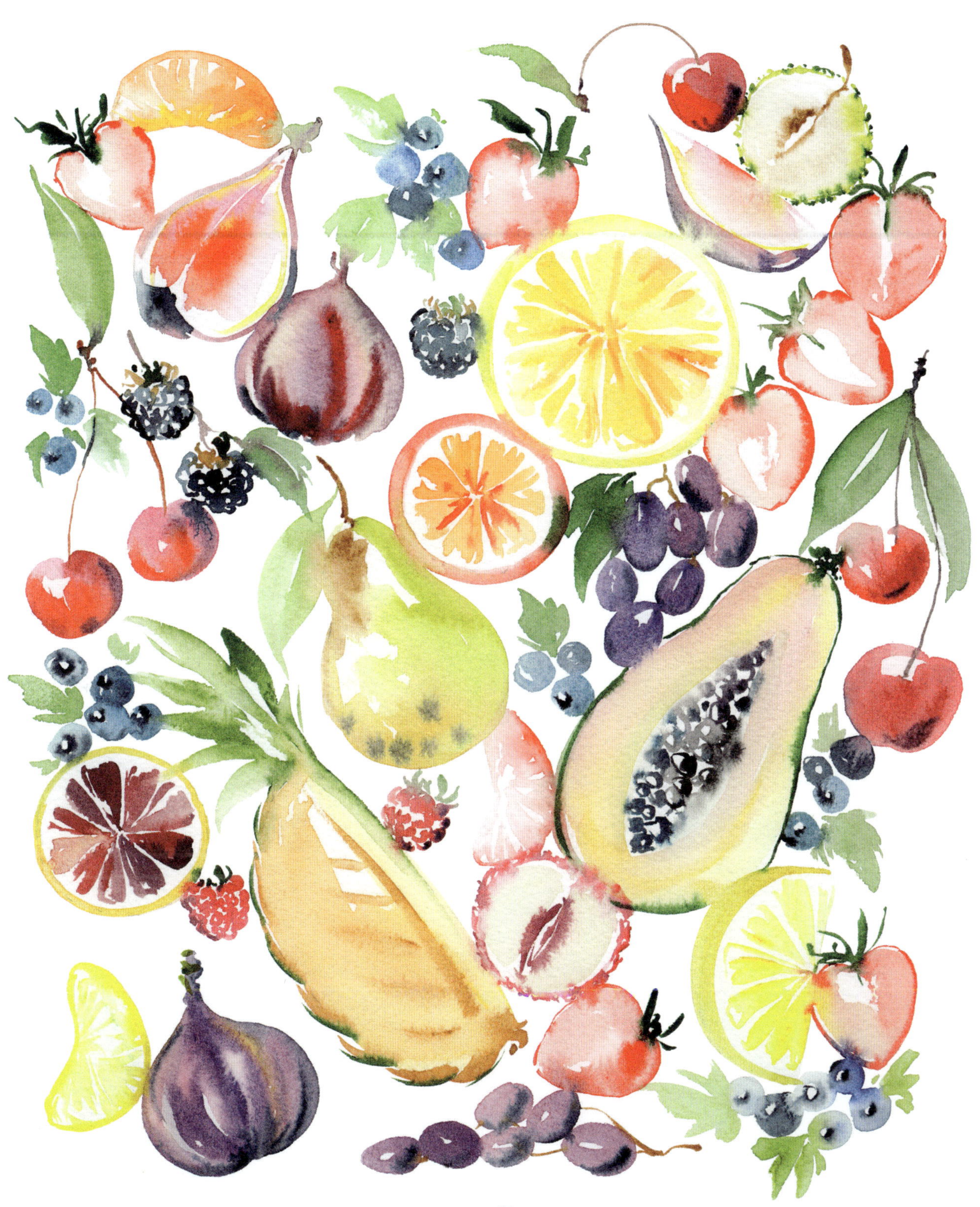

Drawing then Painting

I view pencil drawings as the supporting act for my watercolour paintings. If your pencil drawing includes every single detail, your watercolour painting is in danger of being reduced to mere colouring in, which inhibits the painting style and leads to overworking.

Level
Beginner

You will need
HB pencil, soft and hard erasers, paints in your choice of colours

Can you look at an object and simplify it into shapes and lines?
A pared-back drawing of a cat, for example, will give you the basic body shape as well as plenty of motion by curving, squashing and elongating those same shapes for different poses.

The most important thing to remember is everything is interconnected. Each line or shape you draw provides a clue to finding the next piece of the puzzle. This cat drawing is the same method I use to create all four-legged animals, using uneven circle shapes for the torso and hips. These are then connected by a spine line which elongates to a tail at one end and the neck at the other. The tummy undercarriage line helps us find the legs.

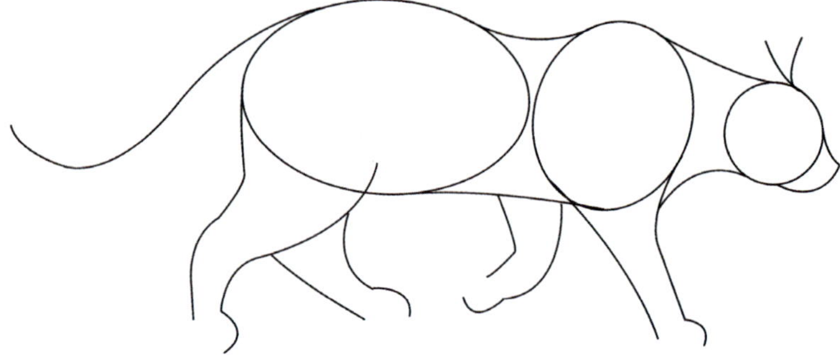

Once you have this very basic block shape, you can flesh it out, following the natural curves of the ovals to produce legs, ears and tail. Now let your watercolour painting create the unique character of the animal.

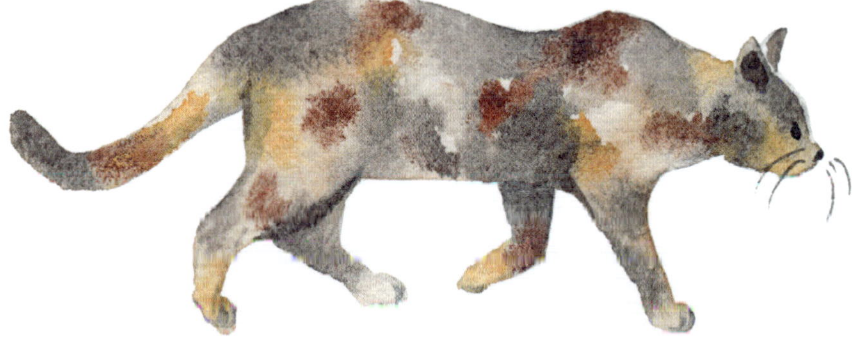

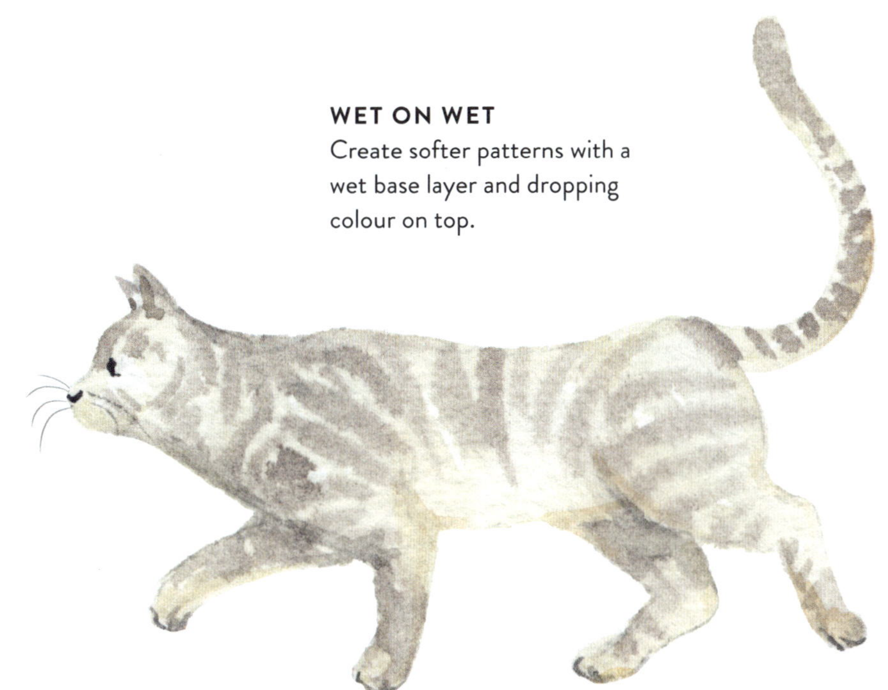

WET ON WET
Create softer patterns with a wet base layer and dropping colour on top.

FUZZY WET ON WET
Wetting the whole page can create amazing fur detail. Check out the washes instructions on page 37 to see how the wetness of your paper will affect the feathering of the paint.

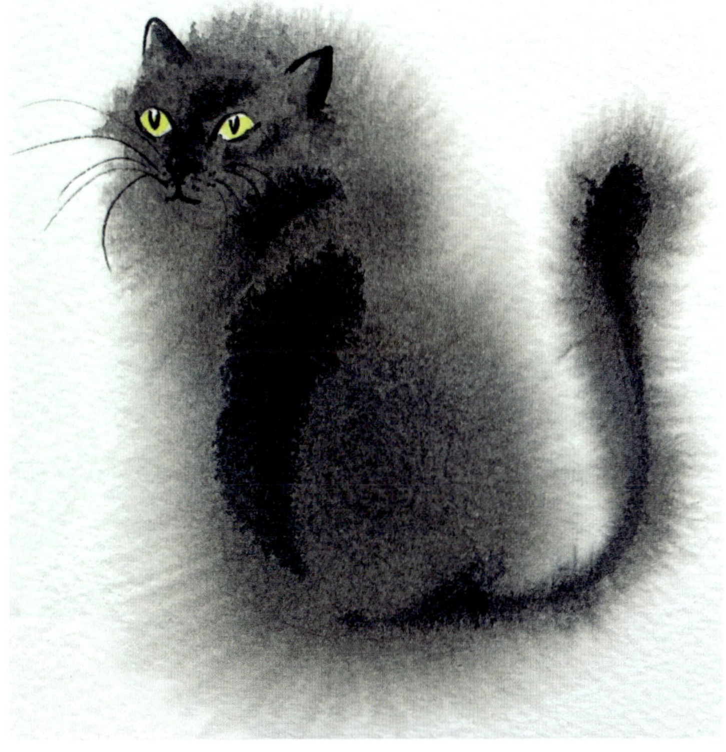

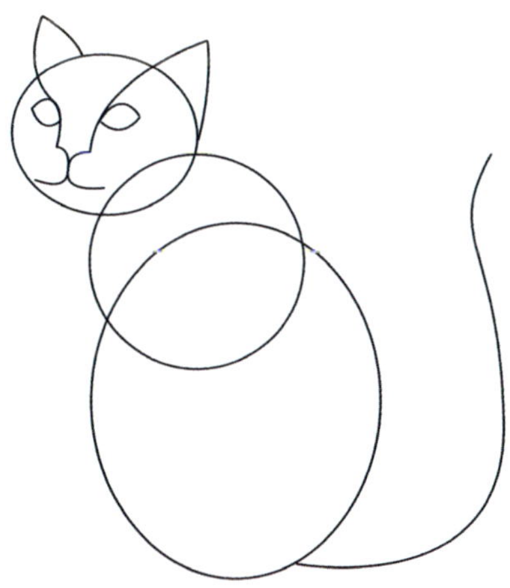

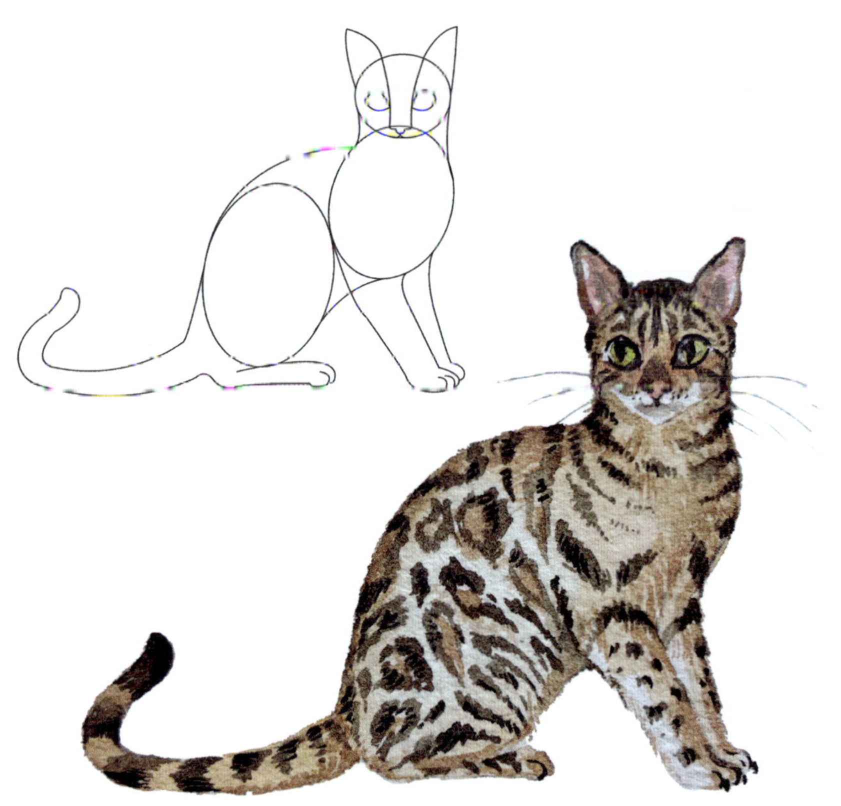

LAYERED

Layer up colours to create a detailed fur pattern as in this Bengal cat.

Both the fuzzy cat and Bengal cat give a good example of a simple face drawing: again everything is interconnected. The ears curve up from the side of the skull, and the inner ears extend down to make the side of the nose and then the muzzle. The eyes sit either side of those lines.

GLAZES

For a sleek coat, try glazing the contours of the body to flesh out your simple drawing.

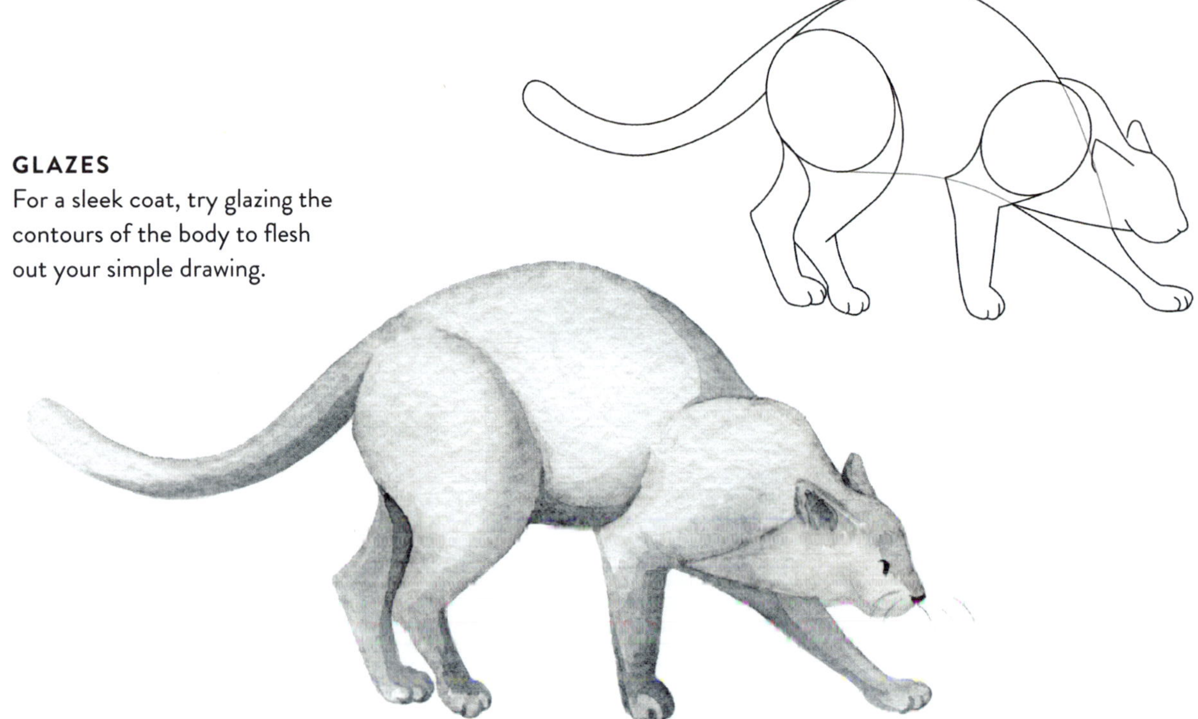

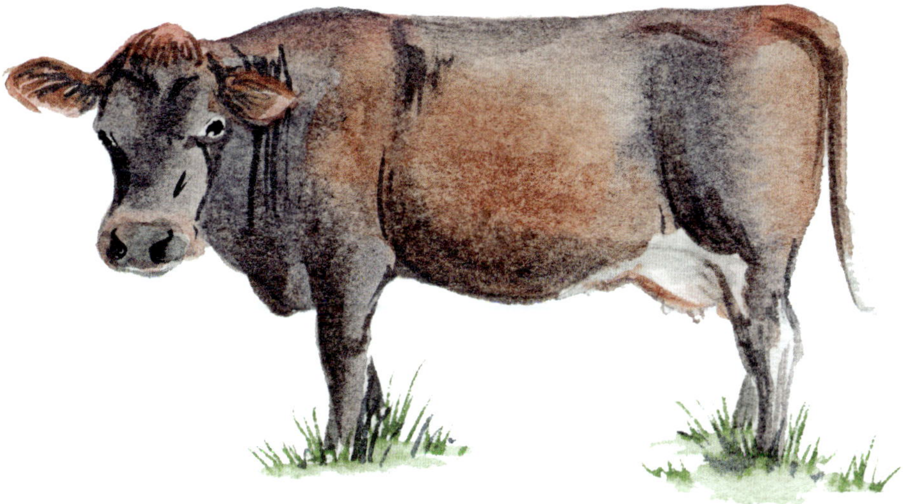

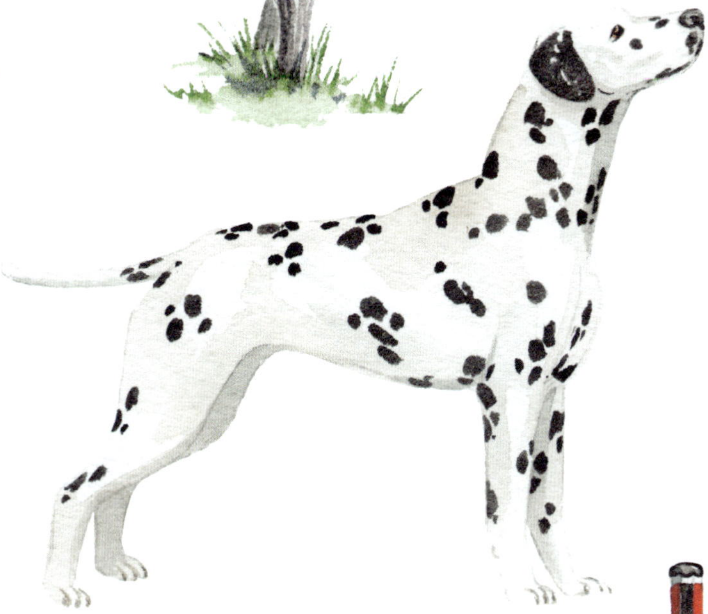

CAN YOU ERASE PENCIL AFTER YOU'VE PAINTED OVER IT?

YES! If you follow these top tips:

• Use a soft or HB pencil and draw lightly so you don't score the paper with your lines.

• Draw the simplest, most minimal line drawing you can.

• Before you paint, roll a soft eraser over the pencil lines to fade them out.

• After painting your basic wash stage (everything has at least one layer on it) and allowing it to become bone dry, rub out visible pencil with a hard eraser.

• If you've followed the steps, there shouldn't be any visible pencil, but after finishing the painting, let it dry completely and do one last rub with the hard eraser.

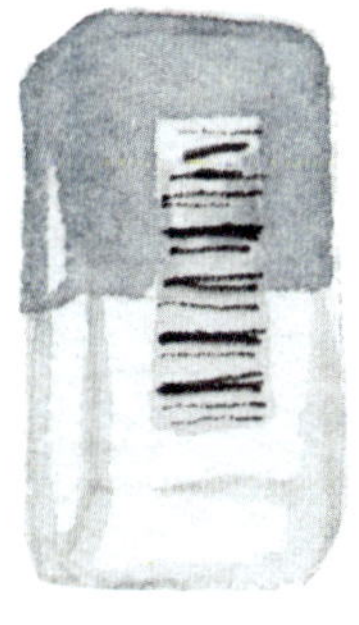

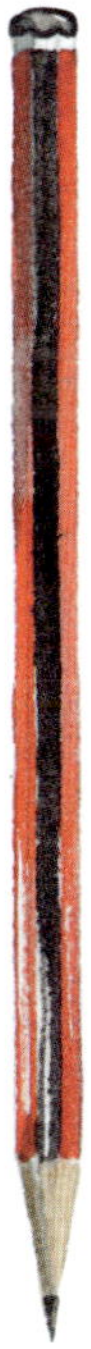

Loose Watercolour: Drawing with the Brush

For successful watercolour paintings we want a happy medium where control meets flow. For me this comes with warming up my brain, my brush and my hand with some low-stakes painting (playing on a page with no plan) before embarking on my project.

After filling that practice page I'll look down and be surprised to see all kinds of familiar shapes, lovely flowers, animals and so on. It's as if I was painting in what is known as the loose watercolour style.

Loose watercolour painting is a style that can intimidate and confuse people: why does it look so simple – even childish at times – and yet is so difficult to master?

Essentially, loose watercolour painting is about having an instinct for shape and form using as few brushstrokes as possible; boiling down the subject matter into a more expressive shape.

I call it drawing with the brush.

Drawing with the brush is a core feature of how I like to paint – be it loose or detailed. If I can keep my pencil lines to a minimum and instead use the brush to create as much of the shape as possible, it will result in vibrant colours and seamless blends. Too many brushstrokes can lead to overworking a piece and muddy colours.

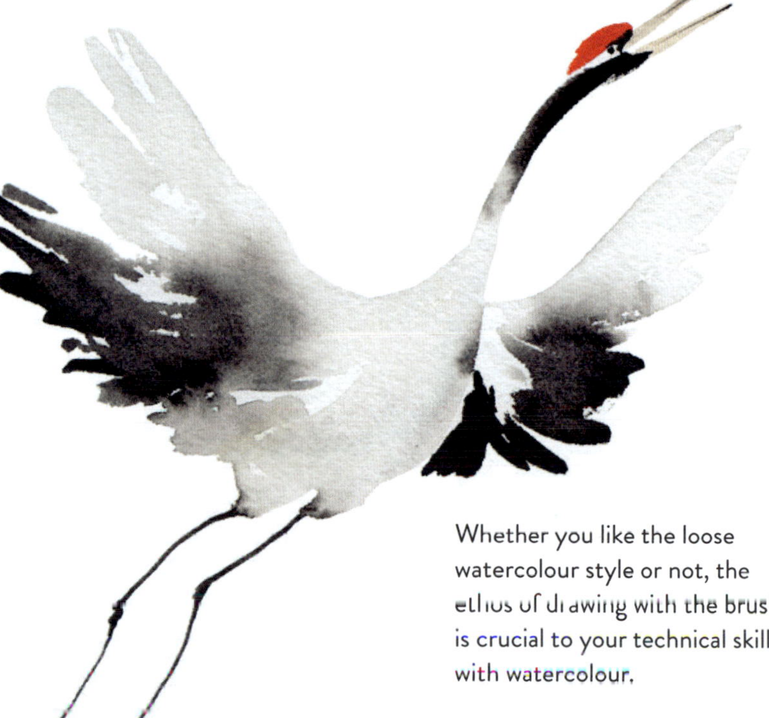

Whether you like the loose watercolour style or not, the ethos of drawing with the brush is crucial to your technical skill with watercolour.

TUTORIAL: Sweet Peas with Loose Lines

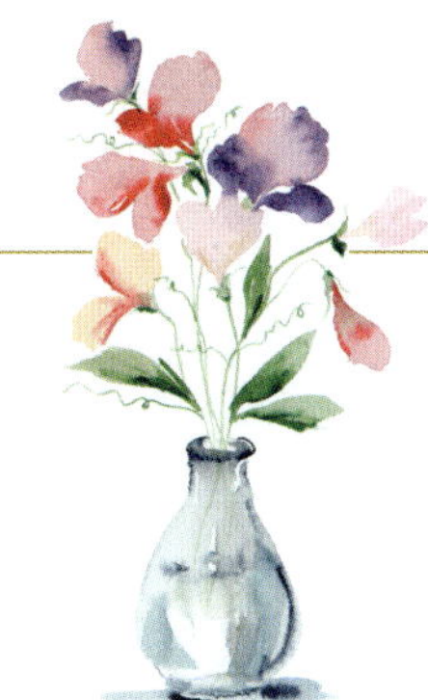

The petals, leaves and stems of sweet peas have a wonderful wispy and wobbly quality, perfect to be painted loose. My instructions are minimal so that you can paint instinctively after looking through the steps.

Level
Beginner

Colours
Alizarin Crimson
Aqua Green
Cadmium-Free Orange
Cadmium-Free Yellow
Imperial Purple
Green Gold
Opera Rose
Payne's Grey
Sap Green

Brushes
Pointed round size 8
(or your large brush of choice)

Constantly swapping brushes is another barrier to going with the flow of a loose watercolour piece. This vase of flowers has been painted with a single brush. A large pointed round brush should be able to make a fine line with the point, but look closely and you'll see how the stems wobble and change thickness; this is all part of the charm of loose watercolour painting. Challenge yourself to pick a brush and stick with it.

Single stroke
Try painting a petal shape with a size 8 (or larger) pointed round brush: load the brush with plenty of coffee-consistency paint, press and fan the bristles out on the page and twist the brush as you drag it down and off the page. It will leave you with a lovely ballooning petal shape that wiggles off into a fine point.

Outline and fill
Try to recreate that petal by painting the outline and colouring it in. It may not look all that different but the time this second technique takes will reduce the chances for a seamless wet-on-wet colour blend. It also runs the risk of leaving a hard-edge outline and causing the colour to feel flat and overworked. It just doesn't feel right.

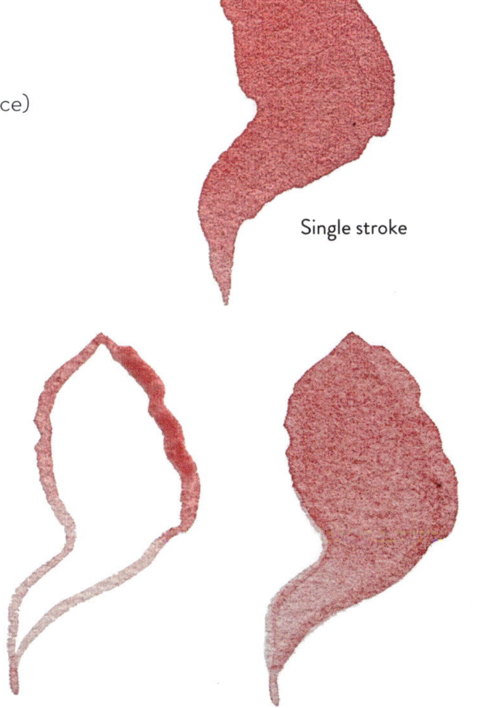

Single stroke

Outline and fill

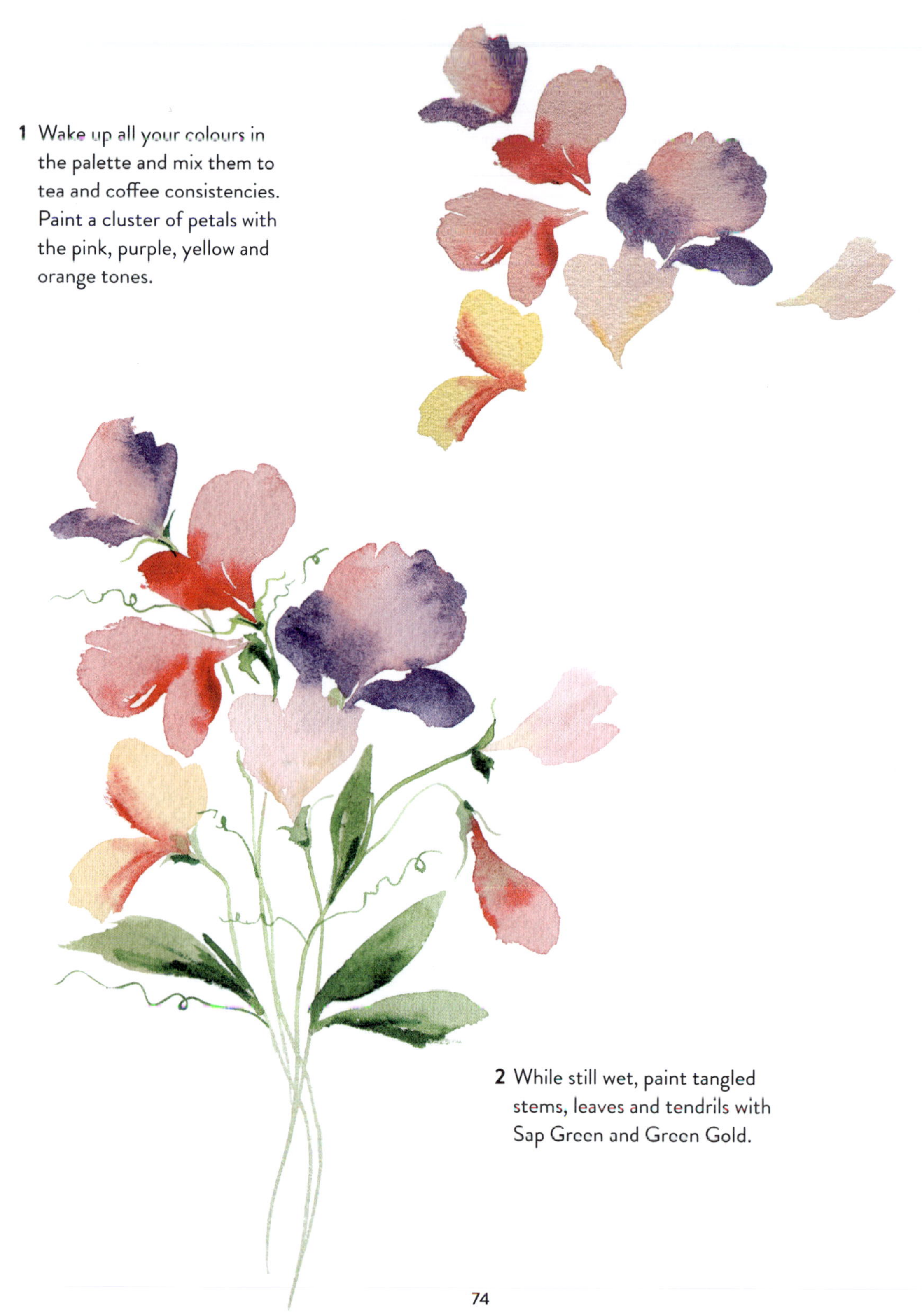

1 Wake up all your colours in the palette and mix them to tea and coffee consistencies. Paint a cluster of petals with the pink, purple, yellow and orange tones.

2 While still wet, paint tangled stems, leaves and tendrils with Sap Green and Green Gold.

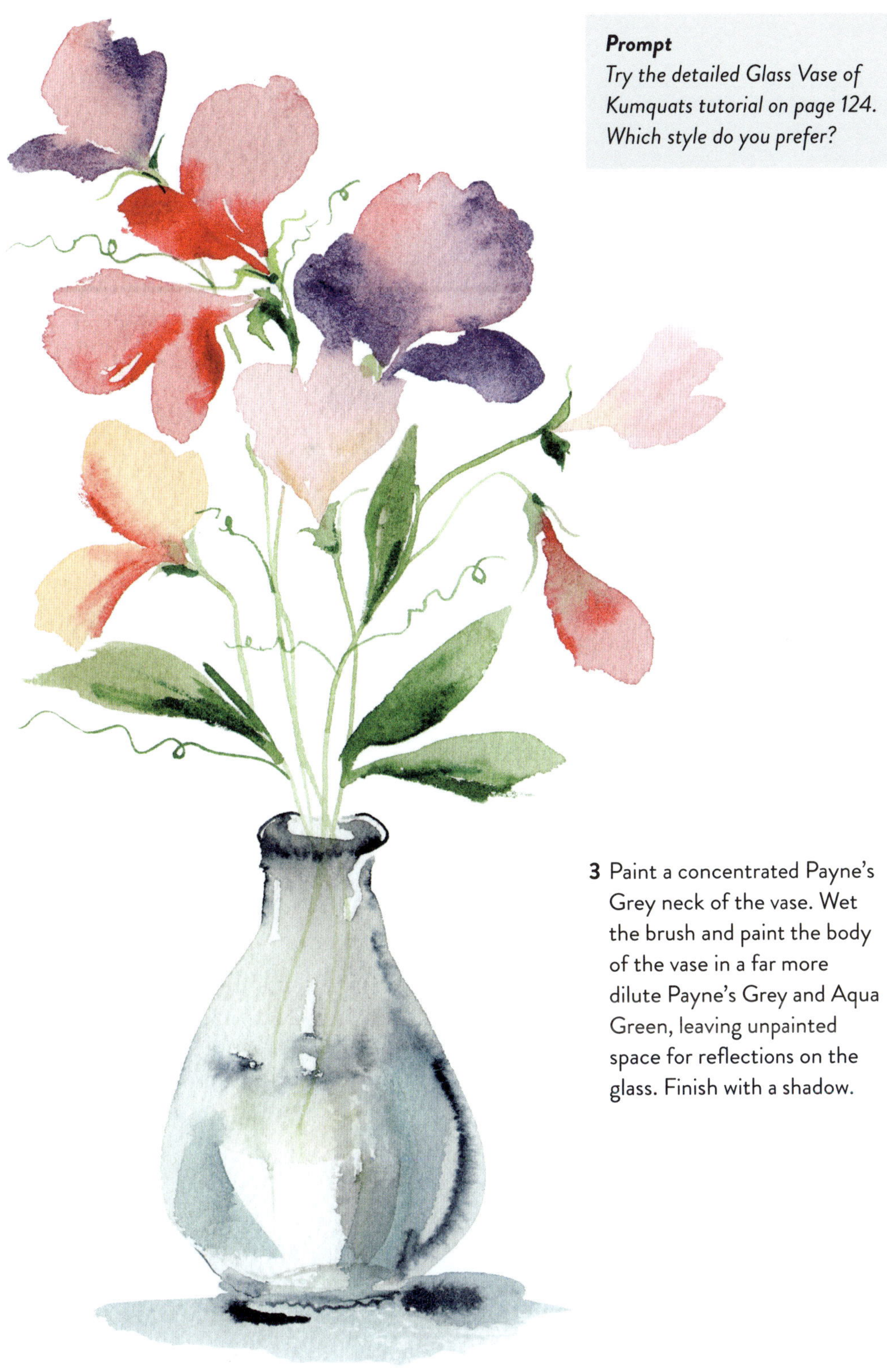

3 Paint a concentrated Payne's
Grey neck of the vase. Wet
the brush and paint the body
of the vase in a far more
dilute Payne's Grey and Aqua
Green, leaving unpainted
space for reflections on the
glass. Finish with a shadow.

Finding Your Style

Watercolour is a wonderfully diverse medium but the choice of styles it offers can be overwhelming. Some watercolour artists are recognized for a particular style but in the early stages of your watercolour journey try not to wed yourself to one way of painting – it can stunt creative development.

Exploring your painting style shouldn't narrow down your options; it's about experimenting with different means and mediums with the aim of exploring all the ways you can put paint to paper. In time, a style might emerge that feels right for you.

Choose something you can paint fairly easily: an object, an animal, a plant. Gather your paints, different brushes, and even some pens and pencils and play.

The tomato has popped up already in this book, so it seems like a good subject to play with.

Compare extremes: Use your largest and smallest brushes, painting slow and detailed and then as fast as you can. Try unexpected colour palettes and art styles.

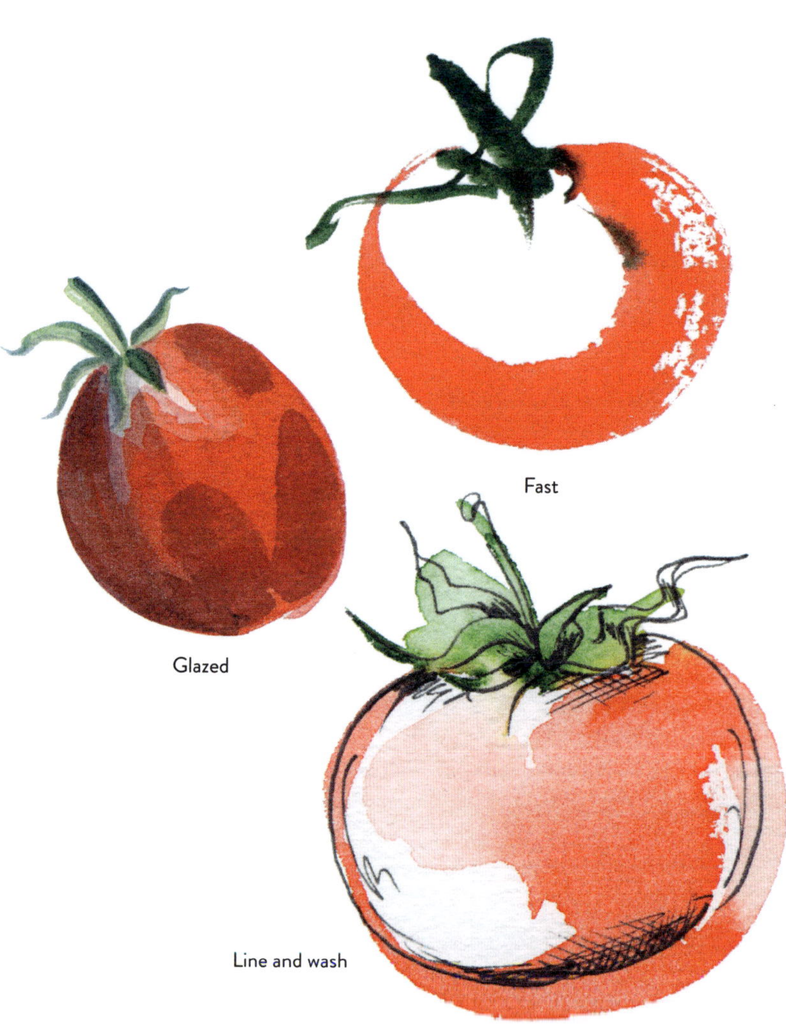

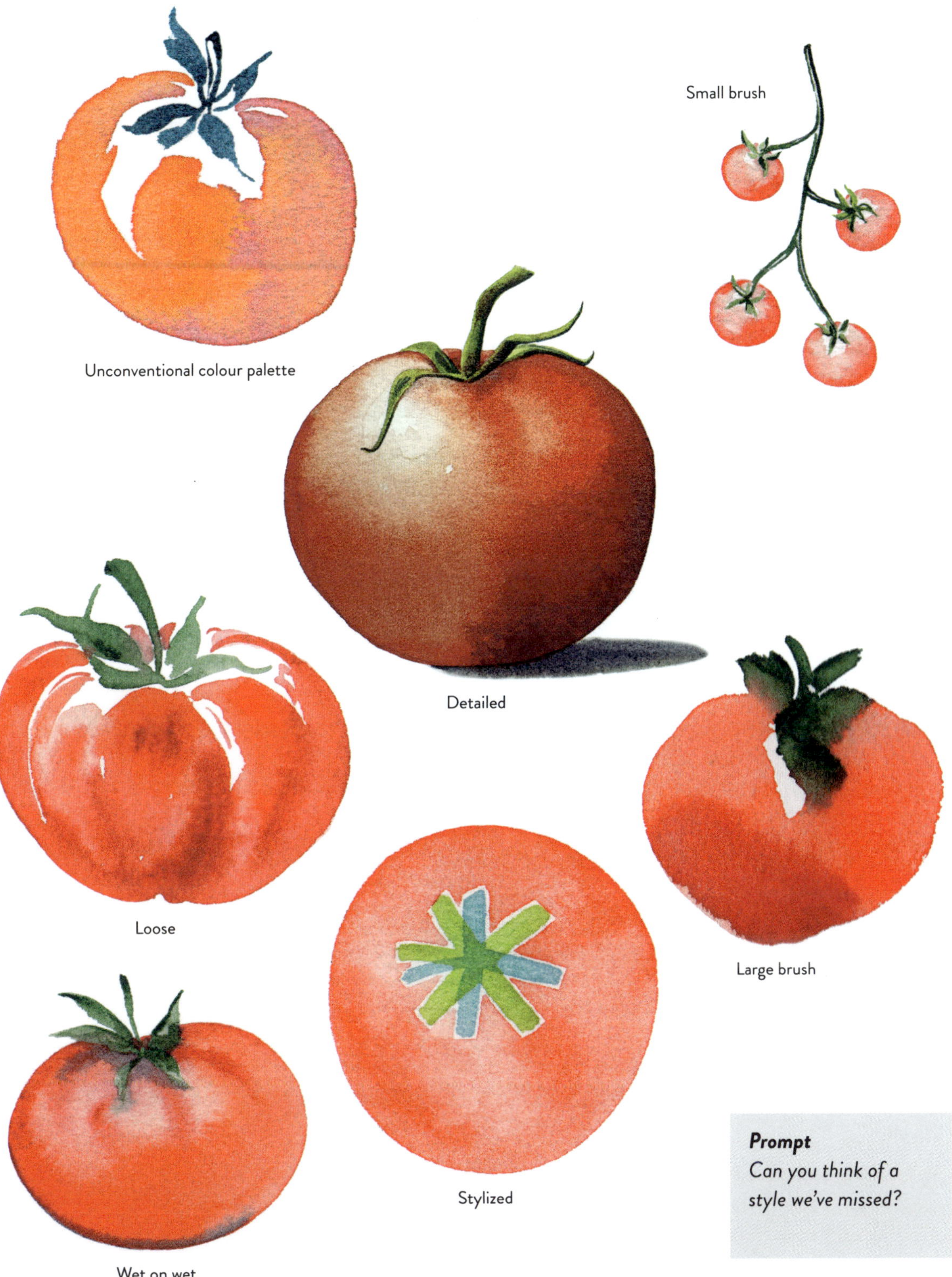

Unconventional colour palette
Small brush
Detailed
Loose
Large brush
Stylized
Wet on wet

Simple vs Detailed Trees

We learn the basics of watercolour because sometimes the basics are all we need. In addition to establishing your own painting style, it's worth remembering that there are times when simplicity is key.

I find that when a painting isn't working, the common reason is that I've overcomplicated things – I'm trying too hard! Success doesn't have to mean hours of toil and technical skill. Beauty often lies in the painting that took you 30 seconds and five sweeps of the brush.

The same tree can be taken in very different directions purely by how much detail you choose to add. These are the choices I made that led to two very different tree paintings.

SIMPLE TREE
A large (size 8) brush gives me voluminous, smooth foliage with looping strokes. The big brush can cover a large amount of distance, meaning I have enough time to paint wet-on-wet green accents before it dries.

A one-colour trunk matches the simplicity of the greenery and complements the piece as a whole. I've chosen to stop at this point. Its purposeful simplicity gives it charm.

Green Gold

Sap Green

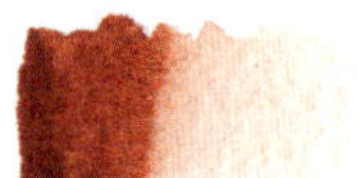

Burnt Sienna

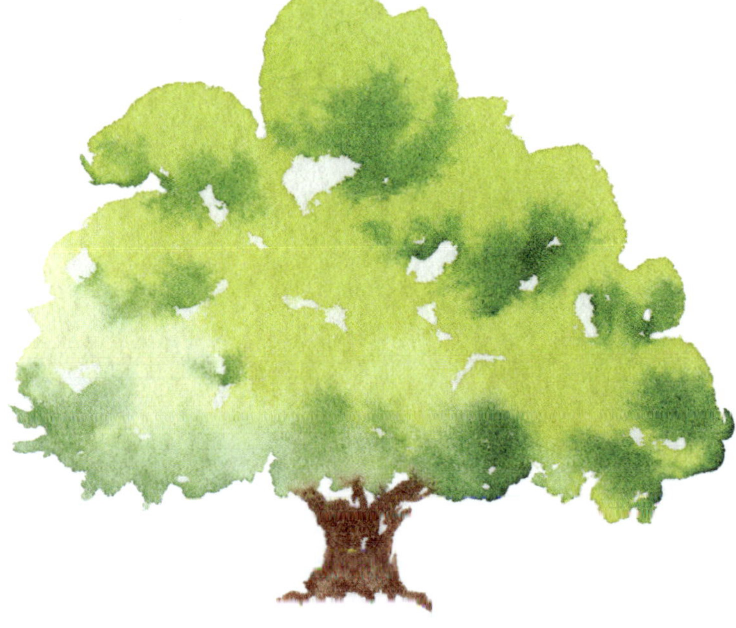

Size 8 brush

DETAILED TREE

I set out with the same colour but chose a much smaller brush (size 0). The smaller marks give a more realistic impression. Painting the leaves takes a lot longer, so the paint has almost dried by the time I've finished. I can get partial blends with the darker green but it's mainly a new textural layer.

I've established this painting has more detail and texture, so I'll paint the trunk with my small brush and add in a secondary lowlight colour. In every gap of foliage I paint a glimpse of branch and add a few more leaves here and there.

Finally, I add a glaze of dappled shadow to enhance the roundness of the shape and a shadow across the ground to place it in context.

There's a time and a place for both styles but it's wise to start your painting with a plan of which style you want to achieve.

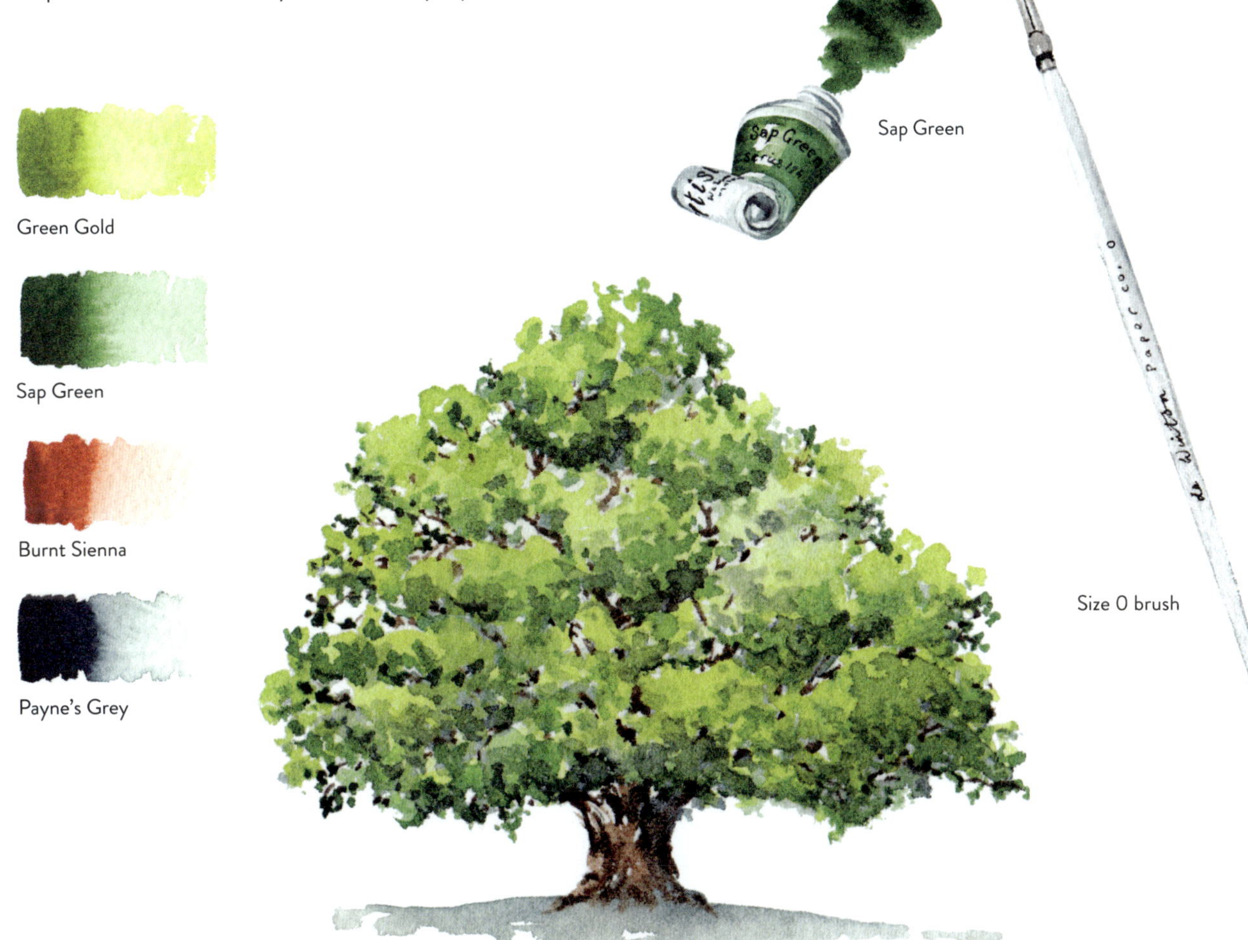

Green Gold

Sap Green

Burnt Sienna

Payne's Grey

Sap Green

Size 0 brush

Angled Flowers

The most natural and realistic-looking floral compositions will have flowers at a number of angles. It's vital to have the basic structure to ensure the petals are anchored into the middle regardless of whether you paint in a detailed or loose style.

Imagine holding a saucer with the circular indentation where the cup goes. Notice how the round saucer becomes oval shaped the more you tilt it away from you. This pairing of one circle centred inside the other is a perfect analogy of a flower face.

OPEN FACE

For an open-face flower, intersect the stem with a small circle for the flower centre. The larger circle indicates the outer tips of the petals.

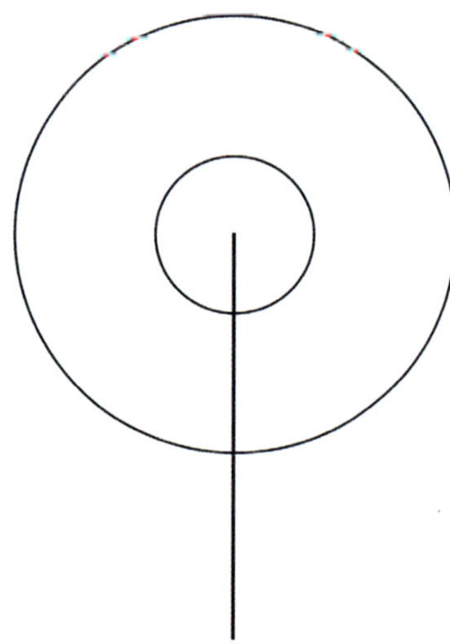

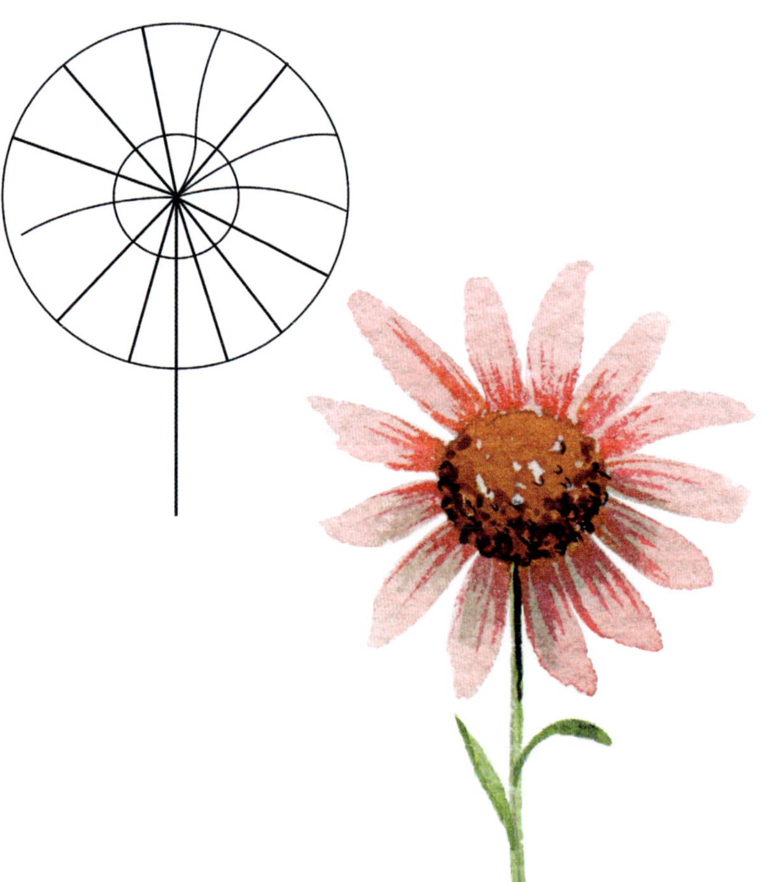

Draw radius lines from the central point to the outer circle for each petal. You won't see the petal lines within the central circle when painting but it's good for visualizing them. With this technique your petals will be anchored even if they curve and bend. You can then paint all of your petals in.

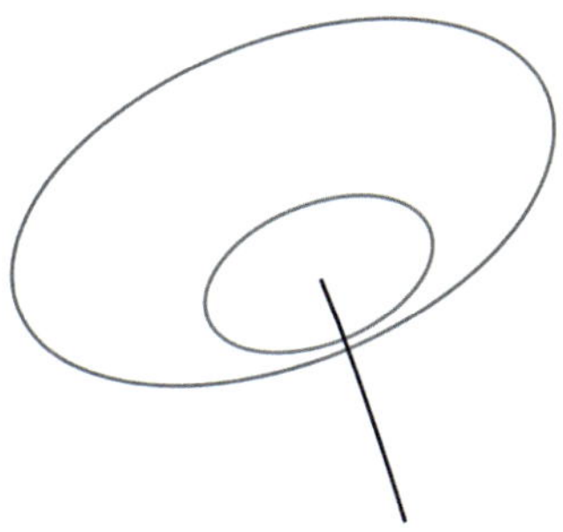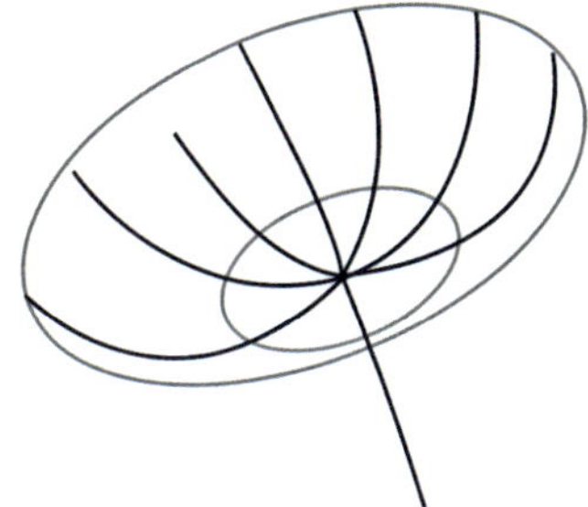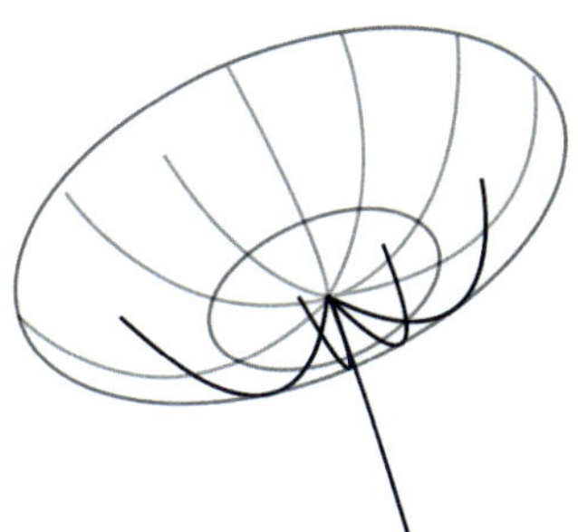

THREE-QUARTER ANGLE

As the flower tilts, the circles become ovals, still intersecting the stem and ending at the outer oval. Notice how this large oval sits closer to the base of the small oval.

This angle gives a 3D view of the petals. Draw radius lines curving from the central point to the outer oval on the far side of the flower.

The petals in the foreground are foreshortened: They have a tighter curve and a squashed appearance as they are growing in the direction of the viewer. Draw radius lines curving from the central point to the outer oval and bouncing up.

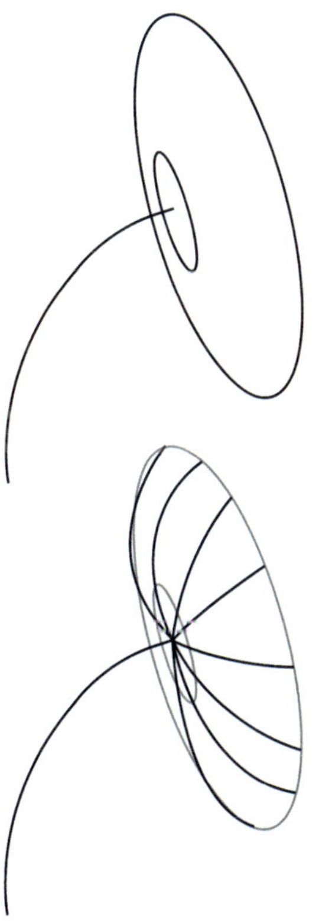

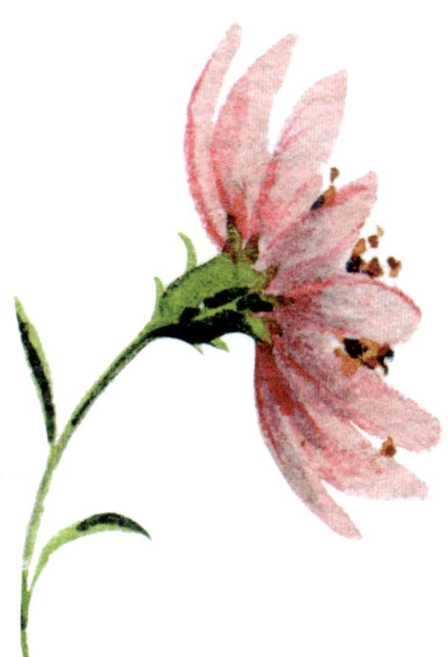

SIDE ON

As the flower tilts further, the circles become flatter ovals.

At such a tight angle, you're only going to see the petals on the near side of the flower. Draw radius lines curving from the central point to the outer tips on the near side of the flower.

Level
Beginner

Colours
Burnt Sienna
Cadmium-Free Orange
Cadmium-Free Yellow
Cerulean Blue
Imperial Purple
Payne's Grey
Sap Green
Yellow Ochre

Brushes
Pointed round sizes 0, 4/0

You will also need
HB pencil, soft and hard erasers

Mixes
Petal mix: Imperial Purple (50%)
and Cerulean Blue (50%)
Stem mix: Payne's Grey (30%),
Burnt Sienna (30%), Sap Green
(40%)

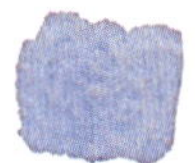

Petal　　Stem

Prompt
*Paint your favourite flower
using this angling technique.
Can you use this technique to
draw and paint other objects?*

1 Draw a sprig of stems and
flowers with concentric circles/
ovals for flower centre and petal
radius. Roll with a kneadable
eraser to fade the drawing.

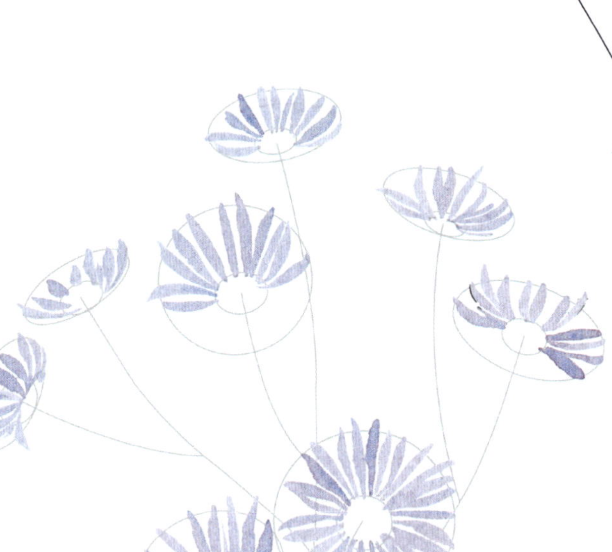

2 With your size 0 brush paint
slender petal-mix (coffee-
consistency) petals all the way
around the open-face flowers,
around the back side of the
angled flowers, and across
the visible half of the side-on
flower. Allow to dry.

3 Paint the foreshortened petals around the front side of the angled flowers. While they dry, paint in slender stems and sepals in stem mix.

4 Use your size 4/0 brush to paint tiny C-curve leaves of Sap Green up and down the stems. With your size 0 brush dab cream consistency Cadmium-Free Yellow flower centres. While still wet, dab Cadmium-Free Orange and Yellow Ochre around the edges. Dome the shape of the angled flower centres.

5 Once dry, add a few lowlights of milk-consistency petal mix to help define certain petals that need it. With your size 4/0 brush dab cream-consistency Burnt Sienna around the edges of the flower centres, and finally dab some Payne's Grey along the edge of the lower half of the more open flower centres.

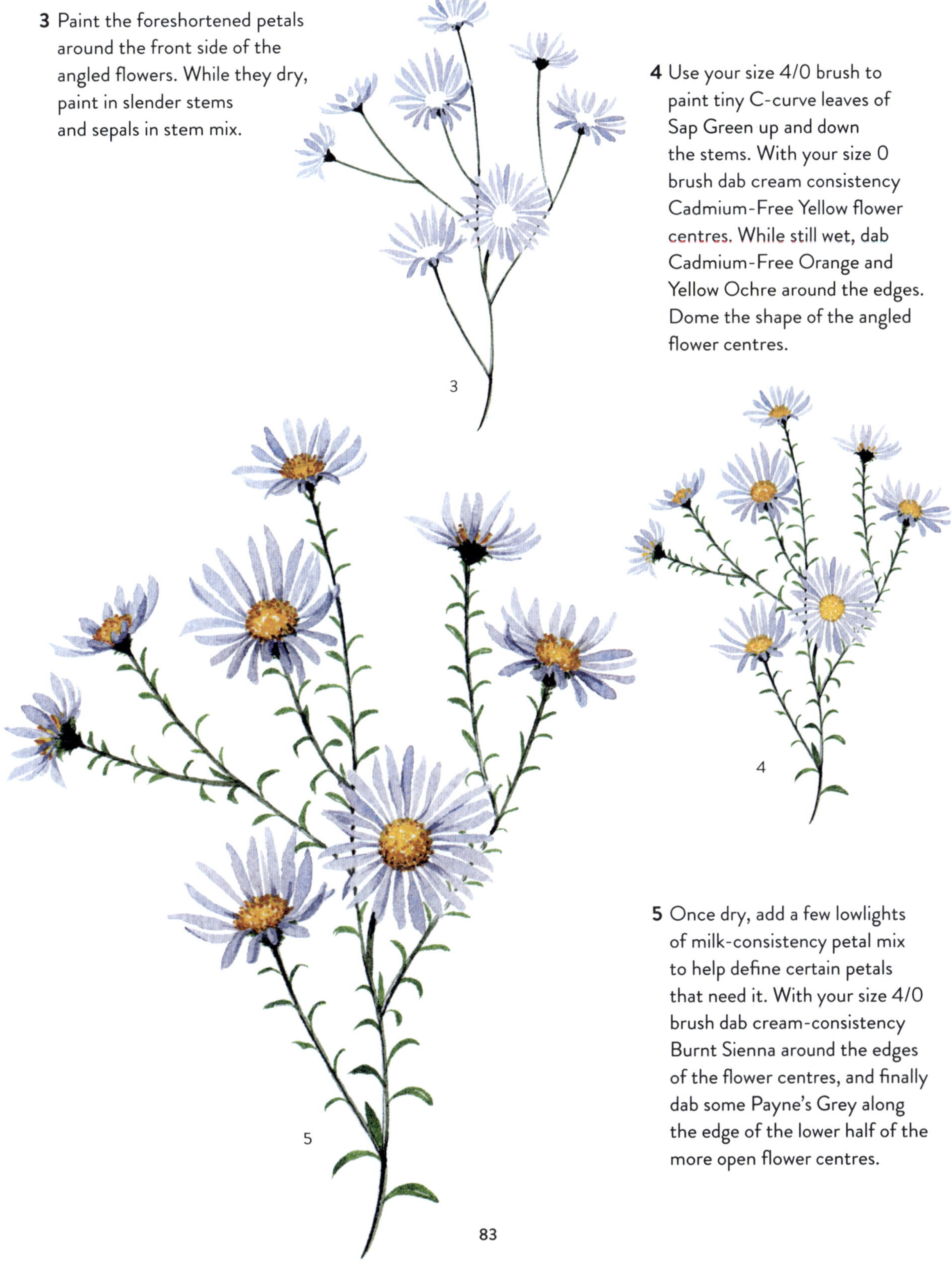

Layers

This cosmos begins with a light base layer and comes to life with a combination of detailed layers and glazes. I particularly love the unexpected green glaze that brings a luminosity to the petals. Keep your glazes transparent (tea, coffee) and your layers concentrated (milk, cream).

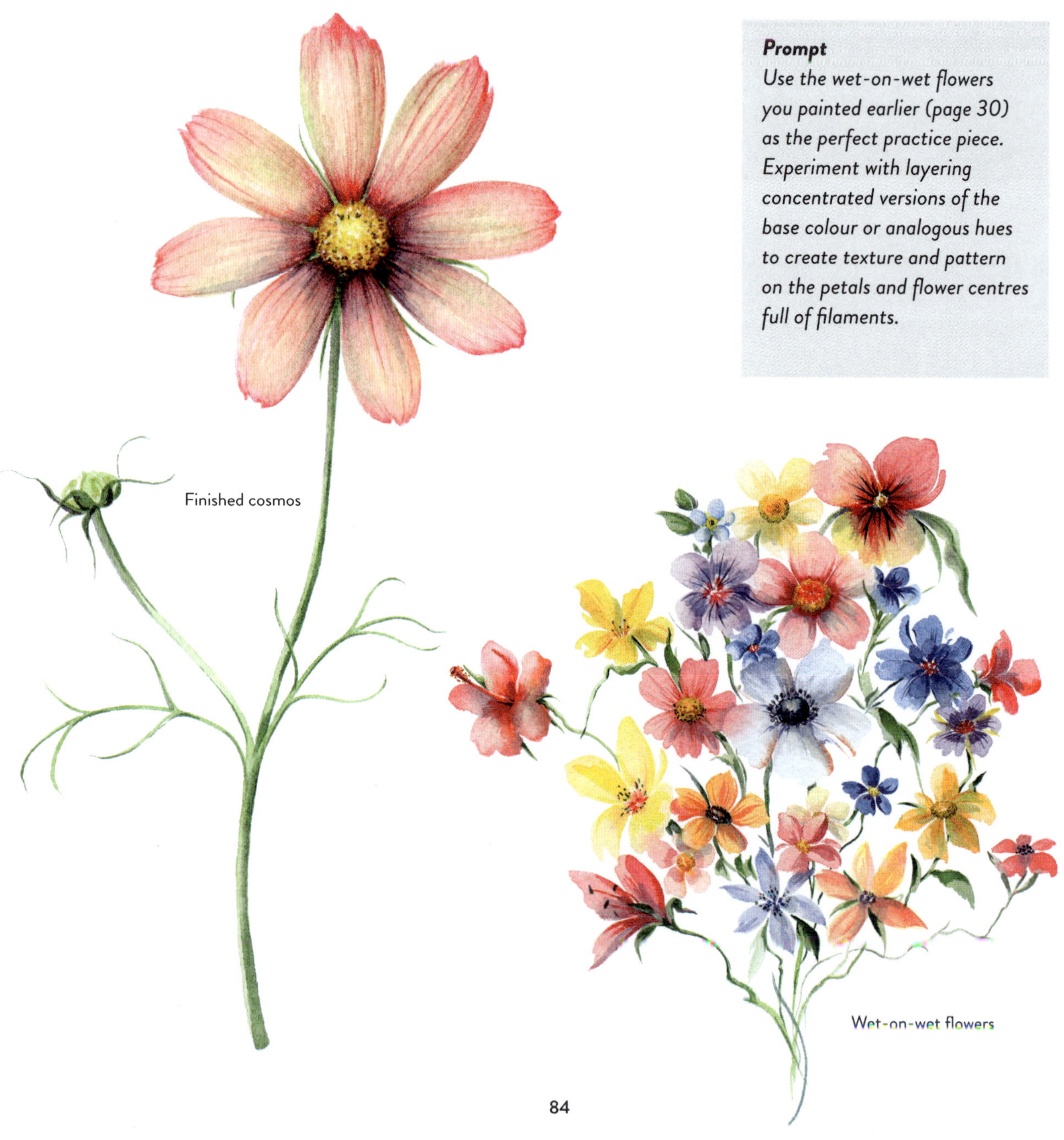

> **Prompt**
> Use the wet-on-wet flowers you painted earlier (page 30) as the perfect practice piece. Experiment with layering concentrated versions of the base colour or analogous hues to create texture and pattern on the petals and flower centres full of filaments.

Level
Intermediate

Colours
Alizarin Crimson
Burnt Sienna
Cadmium-Free Yellow
Green Gold
Payne's Grey
Permanent Rose
Sap Green
Yellow Ochre

Brushes
Pointed round sizes 2, 0, 4/0
Rigger size 0

You will also need
HB pencil, soft and hard erasers

Mixes
Petal mix: Alizarin Crimson (60%)
and Yellow Ochre (40%) (diluted)
Stem mix: Green Gold (50%) and
Sap Green (50%)
Shadow mix: Burnt Sienna (50%) and
Payne's Grey (50%)

Petal

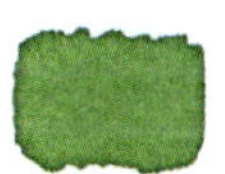
Stem

Shadow

1 Draw a stem and a small circle
for an open-face flower. It can
be useful to draw a larger circle
for the petals' outer tips. Roll
with a soft eraser to fade the
pencil.

2 Paint streaks of tea-consistency
petal mix with your size 2 brush
to create the cosmos petals.
Each petal should overlap into
the small centre circle but try
to keep them separated from
each other. Allow to dry.

3 Glaze streaks of petal mix
up and down the petals with
your size 0 brush to create
the creases (even with the
same paint consistency
they will be visible on a dry
background). Dab a layer
of Cadmium-Free Yellow in
the flower centre, and edge
with dabs of Yellow Ochre.
Allow to dry.

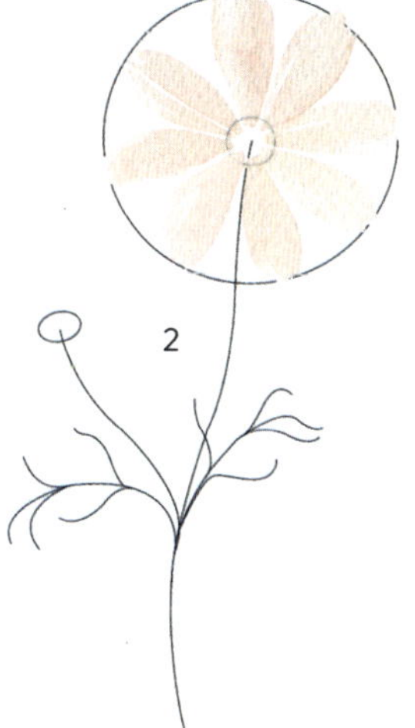

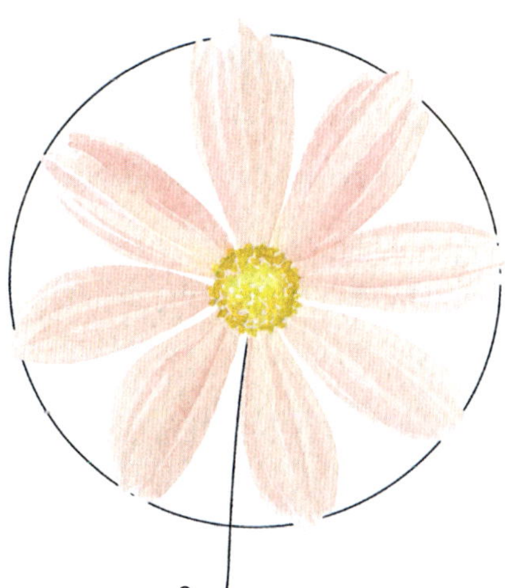

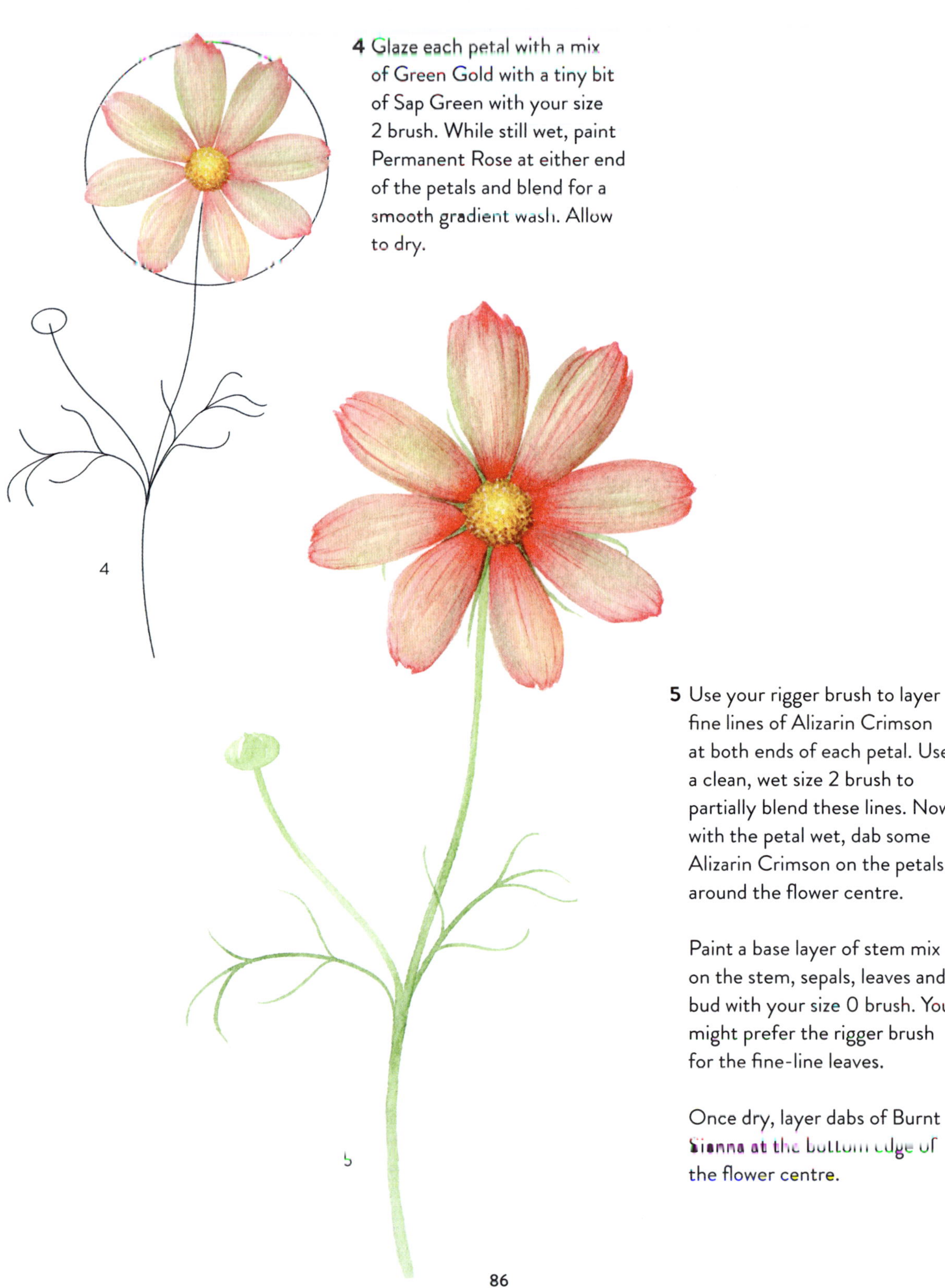

4 Glaze each petal with a mix of Green Gold with a tiny bit of Sap Green with your size 2 brush. While still wet, paint Permanent Rose at either end of the petals and blend for a smooth gradient wash. Allow to dry.

5 Use your rigger brush to layer fine lines of Alizarin Crimson at both ends of each petal. Use a clean, wet size 2 brush to partially blend these lines. Now with the petal wet, dab some Alizarin Crimson on the petals around the flower centre.

Paint a base layer of stem mix on the stem, sepals, leaves and bud with your size 0 brush. You might prefer the rigger brush for the fine-line leaves.

Once dry, layer dabs of Burnt Sienna at the bottom edge of the flower centre.

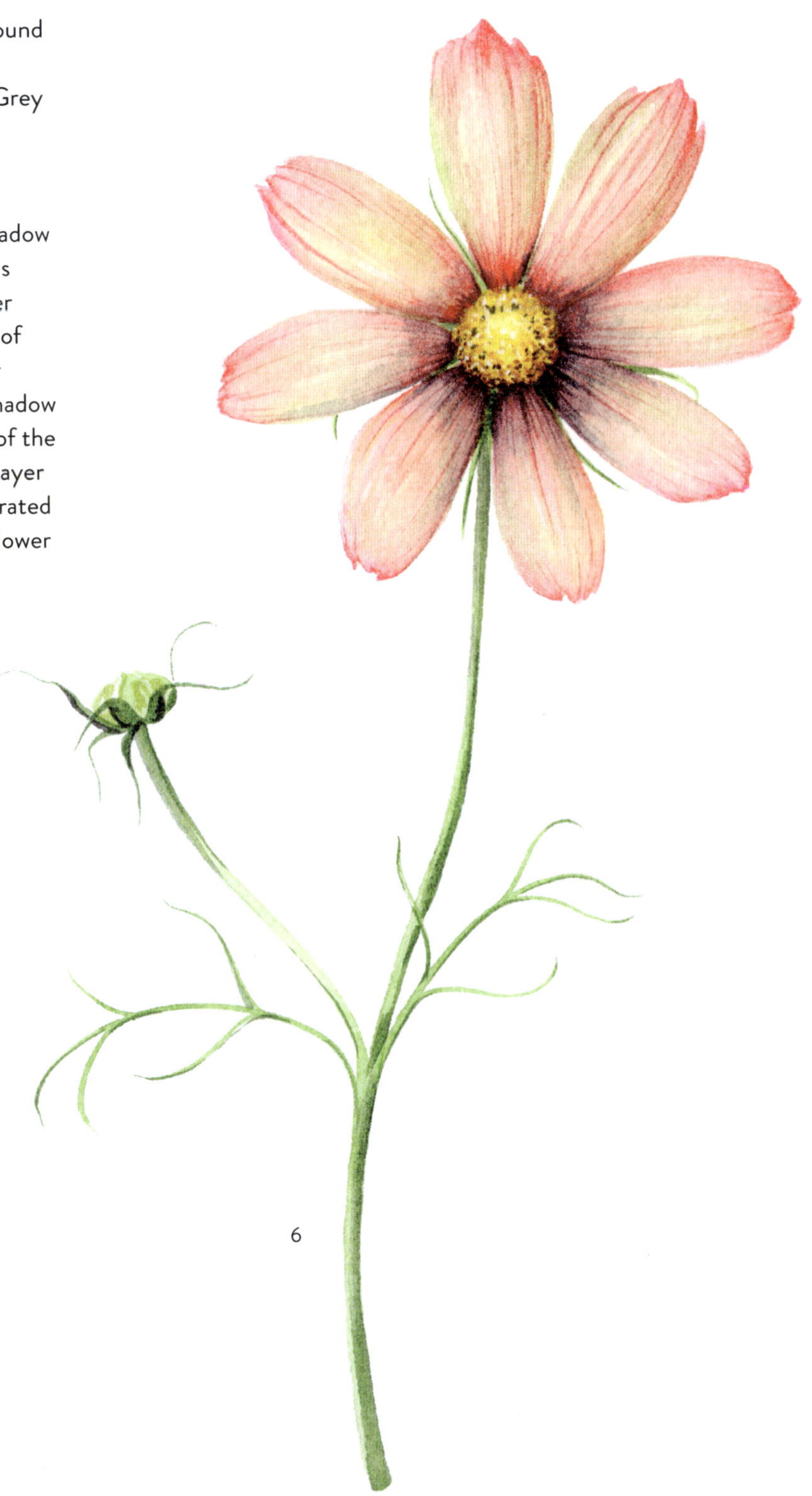

6 Layer Sap Green sepals around the bud with your size 4/0 brush, then glaze Payne's Grey up and down the full stem and leaves.

Layer a few fine lines of shadow mix (page 89) on the petals where they meet the flower centre on the bottom half of the flower with your rigger brush. Then glaze a little shadow mix on the shadowy parts of the petals and flower centre. Layer a few tiny dabs of concentrated shadow mix seeds on the flower centre.

Shadow and Shade

There is no denying that the idea of painting a dark colour over a piece you've spent hours creating feels reckless. But it's quite the opposite: adding shadow heightens your painting's contrast and brings it to life on the page.

Black might seem the obvious shade choice but it has the opposite effect – its deadening quality can shroud a piece in heavy darkness. Instead, why not try the options below? The colour of the object can influence what best shade colour to use. Throughout the book, my choice of colours for shadow mixes will change according to the subject matter.

SHADE
Draw three cherries and paint them with a flat Alizarin Crimson, leaving a little unpainted 'shine' so you know where the light source is coming from.

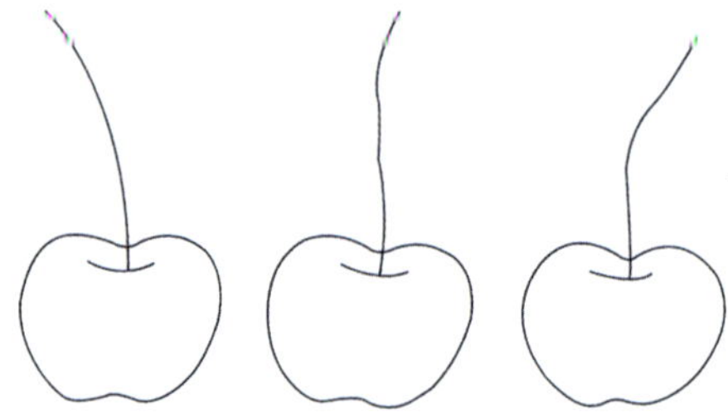

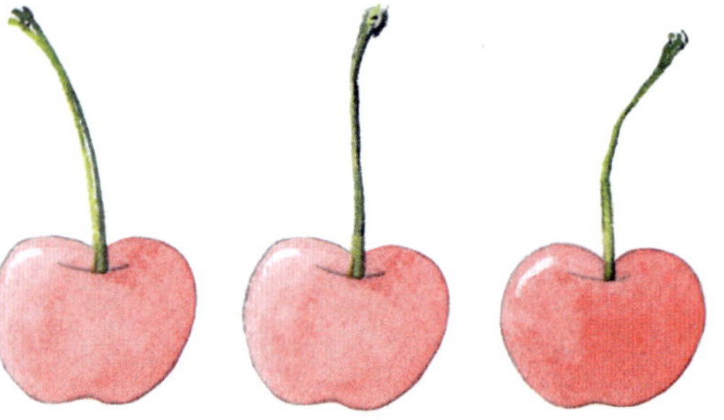

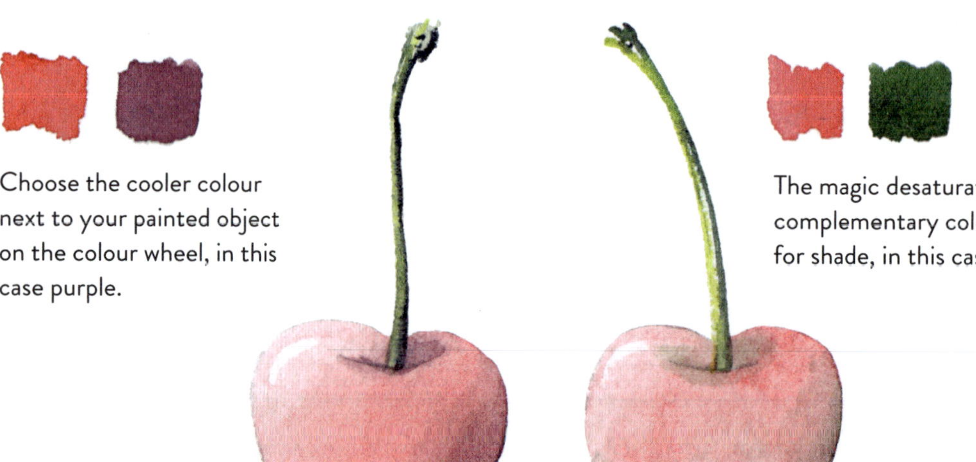

Choose the cooler colour next to your painted object on the colour wheel, in this case purple.

The magic desaturation of a complementary colour is brilliant for shade, in this case green.

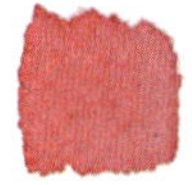 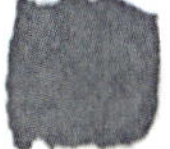

I love an inky mix of Payne's Grey (50%) and Burnt Sienna (50%) when applying shadows and shade. When applied as a glaze it allows the underneath colour to shine through with a wonderful darkness.

Once you've painted your shadows, it can be a good idea to add a final glaze of the original shape's colour (Alizarin Crimson) to tie it all together.

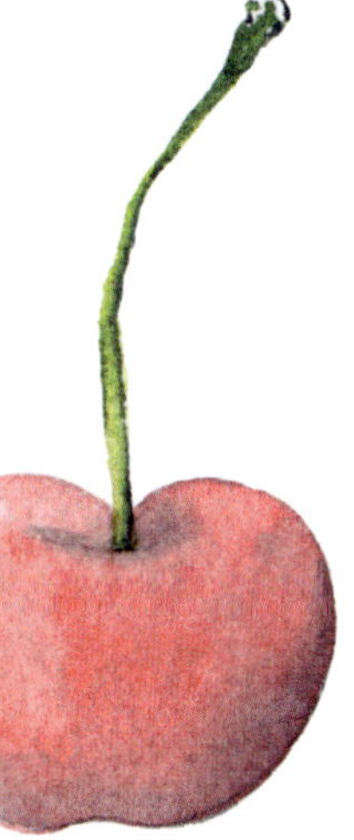 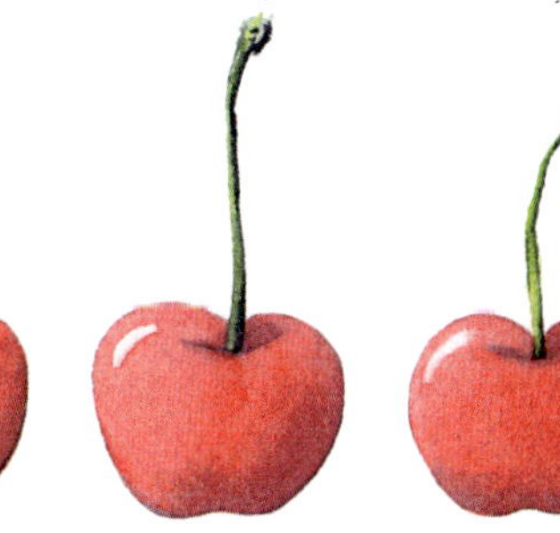

CASTING SHADOWS

I use shadow mix (Burnt Sienna and Payne's Grey) to paint shadows cast along the ground. Keeping the shadow colours simple allows the object casting the shadow to stand out. A shadow can tell us many things about the light source.

Shadow

Wet on dry: A hard-edged pool of dilute shadow around the base of an object indicates a focused but gentle spotlight. Once you've painted in your shadow, you may feel the shade on the object needs boosting to match the shadow cast. For this cherry I added a glaze of shadow mix to match the hard edge.

Wet on wet: Soft-edged shadow comes from a frosted or softened light source.

Dark and long: These shadows tell us the angle of the light source that might capture some of the protruding features of the shape, like the stem of the cherry. The dark shadow demonstrates a stronger light source.

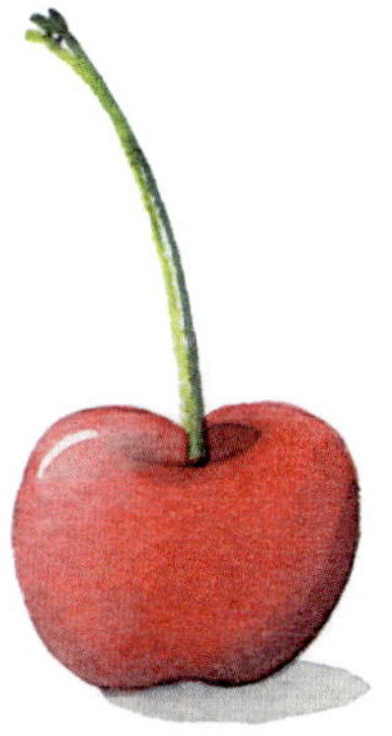

Wet on dry

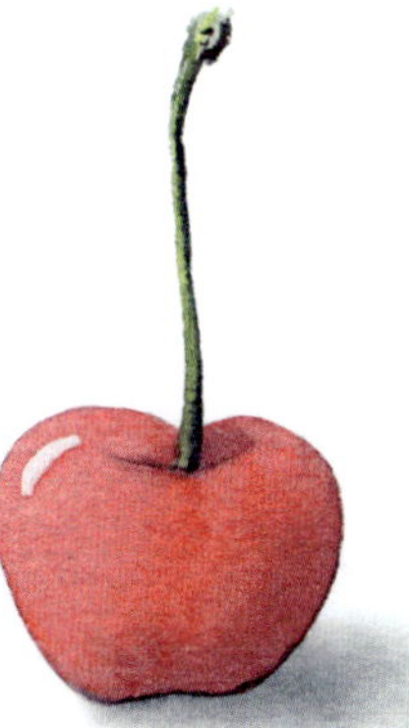

Wet on wet

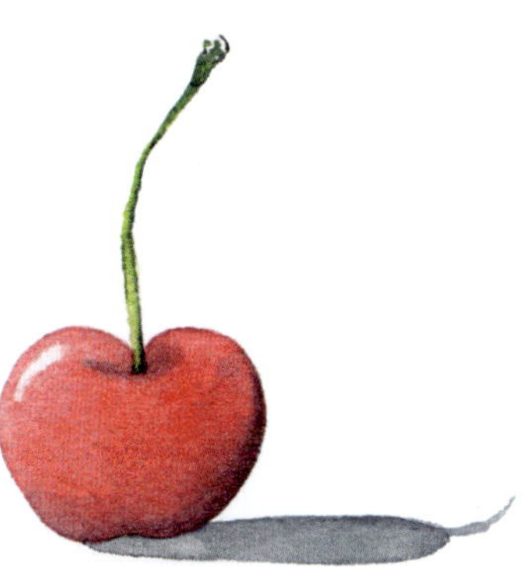

Dark and long

Highlights and Lowlights

Highlights (unpainted space, pale warm tones and glowing yellows) and lowlights (shadows, concentrated accents and layered details) help objects jump off the page.

TUTORIAL: Garlic Bulb

A pale neutral garlic bulb is the perfect subject to paint entirely in highlights and lowlights. Your shadowy glazes will feel shockingly dark to put on such a delicate painting but remember that watercolour dries 30% lighter.

Level
Beginner

Colours
Alizarin Crimson
Buff Titanium
Burnt Sienna
Lemon Yellow
Payne's Grey
Yellow Ochre

Brushes
Pointed round sizes 8, 4, 0

You will also need
HB pencil, soft and hard erasers

Mixes
Highlight mix: Lemon Yellow (50%) and Buff Titanium (50%)
Shadow mix: Payne's Grey (80%) Alizarin Crimson (20%)

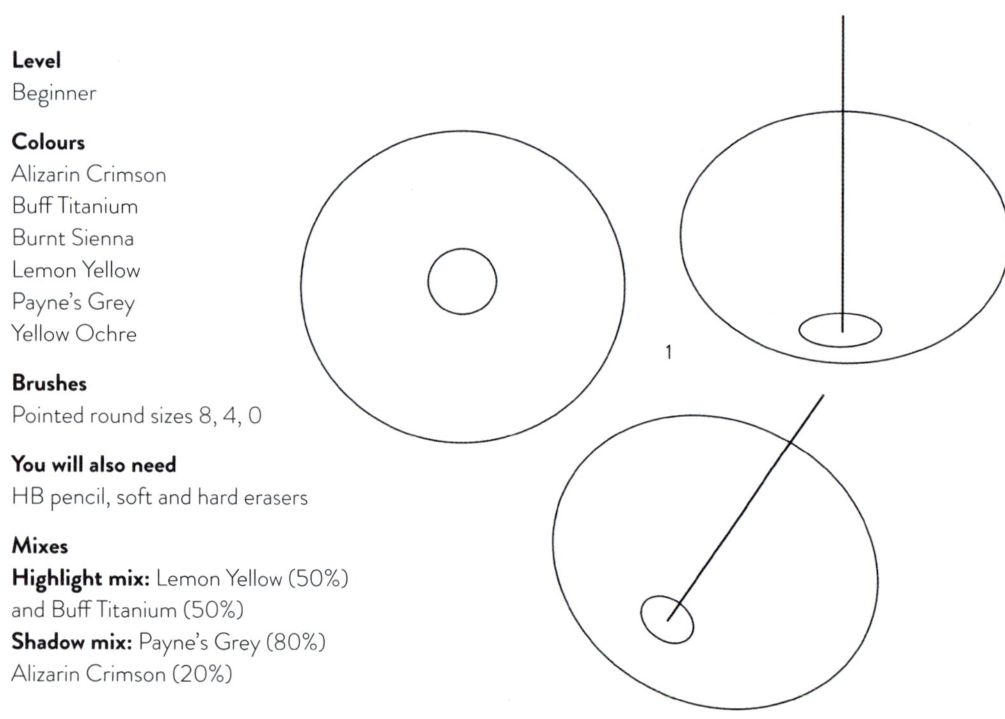

Highlight

Shadow

1 Follow the drawing guide to draw a faint pencil garlic bulb.

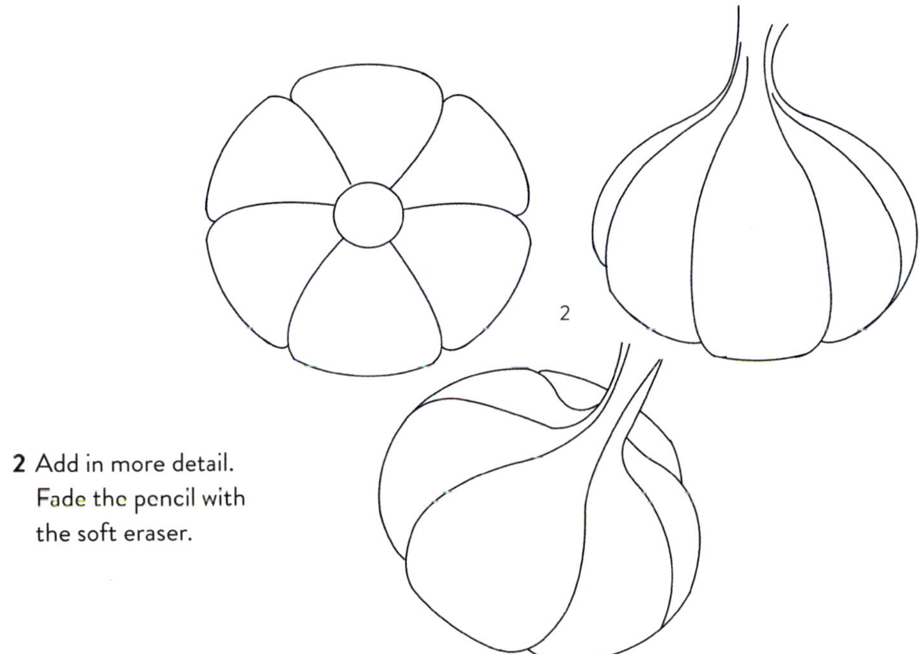

2 Add in more detail.
Fade the pencil with
the soft eraser.

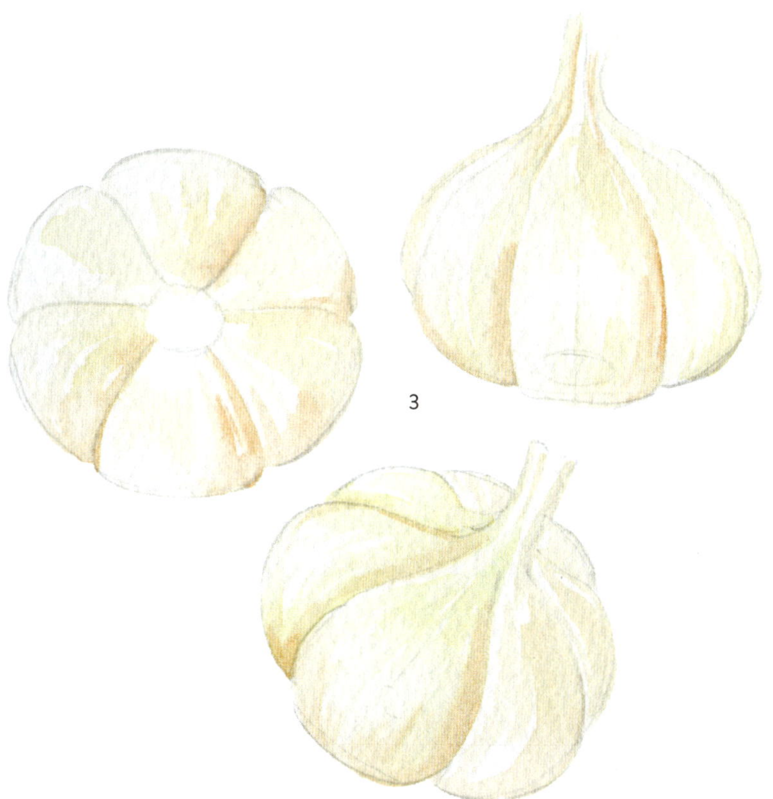

3 Paint each clove of the garlic
bulb in streaks of highlight mix
with your size 4 brush. Follow
the curve of the shape, leaving
unpainted lines to give the
surface some texture. Add some
Yellow Ochre in the crevices to
help achieve roundness.

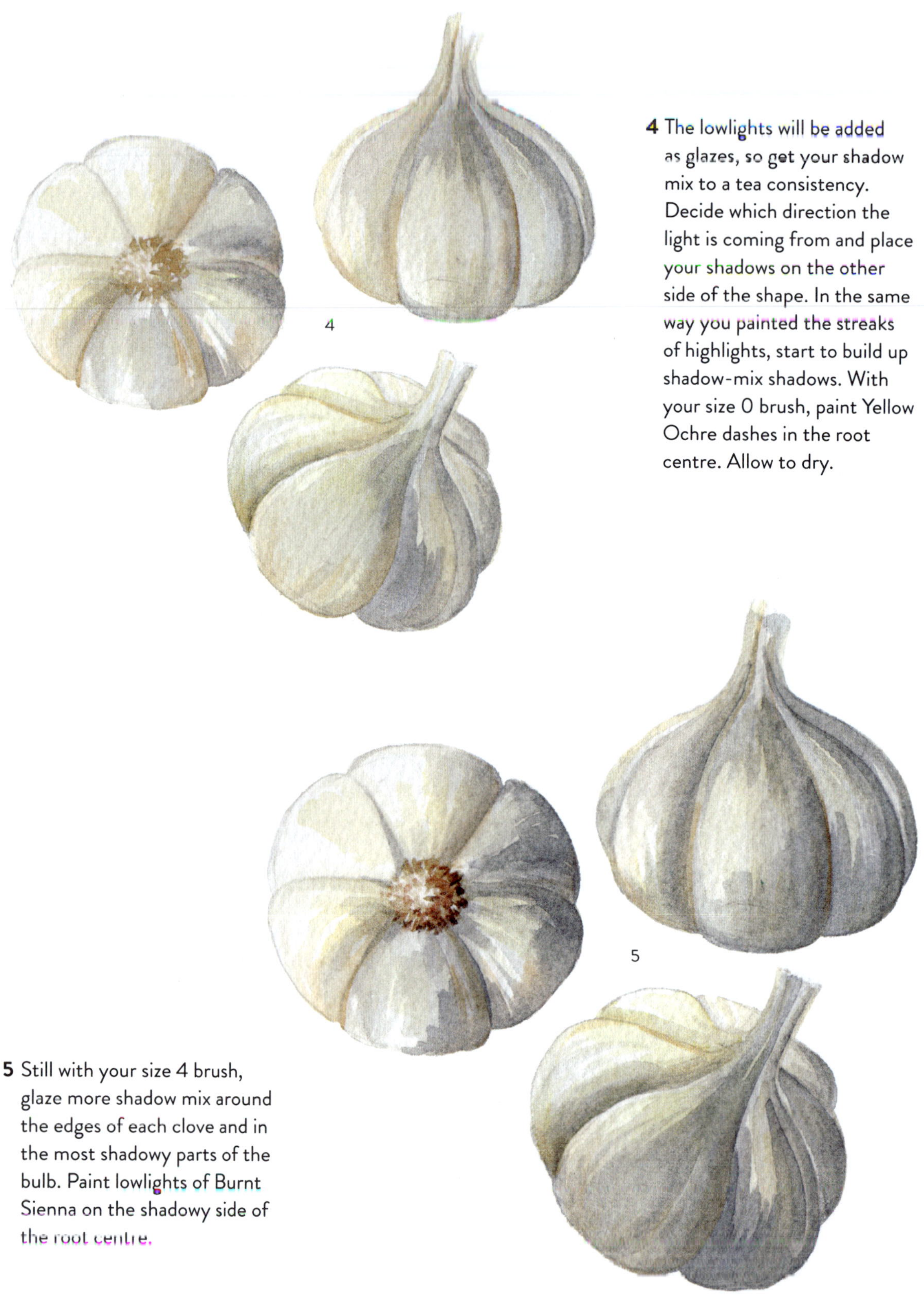

4 The lowlights will be added
as glazes, so get your shadow
mix to a tea consistency.
Decide which direction the
light is coming from and place
your shadows on the other
side of the shape. In the same
way you painted the streaks
of highlights, start to build up
shadow-mix shadows. With
your size 0 brush, paint Yellow
Ochre dashes in the root
centre. Allow to dry.

5 Still with your size 4 brush,
glaze more shadow mix around
the edges of each clove and in
the most shadowy parts of the
bulb. Paint lowlights of Burnt
Sienna on the shadowy side of
the root centre.

6 Slightly increase the
concentration of your shadow
glazes and add some darker
detailed streaks with your size
0 brush. Allow to dry and dilute
the shadow mix right down.
With your size 8 brush, paint
one last glaze over the darkest
areas. Allow to dry fully and rub
out any visible pencil with your
hard eraser.

6

Is Black the Darkest Colour?

I currently have Ivory Black in my palette, but it's rarely the colour I reach for when painting black feathers on a bird or fur on an animal and I don't use it for shadow painting at all. When you look more closely at the feathers on a toucan, you'll see they are flashed with electric blue. Similarly, a black Labrador's fur is full of warm tan tones and highlights. A great way to give black tones a lift is to incorporate a dark value like Payne's Grey.

Ivory Black

Payne's Grey

TUTORIAL: Panda

Level
Beginner

Colours
Burnt Sienna
Ivory Black
Payne's Grey
Permanent Rose
Yellow Ochre

Brushes
Sizes 4, 2, 0, 4/0

You will also need
HB pencil, soft and hard erasers

Mix
Shadow mix: Burnt Sienna (50%) and Payne's Grey (50%), heavily diluted

Shadow

1 Draw a pencil panda, making sure you draw in all the black and white sections. Roll with a soft eraser to fade the lines.

2 Mix an extremely dilute shadow
mix with Yellow Ochre and
paint highlights and lowlights on
the white fur with your size 2
brush. Allow to dry.

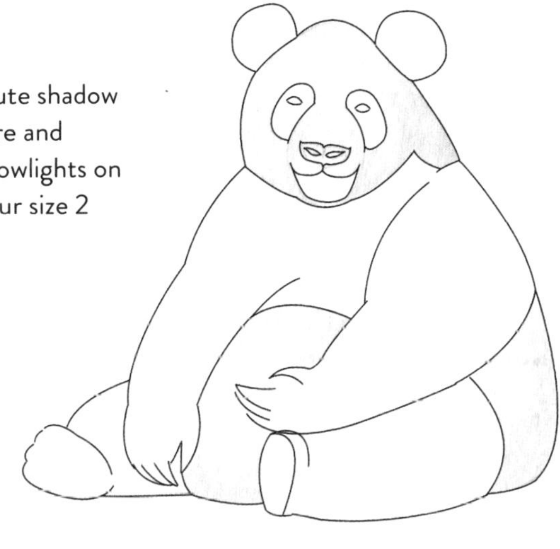

3 Paint a flat Ivory Black coverage
on the black sections with
whatever brush you prefer
for best control. Paint some
dilute Permanent Rose for the
tongue. Allow to dry.

4 With your preferred size of brush,
use Payne's Grey to add lowlights
to the black sections and see how
much darker and richer the black
now appears. Rub out any visible
pencil with your hard eraser.

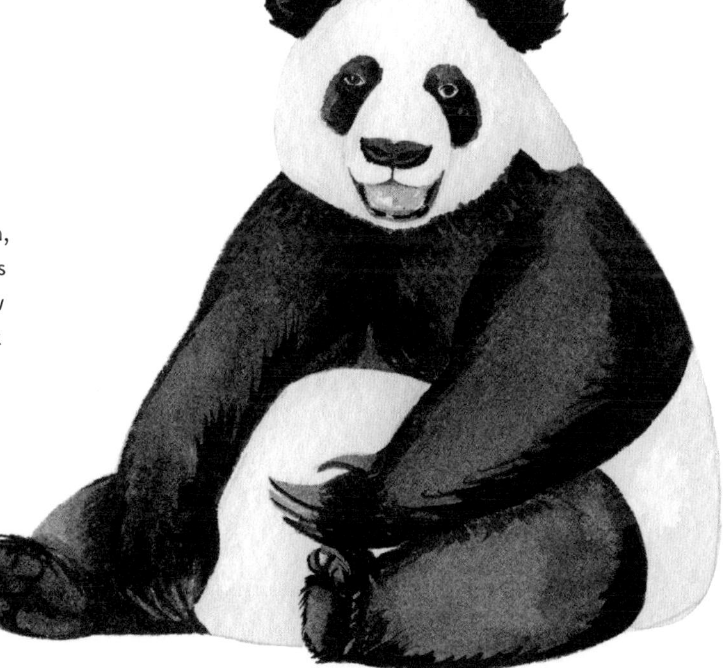

Underpainting

Underpainting – the base layer of watercolour – lays a foundation for your piece. Your choice of colour can drastically alter a painting's mood and appearance.

The butterfly below is underpainted with dilute Cadmium-Free Yellow on one side and Payne's Grey on the other. The golden rule with watercolour is to start with light colours and build up in concentration. These washes are dilute enough to be painted over, but you can see they still have an impact on the piece.

Compare the paintings below with the same butterfly painted on clear white paper and you can see how every colour is affected by that base wash.

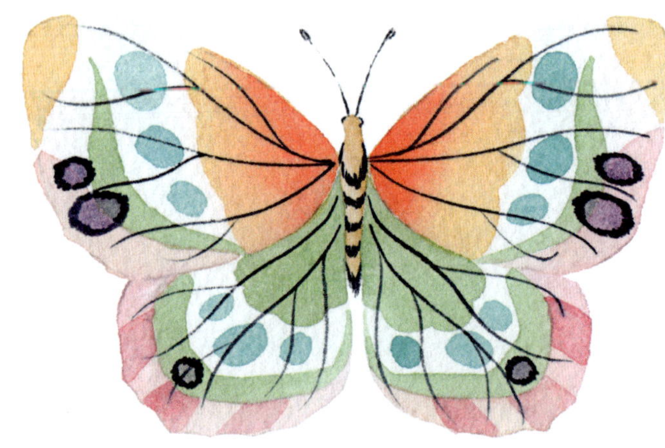

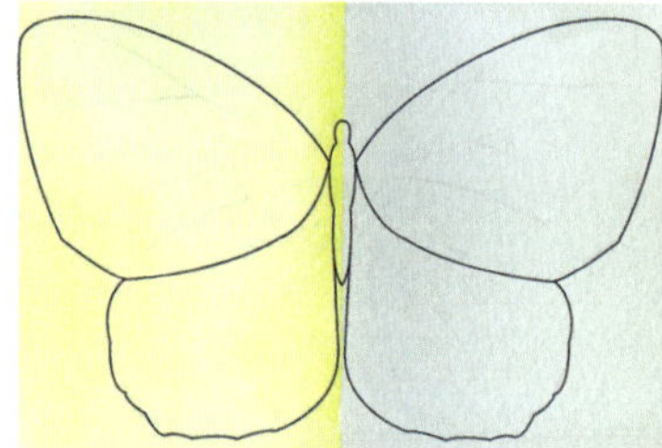

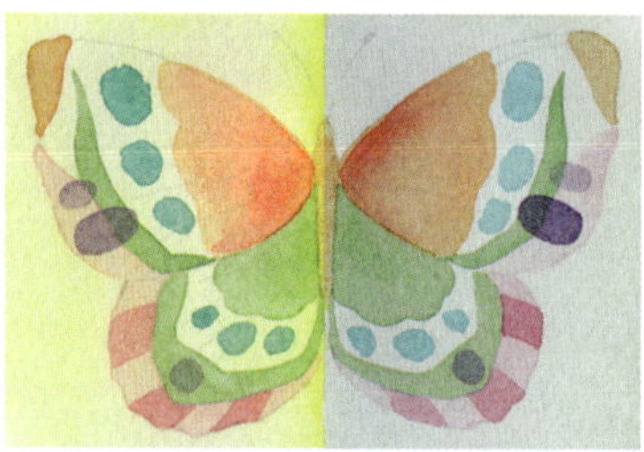

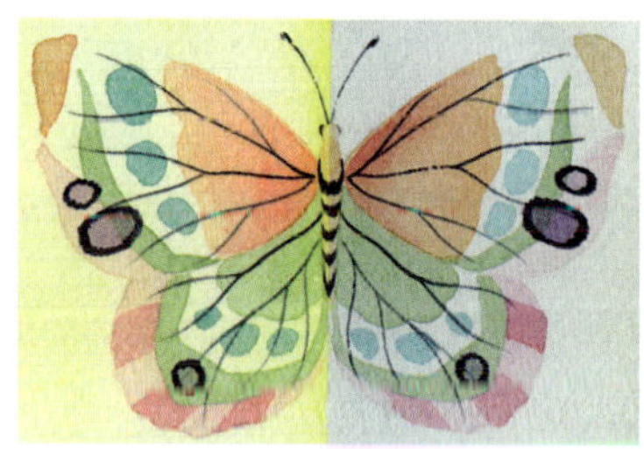

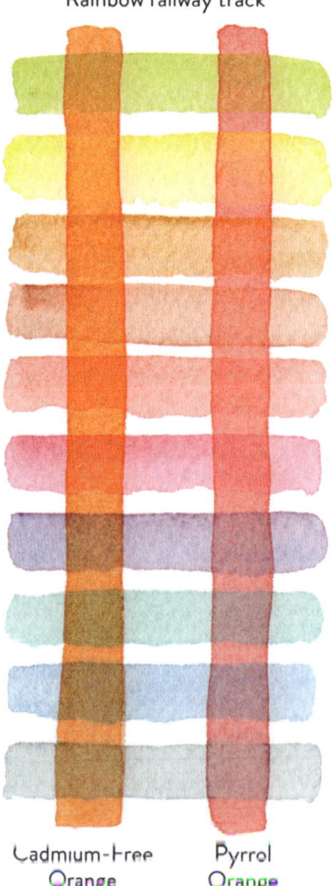
Rainbow railway track

Cadmium-Free Orange (left) is opaque, and Pyrrol Orange (right) is transparent. Look how Pyrrol Orange enhances each swatch when Cadmium-Free Orange feels a bit heavy. Test this out with some rainbow railway tracks of your own. Paint dilute lines of colours from your palette. Once fully dry, compare opaque and transparent colours on top (all painted in a tea consistency)

Look through your paints and see if you can detect their opacity information on the tube. Then create your own fanciful butterfly colour combinations to see what impact underpainting can have on the layers on top.

Analogous and complementary butterflies

We've learned that the easiest route to a harmonious colour palette is by choosing a small grouping of colours either side of each other on the colour wheel.

Level
Beginner

1 Draw a pencil butterfly shape.

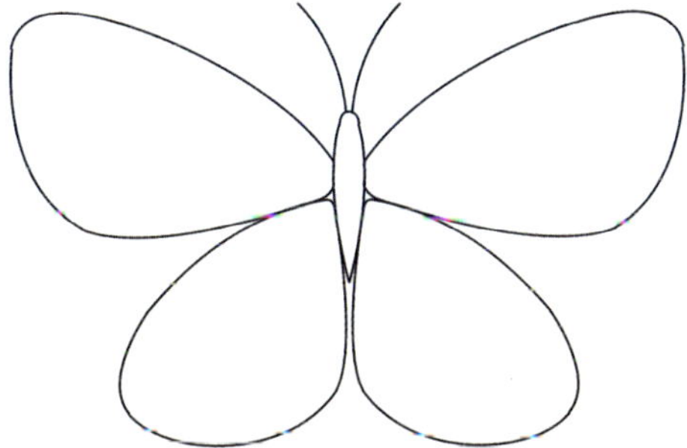

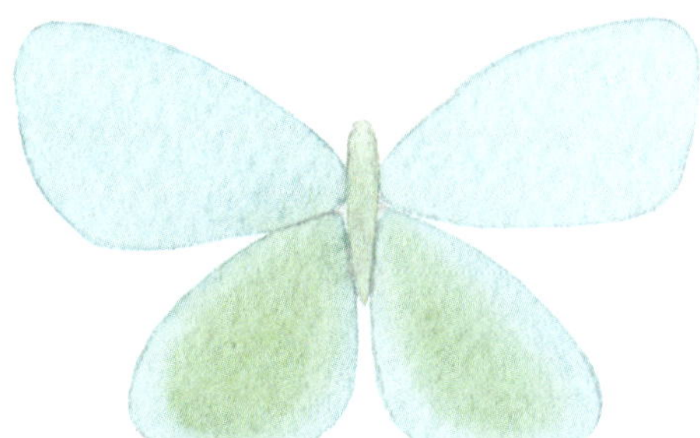

2 Use up to four analogous colours to paint a dilute wash on the butterfly – the underpainting. Allow to dry.

3 Glaze some transparent patterns on top.

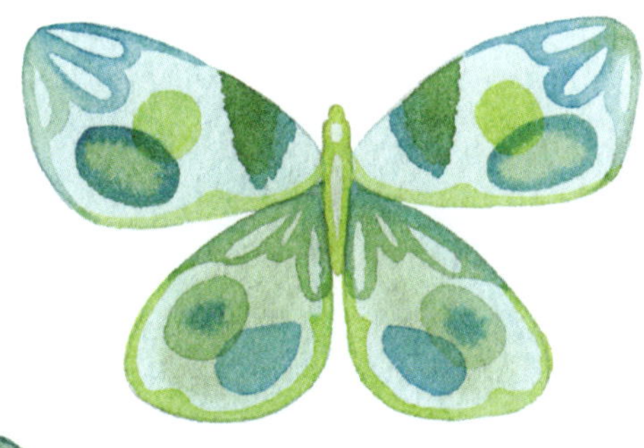

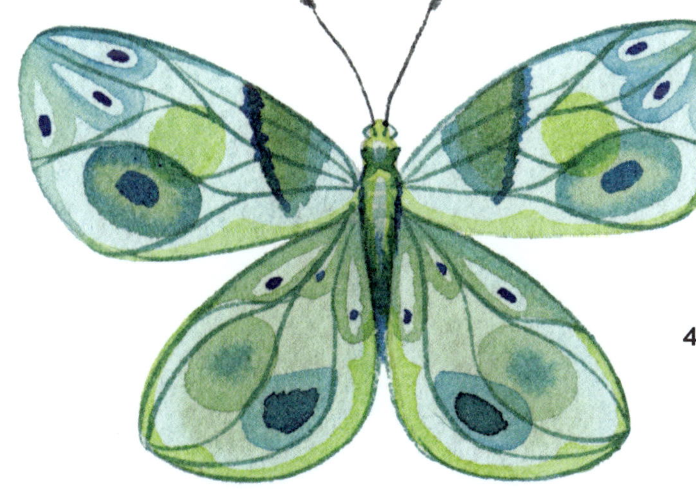

4 Finish with concentrated marks and fine lines, still in your limited colour palette.

COMPLEMENTARY BUTTERFLY

Complementary colours require a little more experimentation to get a harmonious palette. Using the above steps, try a complementary colour butterfly. Do you think this works? When I glazed the green tones onto the underpainted pink wash, it felt dull and lifeless because all the complementary colours were at a similar level of consistency – the piece needed some contrast! With the final layer of concentrated colour it came to life, but I can see that the underpainting of pink gave vibrancy to the bluer green tones while the yellowy green still felt quite dull.

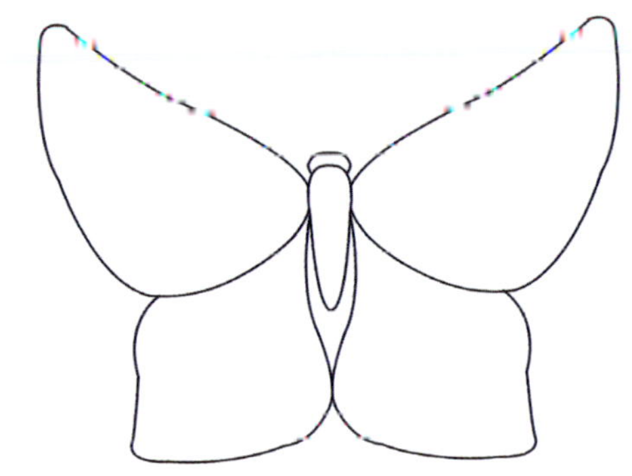

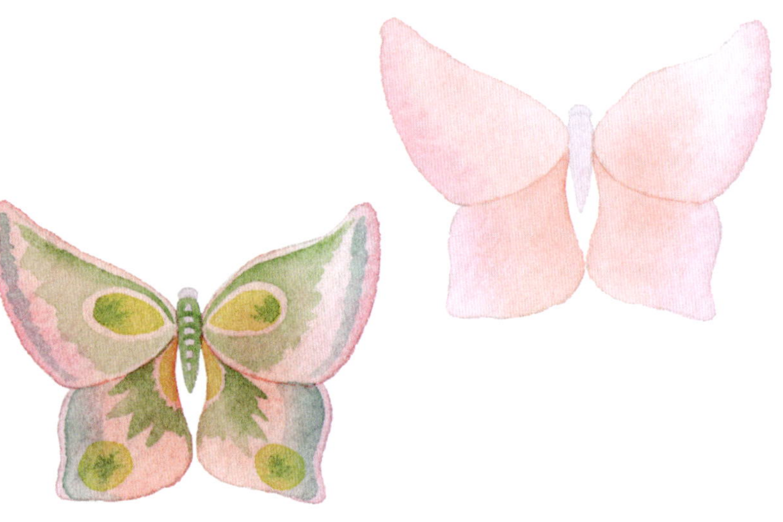

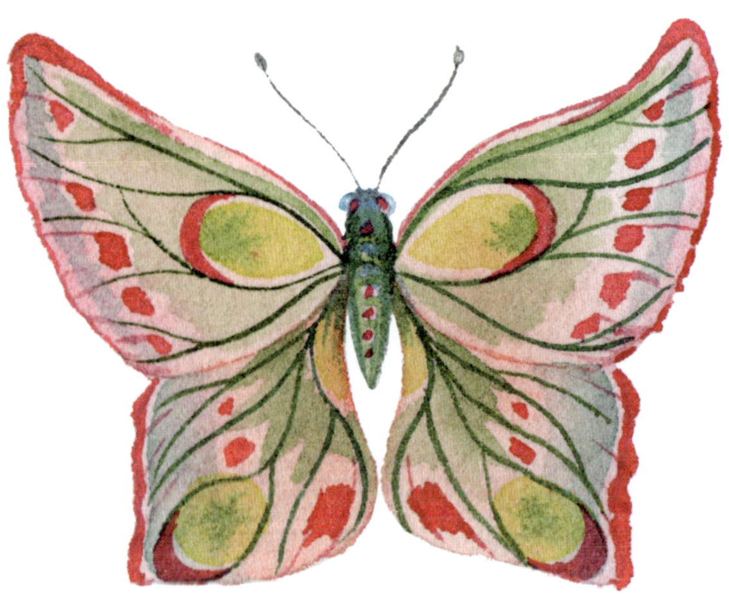

UNDERPAINTING FROM REFERENCES

Underpainting when using a reference photo means you're scanning that photo for the lightest colour you can see. This gives you the first colour to use, before adding the progressively deeper shades you can see in the piece.

 # Meadow Brown Female Butterfly

The pale yellow in the dot of the wings 'eyes' and in the broader pattern of the wings works perfectly as an underpainted layer for this butterfly.

Level
Intermediate

Colours
Buff Titanium
Burnt Sienna
Cadmium-Free Orange
Cadmium-Free Yellow
Payne's Grey
Raw Umber

Brushes
Pointed round sizes 2, 0, 4/0
Rigger size 0

You will also need
HB pencil, soft and
hard erasers

Mix
Shadow mix: Burnt
Sienna (50%) and
Payne's Grey (50%)

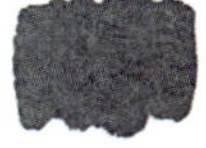

Shadow

1 Draw your butterfly shape in pencil and roll with a soft eraser to fade the pencil.

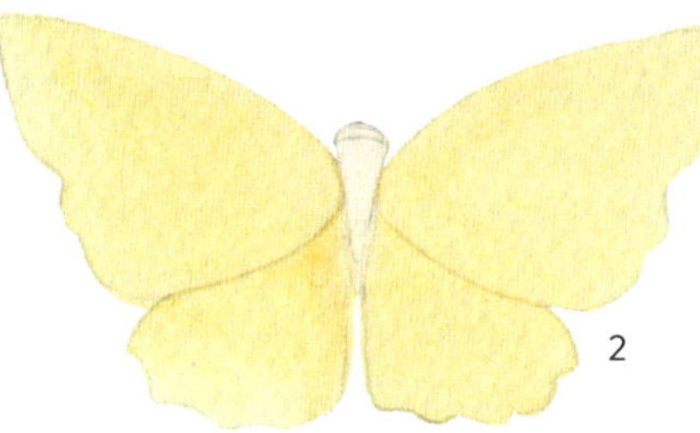

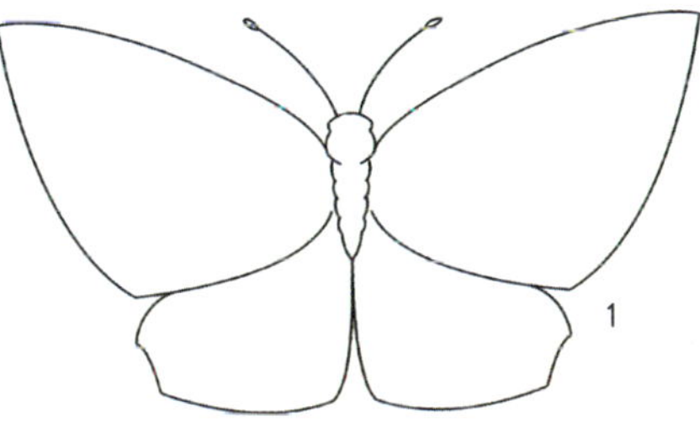

2 Paint a dilute wash of Cadmium-Free Yellow on the wings and Buff Titanium on the body. Allow to dry.

3 Lightly pencil in your wing markings and start to paint brown tones from your palette (coffee in diagonal strokes along each vein, using a size 0 brush. The yellow underpainting will glow beneath these brown shades, giving the painting a cohesive warmth.

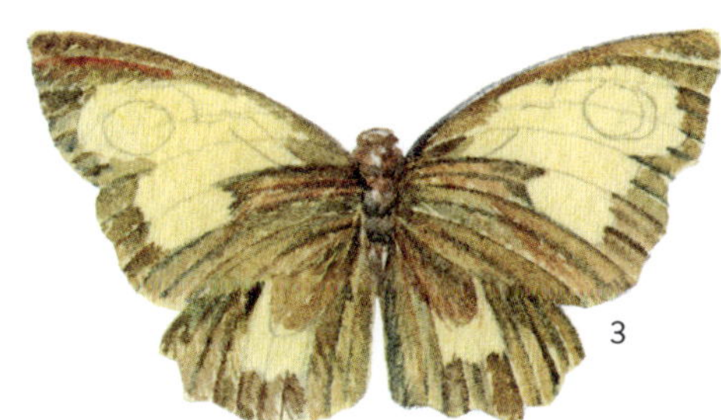

4 Once dry, use a size 4/0 brush to enhance the underpainted yellow patches with some streaks of concentrated Cadmium-Free Orange and Cadmium-Free Yellow and paint a concentrated Payne's Grey eye and details on the body.

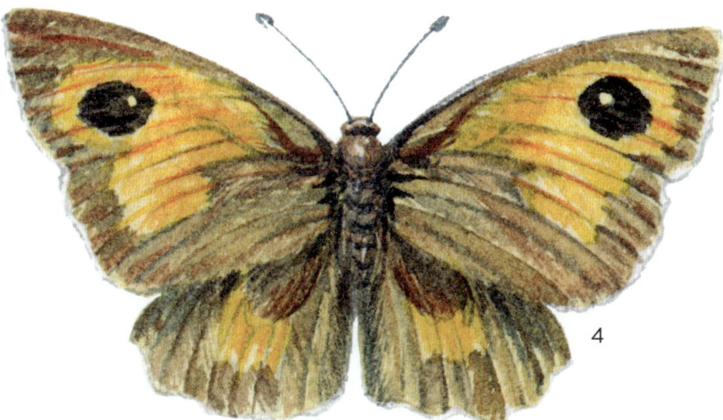

I am forever returning to subjects afresh. This is not the first time I've taught the peacock butterfly. As artists we should be forever learning, so I thought it would be fun to approach something familiar with the focus shifted to underpainting. There are so many subtle colours popping through the bolder red and black layers that this technique is going to work really well.

Level
Intermediate

Colours
Alizarin Crimson
Buff Titanium
Burnt Sienna
Cadmium-Free Red
Cadmium-Free Yellow
French Ultramarine
Ivory Black
Payne's Grey
Winsor Blue
Yellow Ochre

Brushes
Pointed round sizes 4, 2, 0, 4/0
Rigger size 0

You will also need
HB pencil, soft and hard erasers

Mixes
Shadow mix: Burnt Sienna (50%) and Payne's Grey (50%)
Gold mix: Cadmium-Free Yellow (50%) and Yellow Ochre (50%)
Blue mix: Alizarin Crimson (10%), Winsor Blue (50%) and French Ultramarine (40%)

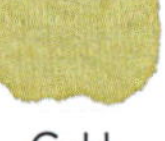
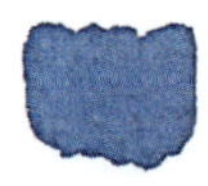

Shadow   Gold   Blue

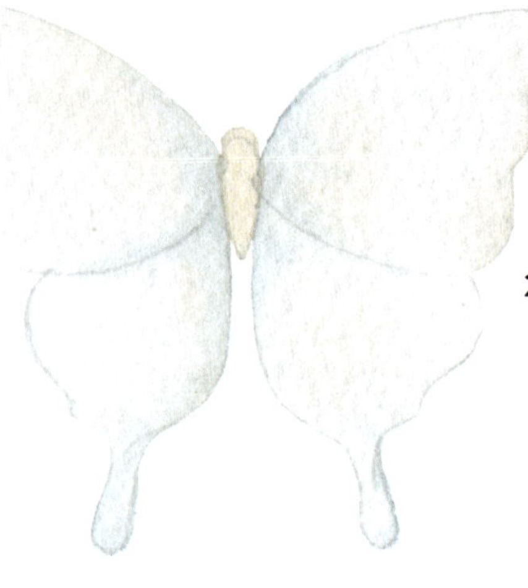

1 Follow the drawing guide to create a faint pencil body shape.

2 With a size 4 brush, paint a wash of Buff Titanium across the wings. While still wet, dab some dilute Payne's Grey where the wings meet the body. Paint the body in dilute Yellow Ochre.

3 With your size 2 brush, paint gold mix (coffee) at the shoulders and blend out with water, following the top line of the wing to the tip. Then continue around the edge of the wings with shadow mix in tea consistency. Paint dilute blue mix in the wing corners and on the hindwing 'eyes'.

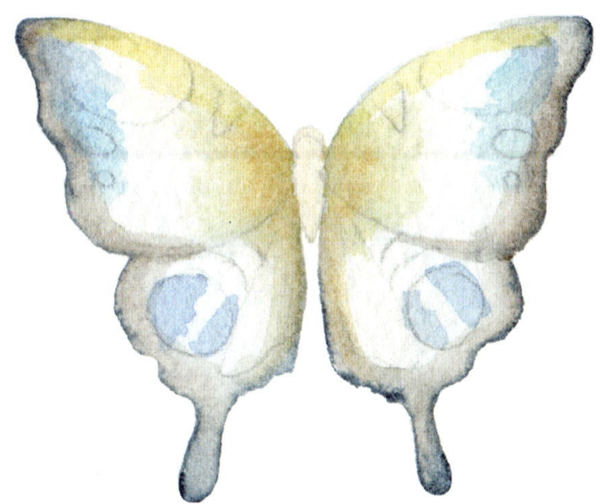

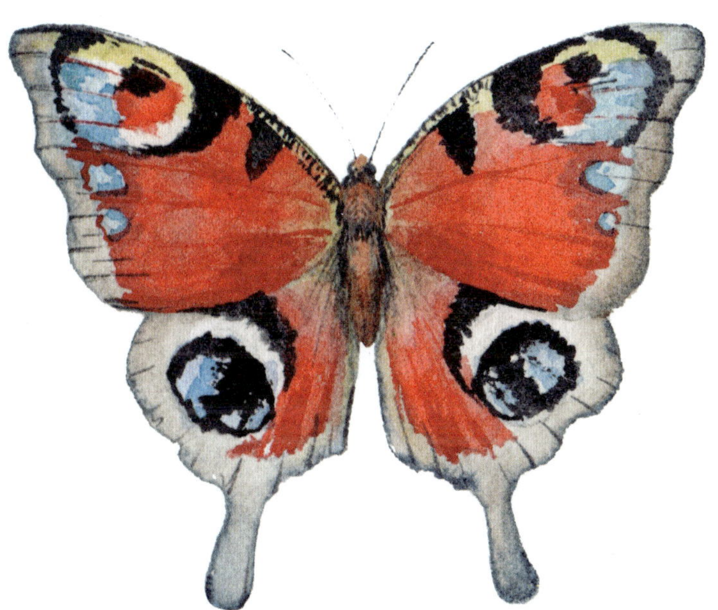

4 Layer each wing with Cadmium-Free Red (milk), fading the colour into the body. Paint in the black details (cream). Once dry, add some Alizarin Crimson to your red and paint the wing veins. Add shadow mix veins to the wing edges and dashes to create hairs on the body. Finish with glazed dots of blue mix on the blue 'eyes' and black antennas with your rigger brush.

I have the luxury of practising and sharing only the best version of my paintings when writing a book or teaching a class. But, in this case, I promise each of these paintings is my first attempt, produced strictly within the time limit.

We spent the first half of the book with limited colours and brushes, looking at how we could push the potential of those colours. Here, your limitation is time: there's no room for doubt and self-criticism, or making too many choices. You just have to go for it.

The worst-case scenario is some wonky paintings. The guaranteed positive is you've taken another step to understanding what you love about painting.

I wrote down my immediate reaction to how I felt throughout and how I evaluated the paintings afterwards.

BEFORE YOU START
Choose a limited colour palette (I went for complementary orange and blue) and have all your colours mixed up and ready to go.

Have your brushes close at hand (large ones will cover more distance and carry more liquid)

Set the timer with an extra ten seconds so you can ready yourself before starting.

Have extra jars of clean water for making a quick transition between colours.

HOW I FARED:

30 seconds
My first feeling was panic! I also realized I wasn't going to be able to waste time with changing brushes, so I did the whole piece with a size 8. I managed to the get the basic shape of the fish down on paper with some colour changes that I liked. I looked forward to trying again with a bit more time.

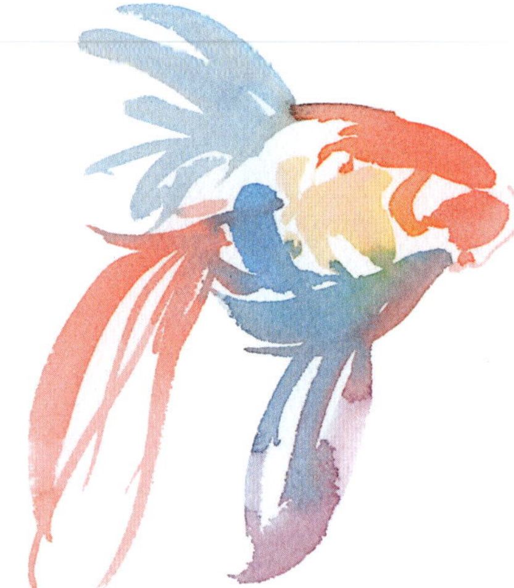

30 seconds

1 minute

1 minute
I still had no time to change brushes, but armed with the knowledge of what I could achieve in 30 seconds I felt a tiny bit calmer trying this version. The limited time forced me to paint instinctively. I even had the time to paint the fish's eye.

5 minutes

This is quite a leap in the amount of time but I still felt in a speedy mode from the previous two paintings. In doing so, I had too much time to fret that my brushstrokes had been unwise and started to make corrections which made things worse. I inadvertently created a green tone by adding blue to my yellow sections, which doesn't really work. I prefer the freedom of my one-minute piece but I feel better prepared going into the 10-minute painting.

10 minutes

This felt wonderful. I had time to apply the knowledge I'd built up from the previous three paintings. I kept the energy of the brushstrokes of the 30-second painting and how I had captured the body shape in the 1-minute painting. I learned from the 5-minute painting when to be fast and when to wait.

In conclusion, my final painting is all the better because I had experienced the previous three. Each session taught me something different and built my confidence with painting in a loose, expressive style. This is the perfect way to warm up your creative muscles!

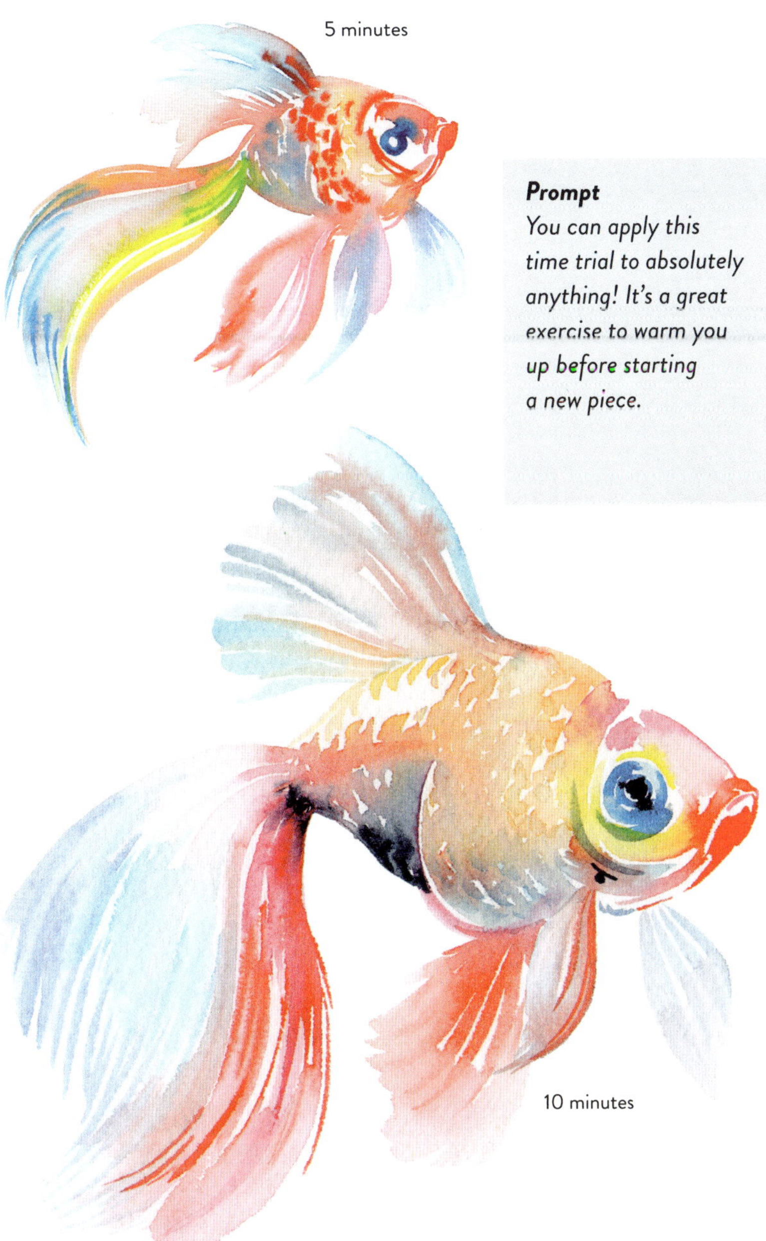

Prompt
You can apply this time trial to absolutely anything! It's a great exercise to warm you up before starting a new piece.

NOW TRY

Find a photo of a single item/animal or a simple landscape. Follow the guidelines above, setting your own time limits. Once you've tried it out, switch things up by starting with the longest time frame and gradually shortening it. Try doing a set with the timer concealed so you don't know how long you have left until the alarm rings.

Loose vs Detailed, or 'Wet vs Dry'

Lovebirds have unbelievably vibrant feathers that lend themselves to a loose, wet-on-wet style of painting just as much as a slow and detailed 'dry' approach.

Loose painting may appear simple but I know many a painter who frets over capturing the freedom of loose watercolour painting, preferring the slow and patient approach with layers of detail.

KNOW YOUR SUBJECT
My personal preference is to spend the time getting to know a subject through the detailed approach before having a go at the loose style. Which order will you choose?

TUTORIAL: Detailed lovebird

Level
Intermediate

Colours
Aqua Green
Buff Titanium
Burnt Sienna
French Ultramarine
Green Gold
Ivory Black
Lemon Yellow
Opera Rose
Payne's Grey
Permanent Rose
Pyrrol Orange
Winsor Blue

Brushes
Pointed round sizes 8, 2, 0, 4/0

You will need
HB pencil, soft and hard erasers

Mixes
Green Mix: Green Gold (50%) and Aqua Green (50%)
Lemon Mix: Green Gold (30%) and Lemon Yellow (70%)
Red mix: Pyrrol Orange (50%) and Opera Rose (50%)
Shadow Mix: Aqua Green (30%), Payne's Grey (40%) Burnt Sienna (30%)
Purple Mix: Aqua Green (20%), Payne's Grey (40%), Burnt Sienna (20%), Permanent Rose (20%)

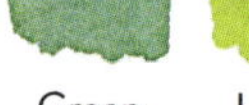
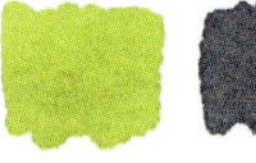

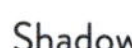
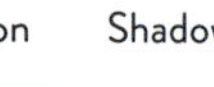

Green   Lemon   Shadow

Red   Purple

1 Follow the drawing guide to create the basic bird shape

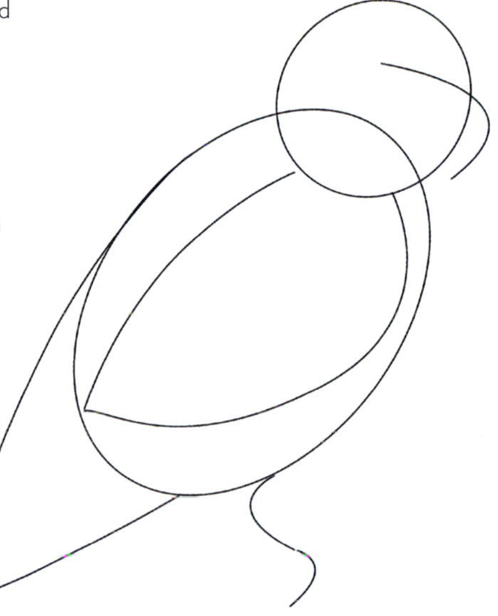

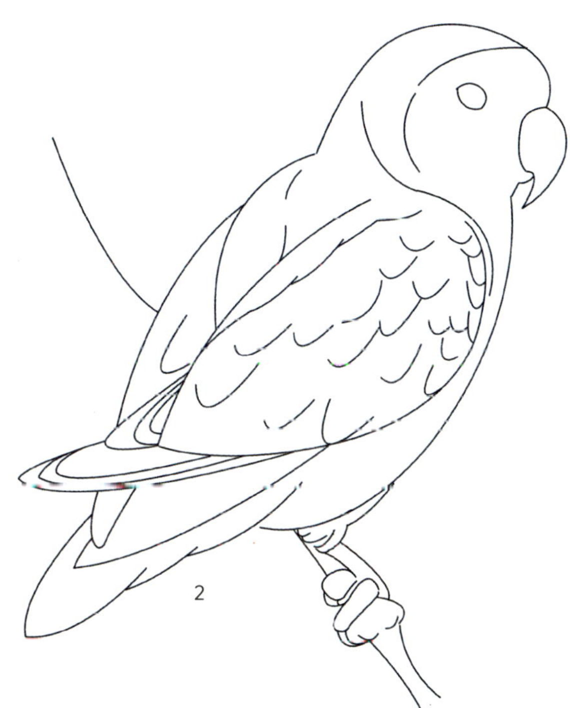

2 Add in more detail of feather and feature placement. Roll with a soft eraser to fade the pencil.

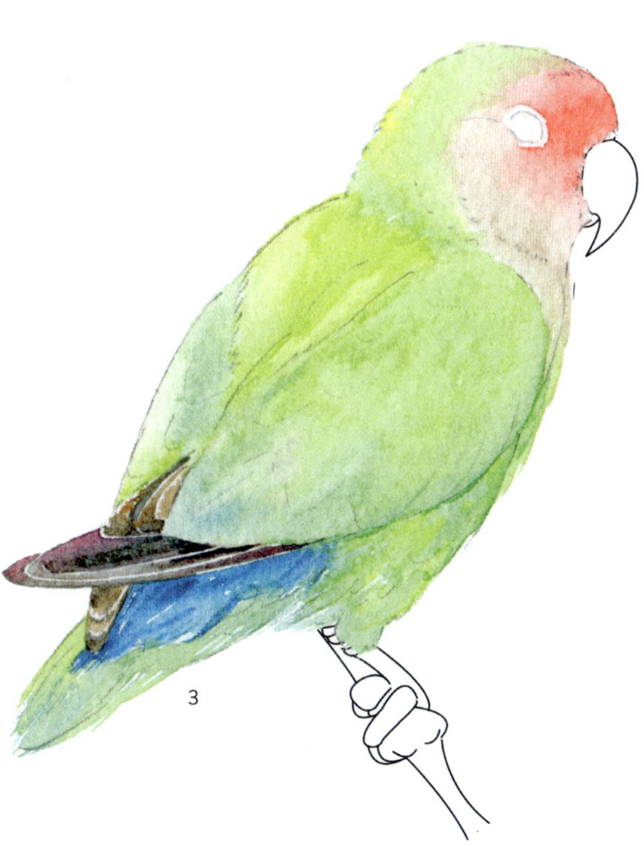

3 With your size 2 brush paint a coffee-consistency red mix on the head and start to fade with water as you pass the eye and move down to the neck. Continue with a dilute Buff Titanium down the chest. Paint lemon mix down the back of the head, onto the back and wings. Add a little green mix towards the legs and tail feathers. Even though you're painting first-layer washes, use the brush strokes to mimic the curve of feathers. With your size 0 brush, paint the wing tips in a range of brown tones, shadow mix and purple mix, leaving tiny lines of unpainted space between the feathers. Allow to dry.

4 Starting at the head again, with your size 4/0 brush, paint fine-line feathers of the corresponding colour in milk consistency in the base layer. Be careful to follow the direction of feathers across the contours of the body.

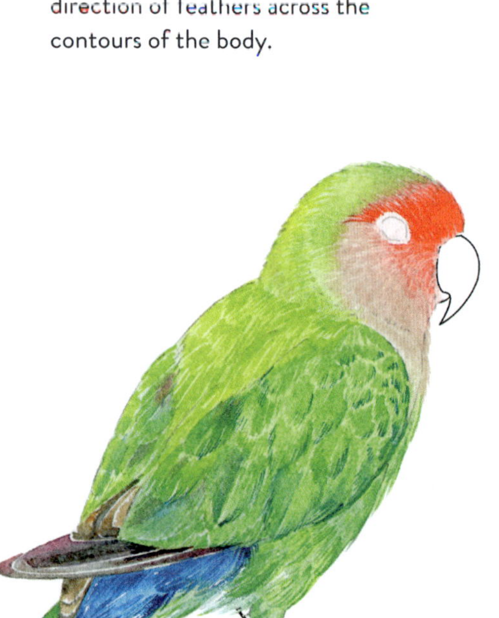

5 Move down the body, creating little fanned feathers with fine lines in your size 4/0 brush in the corresponding colour in the base layer. Add French Ultramarine to your Winsor Blue tail feathers.

6 Paint fine-line feather details along the wing tips with shadow mix and purple mix in your size 4/0 brush. Use these colours to dab dilute texture onto the legs and feet and around the eye. Paint a tea-consistency lemon mix wash on the beak and dab it with some dilute Pyrrol Orange.

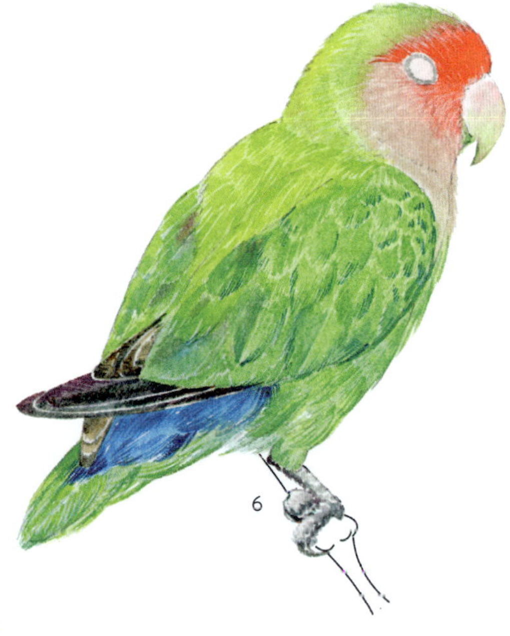

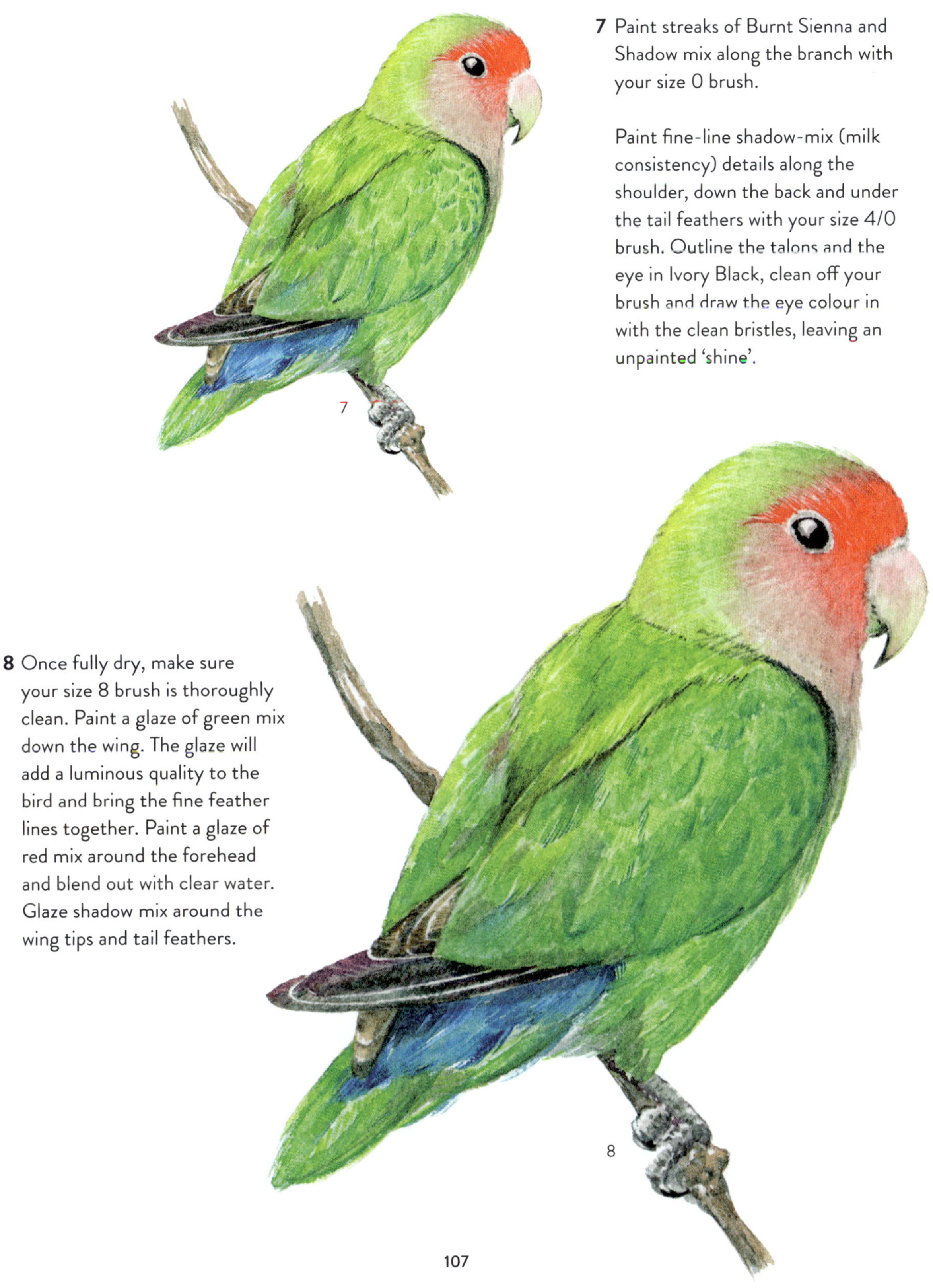

7 Paint streaks of Burnt Sienna and Shadow mix along the branch with your size 0 brush.

Paint fine-line shadow-mix (milk consistency) details along the shoulder, down the back and under the tail feathers with your size 4/0 brush. Outline the talons and the eye in Ivory Black, clean off your brush and draw the eye colour in with the clean bristles, leaving an unpainted 'shine'.

8 Once fully dry, make sure your size 8 brush is thoroughly clean. Paint a glaze of green mix down the wing. The glaze will add a luminous quality to the bird and bring the fine feather lines together. Paint a glaze of red mix around the forehead and blend out with clear water. Glaze shadow mix around the wing tips and tail feathers.

Ideally, you would put brush to paper without any pencil guide but feel free to draw a basic bird shape along the lines of this one. Warm up your brush strokes before painting the bird – the most successful loose paintings are created with a minimal number of confident and swift strokes.

Level
Beginner

Colours
Aqua Green
Cadmium-Free Red
Green Gold
Ivory Black
Permanent Rose
Lemon Yellow
Opera Rose
Pyrrol Orange
Winsor Blue

Brushes
Pointed round size 8

Mixes
Green mix: Green Gold (50%) and Aqua Green (50%)
Lemon mix: Green Gold (30%) and Lemon Yellow (70%)
Red mix: Pyrrol Orange (50%) and Opera Rose (50%)
Purple mix: Payne's Grey (30%), Burnt Sienna (30%), Permanent Rose (40%)

Green

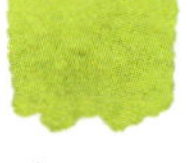
Lemon

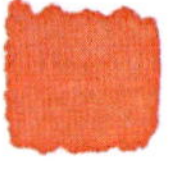
Red

Purple

BEFORE YOU START
For a loose painting, all your paints should have a coffee consistency. Have all your colours ready to go.

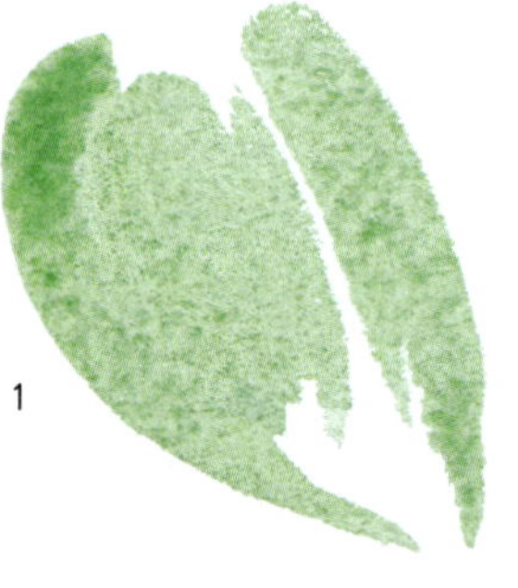

1 Paint the torso, shoulder and wing in the green mix. Try to leave directional sections of unpainted space that might indicate the wing.

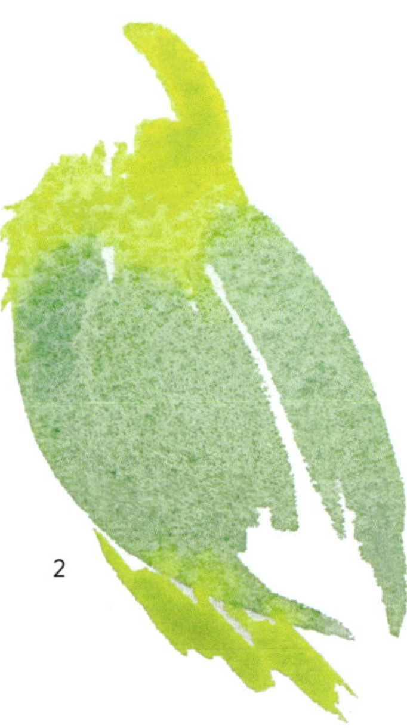

2 While still wet, paint a lemon-mix neck and head and tufts down the belly.

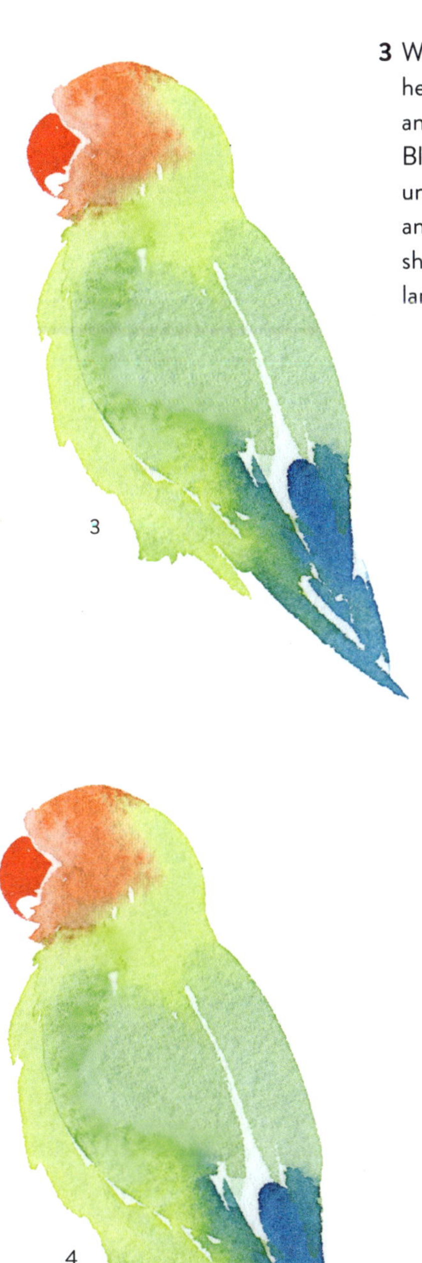

3 While still wet, complete the
head shape with the red mix
and the tail feathers in Winsor
Blue. Paint a red beak, leaving
unpainted space between it
and the head. These last stages
should be easily achieved if your
large brush makes a fine point.

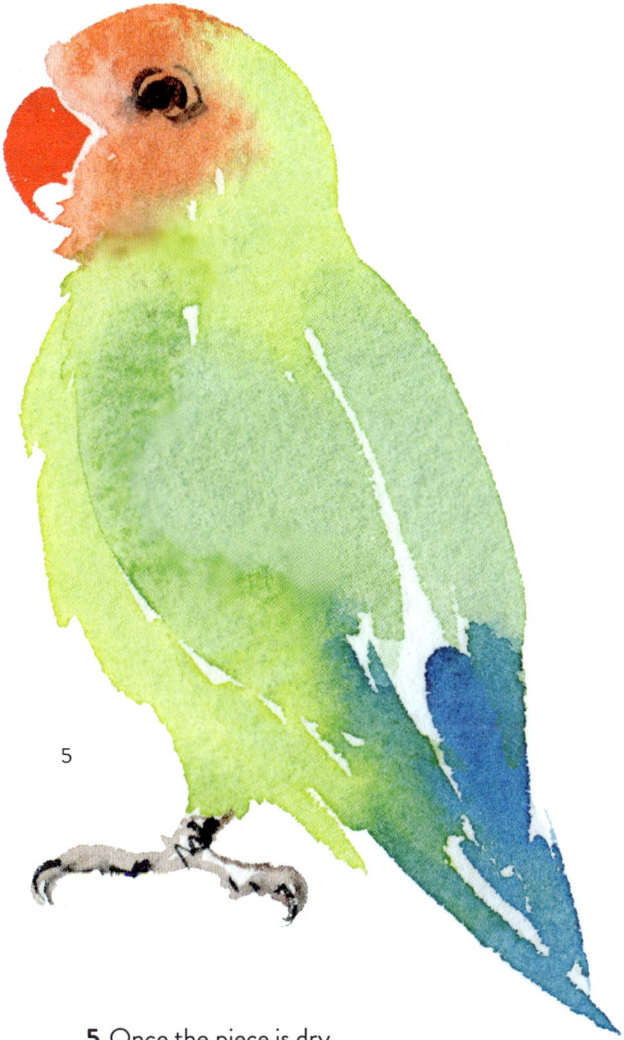

4 Paint a scribbled
claw with purple mix
and Ivory Black.

5 Once the piece is dry,
add an Ivory Black eye.

The Many Shades of Black

Earlier in the book we introduced the notion that black is not necessarily the darkest colour in your palette. Now we are painting with more contrast and texture, let's look further into the colour black to see what other colours we can pick out.

Some of the best black tones come from mixes. I tirelessly use Burnt Sienna and Payne's Grey for shadow tones; Cadmium-Free Red and Prussian Blue make an incredible deep purple that, when concentrated, is my favourite black for poppy and anemone centres. And when I need a colour that seems even darker than black, the inky depth of concentrated Payne's Grey works a treat.

Mixing blacks allows you to control the temperature of the colour with the proportion of warm or cool tones included.

NOW TRY
Primary colours mixed in equal parts
Transparent yellows will make a vibrant black; opaque yellows make a muddier black.

Earth tones
Mixing with soft paint fresh out of the tube allows you to mix a concentrated colour without too much water diluting the mix. Your wet brush will provide the small amount of necessary moisture.

Burnt Sienna

Payne's Grey

Warm Black

Cadmium-Free Red

Prussian Blue

Cool Black

TUTORIAL: Magpie

The Eurasian magpie appears black and white but on closer inspection has flashes of blue and green in its feathers. It's the perfect subject for trying out all sorts of black mixes.

Level
Intermediate

Colours
Ivory Black
Burnt Sienna
French Ultramarine
Payne's Grey
Winsor Blue
Green Gold
Buff Titanium

Brushes
Pointed round sizes 2, 0, 4/0

You will also need
HB pencil, soft and hard erasers

Mixes
Green mix: Green Gold (50%) and Winsor Blue (50%)
Dark green mix: Ivory Black (20%), Green Gold (40%) and Winsor Blue (40%)
Dark blue mix: Burnt Sienna (40%), Payne's Grey (40%) Winsor Blue (20%)
White mix: Burnt Sienna (30%), French Ultramarine (30%), Buff Titanium (40%) (heavily diluted)
Shadow mix: Burnt Sienna (50%), French Ultramarine (50%)
Black mix: Burnt Sienna (50%) and Payne's Grey (50%)

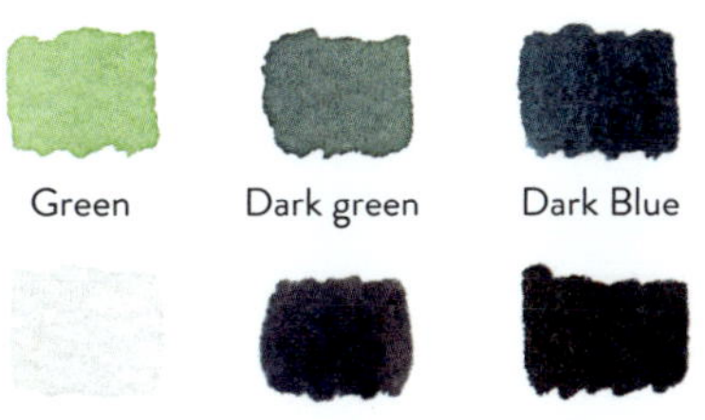

1 Draw the magpie in pencil, and roll with a soft eraser to fade the lines.

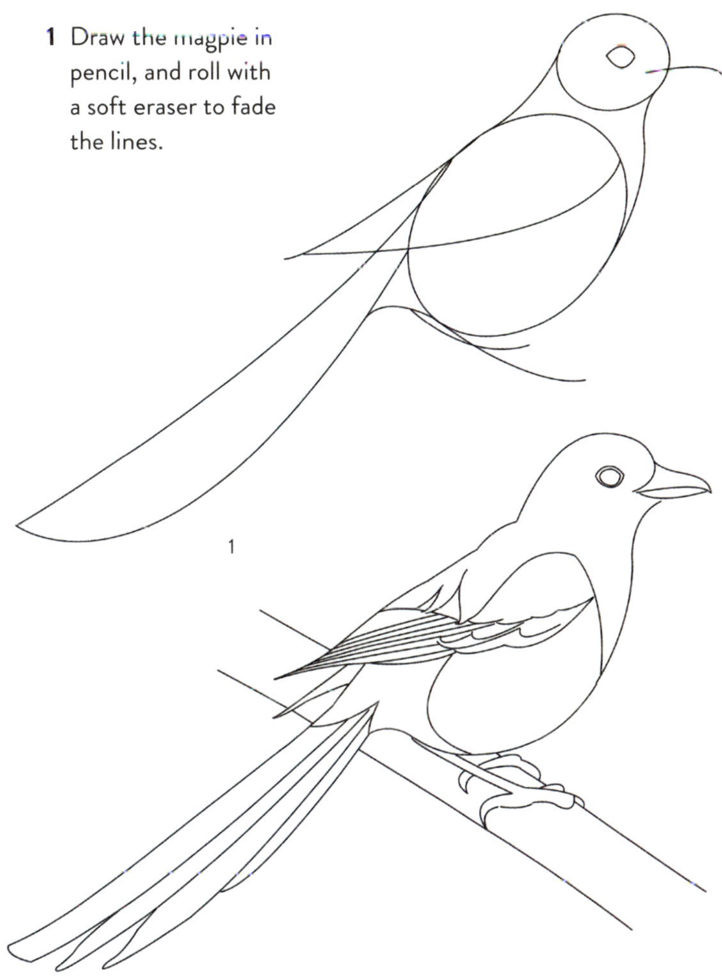

2 Paint C-curves of diluted white mix across the areas of white feathers with your size 0 brush. Paint a dilute shadow mix beak leaving some unpainted shine on the top. Dab shadow mix along the legs and feet for texture.

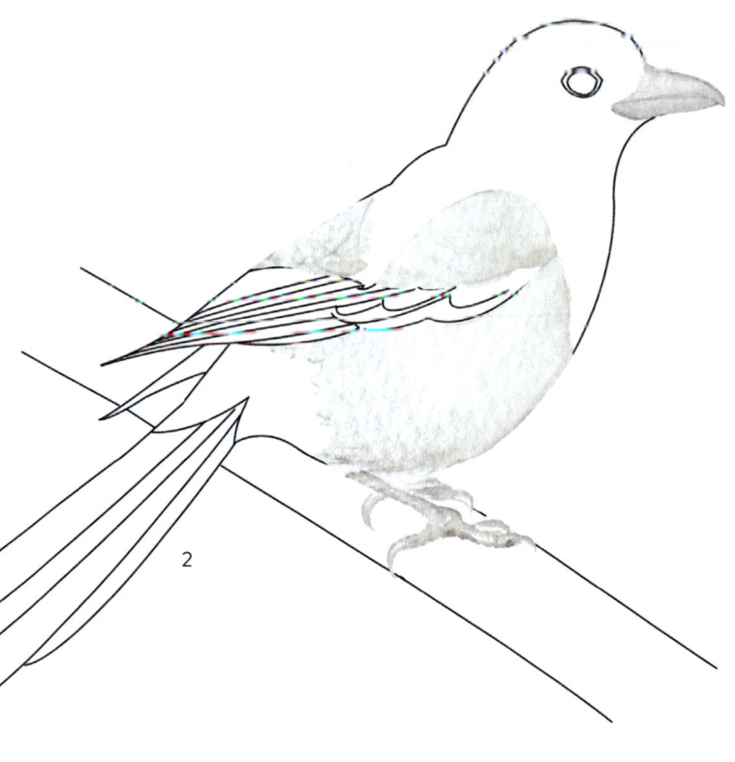

3 Paint Winsor Blue feathers along the most vibrant blue sections of wing feathers with your size 0 brush, allowing for tiny unpainted slivers between the strokes. While still wet, incorporate dark blue mix to paint in the darker blue feathers on the wing.

Paint alternating tail feathers in the green mix (choose the largest brush that still has good control; I started with a size 2 then went down to a 0 for the smaller feathers). While still wet, edge with the dark green mix. Allow tail feathers to dry before painting the one immediately next to it.

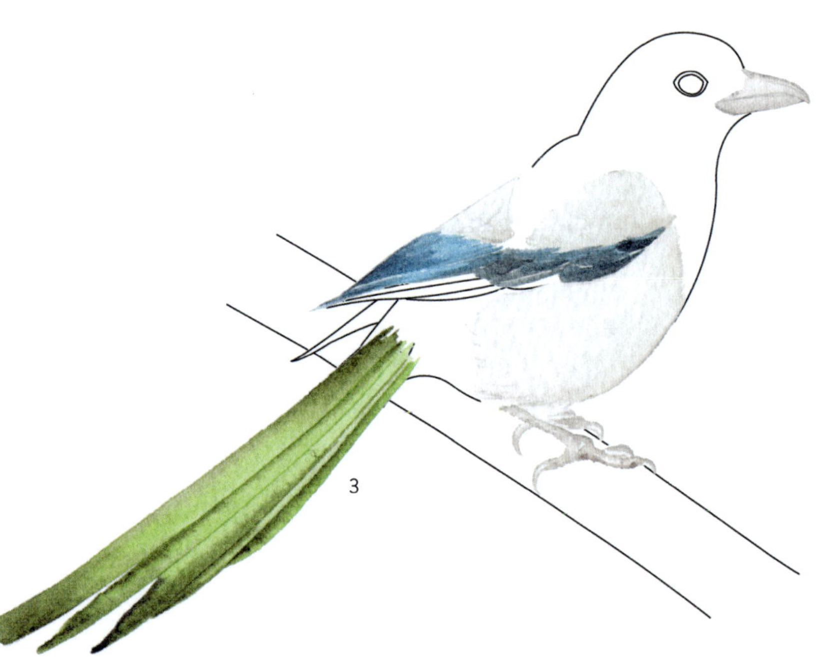

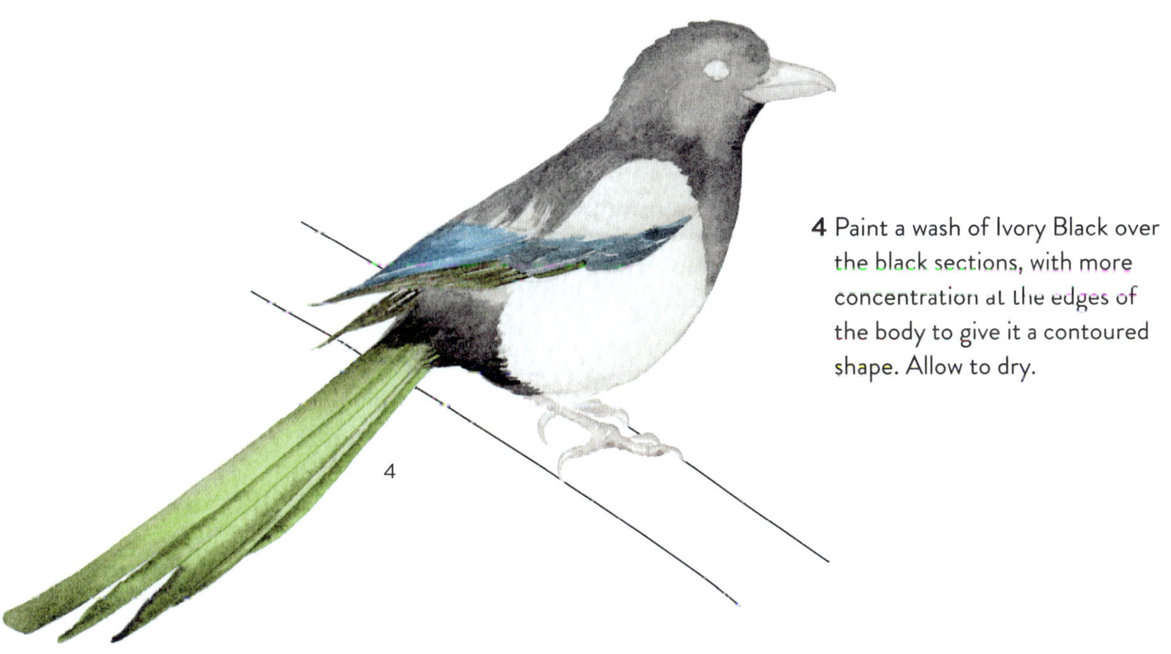

4 Paint a wash of Ivory Black over
the black sections, with more
concentration at the edges of
the body to give it a contoured
shape. Allow to dry.

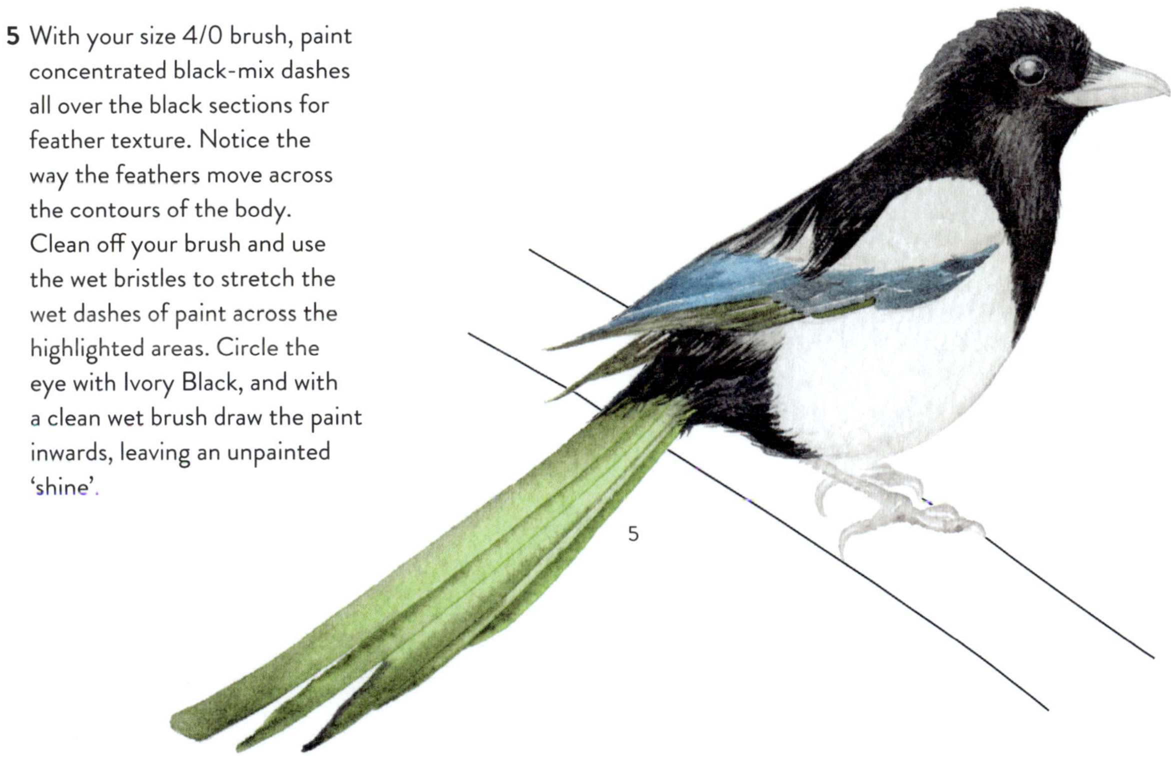

5 With your size 4/0 brush, paint
concentrated black-mix dashes
all over the black sections for
feather texture. Notice the
way the feathers move across
the contours of the body.
Clean off your brush and use
the wet bristles to stretch the
wet dashes of paint across the
highlighted areas. Circle the
eye with Ivory Black, and with
a clean wet brush draw the paint
inwards, leaving an unpainted
'shine'.

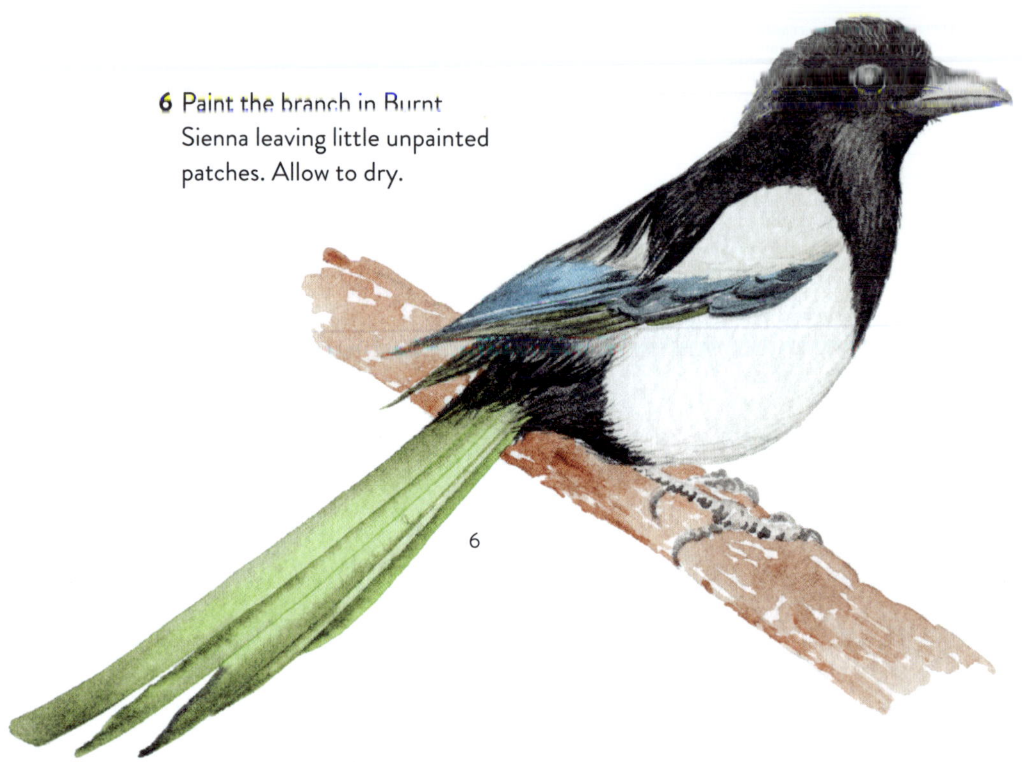

6 Paint the branch in Burnt
Sienna leaving little unpainted
patches. Allow to dry.

6

7 This is where the magic
happens: glazes. Make sure
your painting is 100% dry.
Refresh your water, clean a
space in your palettes and
thoroughly clean your brushes.
Make a fresh diluted green mix,
Winsor Blue and Payne's Grey,
respectively.

Paint a glaze of Winsor Blue
over the blue (and dark blue)
wing feathers with your size 0
brush. Paint a green-mix glaze
along the tail feathers with your
size 2 brush. While still wet, add
Payne's Grey to the tips and a
streak between each feather.

Paint a glaze of Payne's Grey
over the black sections. Watch
them turn to rich velvet as the
diluted colour smooths over
the top. Try to do this in as few
brush strokes as possible, so
use the largest brush you can
control in the tight corners.
Dilute your shadow mix to
almost clear water and glaze
along the white sections, still in
curving strokes.

Glaze dabs of Payne's Grey
along the shadowy side of the
branch. Once it dries, the
feet might need a bit more
definition: paint concentrated
dabs of Payne's Grey on
the legs, feet and along the
shadowy part of the branch.

Once fully dry, gently rub out
any visible pencil.

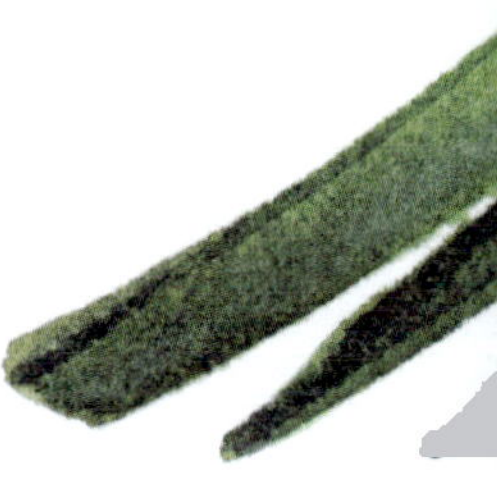

Prompt
Look again at animals you thought were black. Could you paint them with other colours and really bring them to life on the page?

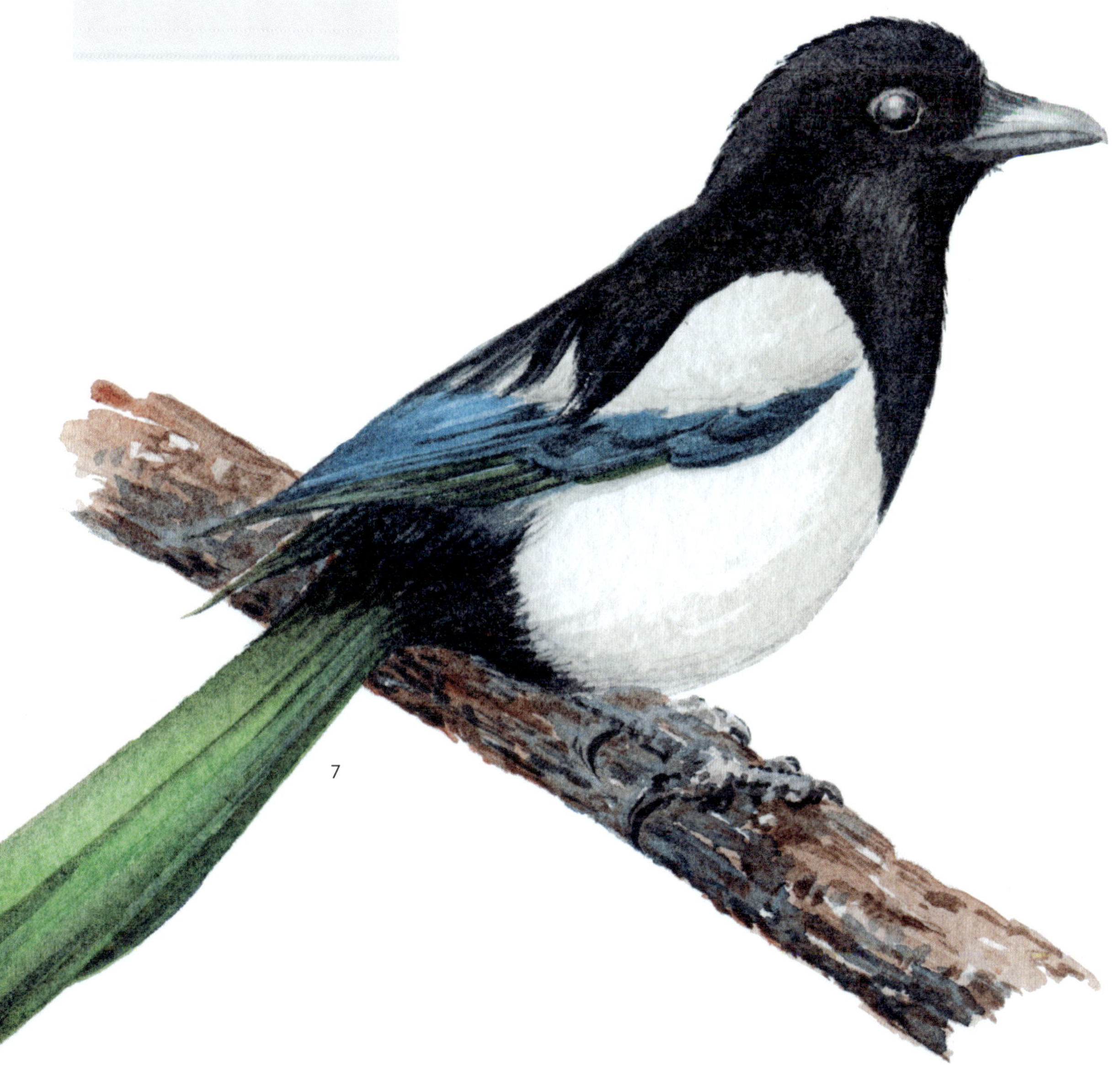

7

Masking Fluid and White Space

Masking fluid is a liquid latex used to mask off certain areas that you don't want watercolour to go. Some have built-in applicators or you can also buy special brushes to apply the fluid. Careful, it can ruin your regular brushes – I save old brushes that are no good for painting any more to use as applicators.

Masking fluid creates delicate and detailed unpainted areas, but the most wonderful thing is you can put it down on a dried painted layer, too.

Never speed up the drying process with heat. Just be patient, then you can peel off the dried fluid with your fingers or using an eraser.

THE COLOUR WHITE

To paint the colour white we can use the value scale and mix heavily diluted colours that are reflected or concealed in the white object. Look closely at a white rose petal and you'll see a faint greenish gold or peachy pink. For snowdrops, I mix Sap Green, Yellow Ochre, Burnt Sienna and Payne's Grey then add plenty of water to dilute it down to almost clear water. It looks invisible when it goes on the page but dries in a beautifully delicate off-white colour.

Zinc White, Titaium White and Chinese White are watercolours used to thicken other colours. These are great for layering highlights, but do note that your colour will lose its natural transparency and become chalky.

Simple highlight method: Wax crayon/pencil crayons create a resistance to watercolour resulting in highlights on the page. It's not particularly precise, and you can't remove it after painting in the way that you can with masking fluid but I've created some of my favourite pieces with this simple and expressive method.

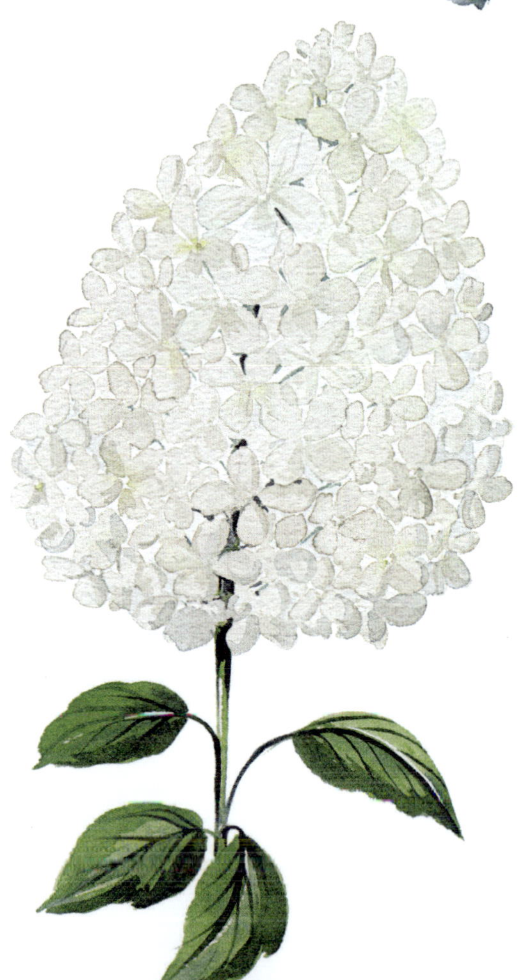

TUTORIAL: Aspen Forest

A forest of Aspen trees is the perfect topic for using masking fluid: the trees in the foreground will be masked before painting to be pure white, the mid-ground trees will have one wash before masking, and the background trees will appear most in shadow with two washes before the application of masking fluid.

Level
Beginner

Colours
Burnt Sienna
Cadmium-Free Orange
Cadmium-Free Yellow
Green Gold
Lemon Yellow
Payne's Grey
Sap Green

Brushes
Pointed round sizes 8, 0, 4/0

You will also need
Masking fluid, masking fluid applicator (I used an old size 0 brush), HB pencil, soft and hard erasers

Mix
Shadow mix: Burnt Sienna (50%) and Payne's Grey (50%)

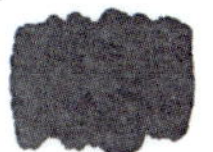

Shadow

1 Draw three horizontal lines: the top one demarcates the background, the middle one the mid-ground, and the bottom the foreground. Your largest tree trunks will hit the foreground line, while the thinnest will hit the background line. Draw a few branches on the trees in the foreground. Roll with a soft eraser to fade the pencil. Paint your foreground trees with masking fluid as well as a few leaf clusters. Allow to dry completely (it will be tacky to the touch).

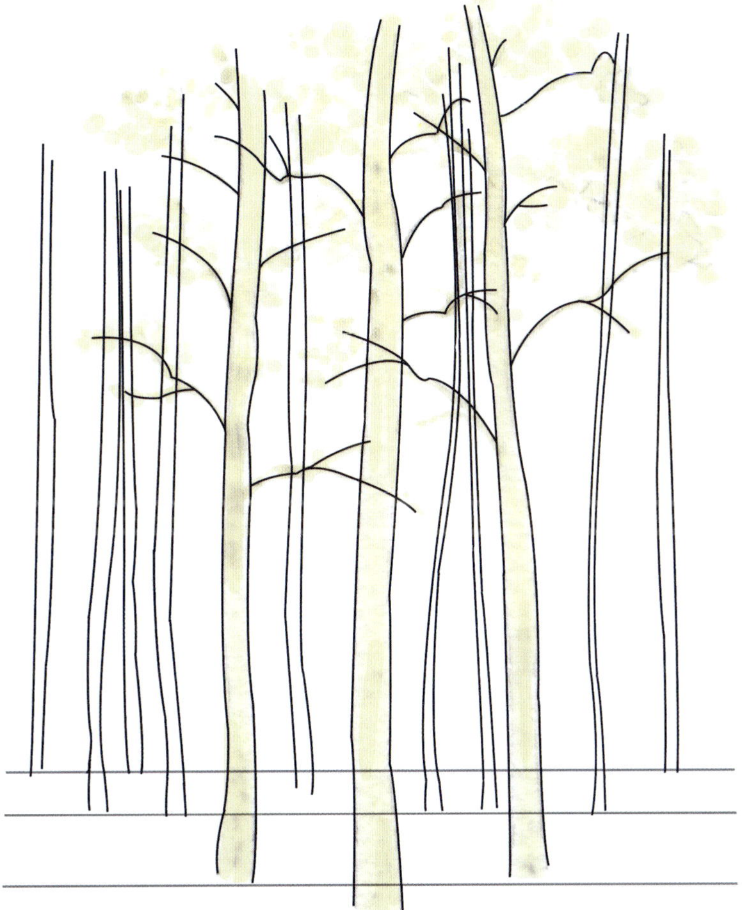

1

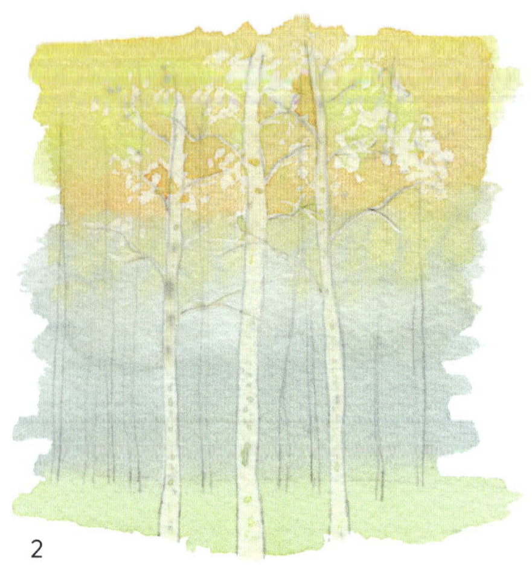

2

2 With your size 8 brush paint a wash of Green Gold along the ground, then a shadow-mix wash two-thirds up the trees. Thoroughly clean your brush and paint dabs of coffee-consistency Lemon Yellow, Cadmium-Free Yellow and Cadmium-Free Orange in the top section of the piece. Allow the yellow to meet the shadow but don't overwork the colours. Allow to dry fully.

3 Paint your mid-ground trees and a few leaf clusters in masking fluid. Allow to dry completely. Repeat the washes – the green can be glazed over the top in streaks but paint a full shadow wash and dabs of yellow leaves. Allow to dry fully.

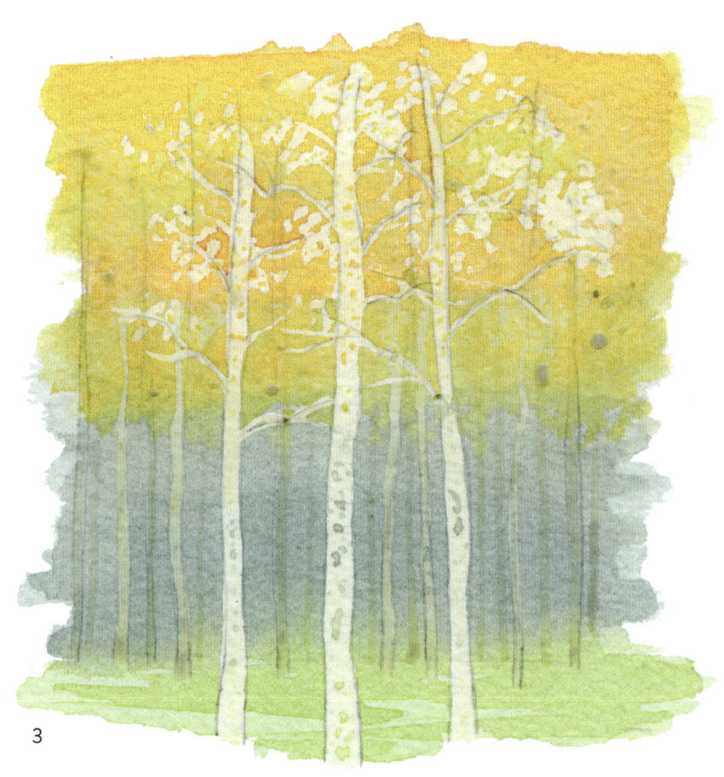

3

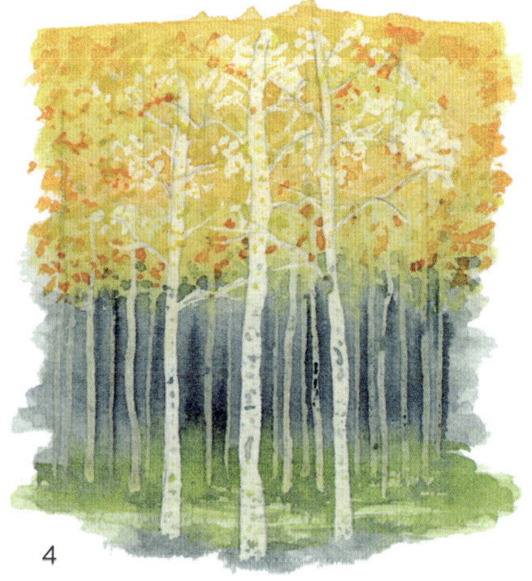

4

4 Paint masking fluid on your background trees and a few leaf clusters (add in more trees if you wish). Allow to dry completely. Repeat the washes, add some shadow mix to the green ground around the tree bases. Paint a shadow wash and add vertical streaks of Payne's Grey to suggest further shadowy trees in the distance. Add milk consistency yellow and orange leaves. Allow to dry fully.

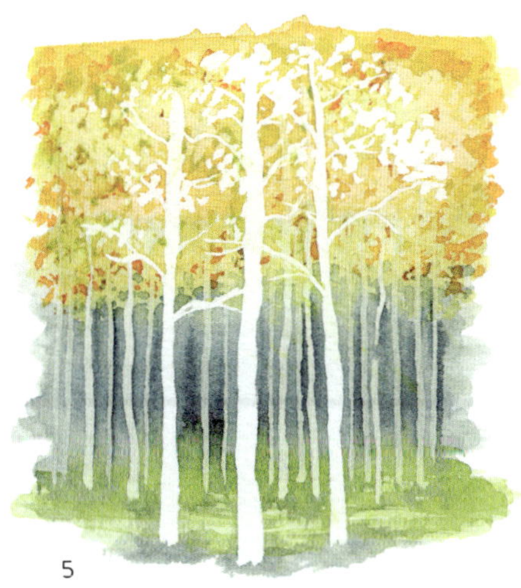

5 Rub off all the masking fluid. I like to use a hard eraser as it will rub out any pencil in the process. Now it's time for some detail! Paint milk-consistency Lemon Yellow dabs among the white leaves. To create more perspective, add the most detail to the foreground, and some to the mid-ground, but leave the background untouched.

6 Paint a dilute glaze of shadow up one side of the trees in the foreground and mid-ground. Add Sap Green tufts of grass and add Payne's Grey to the foreground. With your size 4/0 brush, use a concentrated shadow mix to dry brush bark detail onto the foreground trees and branches. Dilute it and do half as much bark detail to the mid-ground trees.

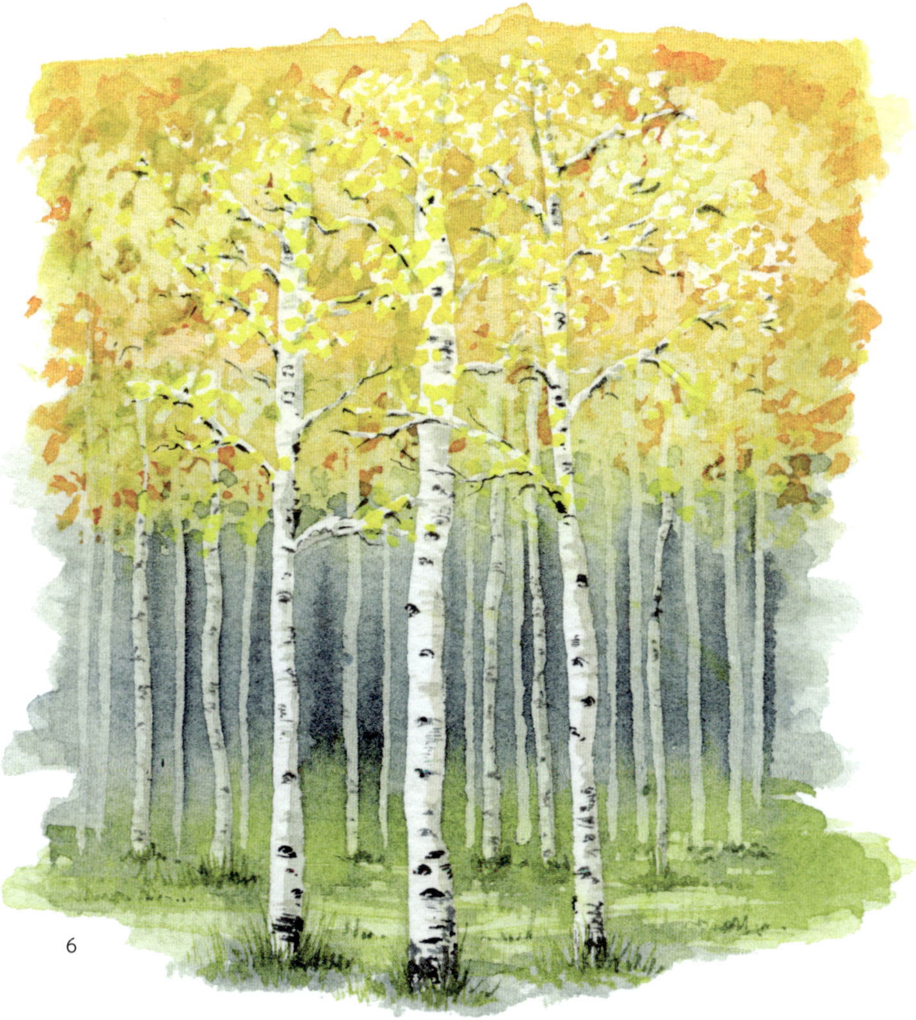

I have taught many snowdrop tutorials, making a new discovery each time. When it comes to painting snowdrops, it's all about the light and how it bounces off the flowers and the snow.

Level
Intermediate

Colours
Burnt Sienna
Green Gold
Lemon Yellow
Payne's Grey
Pyrrol Orange
Sap Green
Yellow Ochre

Brushes
Sizes 8, 2, 0, 4/0

You will also need
HB pencil, soft and hard erasers

Mixes
Petal mix: Sap Green (30%), Yellow Ochre (30%), Burnt Sienna (30%) and Payne's Grey (20%) (dilute)
Light petal mix: Lemon Yellow (20%), Sap Green (20%), Yellow Ochre (20%), Burnt Sienna (20%) and Payne's Grey (20%) (dilute)
Shadow petal mix: Sap Green (20%), Yellow Ochre (20%), Burnt Sienna (20%) Payne's Grey (40%) (dilute)
Stem mix: Green Gold (50%) and Sap Green (50%)

MIXING NOTES
Create the petal mix and swatch it, adding more water to see how pale you can get your colour. When it dries 30% lighter, these watery grey swatches will start to look perfect for snowdrop petals as well as being a perfect base to add Lemon Yellow highlights. Slightly increase the Payne's Grey for lowlights.

Snow is another wonderful example of how white is full of colour. In a vibrant sunset, snow glows with all the warm colours, contrasted with the long blue shadows, so be ready to paint all sorts of colours when you're creating a predominantly 'white' scene. I chose Pyrrol Orange and Lemon Yellow for the warmth on the snow.

1 Draw a cluster of snowdrops. Draw wobbly horizontal lines for the snow. Roll with a soft eraser to fade the pencil.

Petal

Light petal

Shadow petal

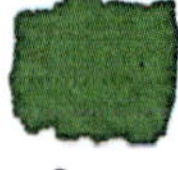
Stem

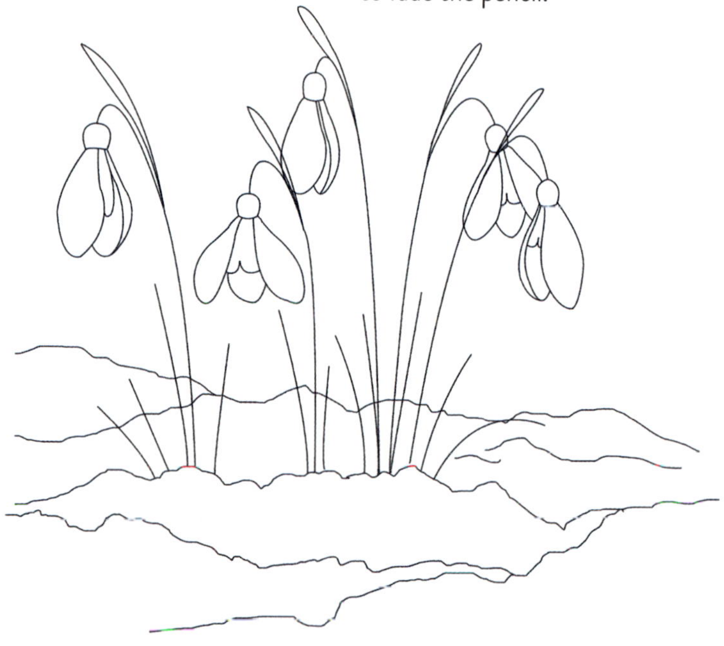

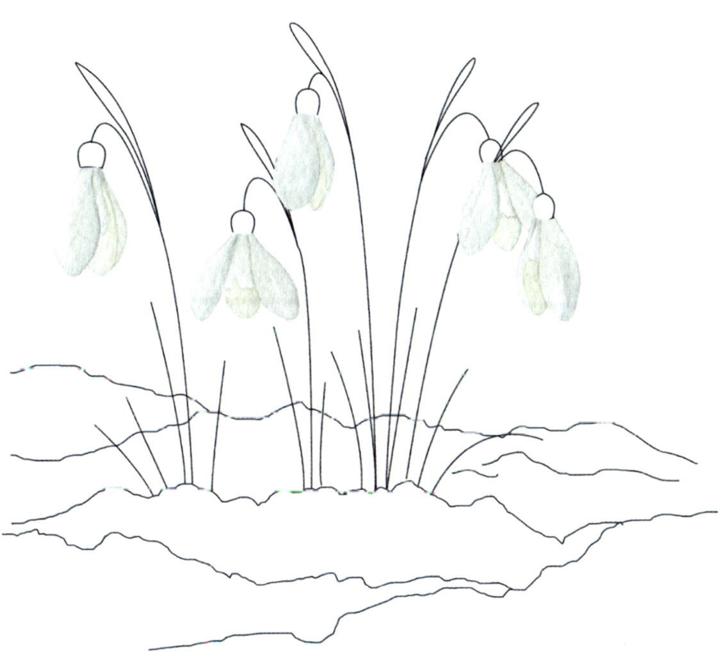

2 Paint each foreground petal in petal mix with your size 2 brush, allowing the sections to dry before painting one immediately next to it. Even at this stage you can add a sweep of shadow petal mix down one side of the petals. The scene is backlit, so paint your background petals in light petal mix. The flower centre needs only a little streak of petal mix, it can be largely left unpainted as a contrast to the other white petals around it.

3 Paint the stem mix details on the flower and spathe with your size 0 brush. Add a little more Sap Green to the mix and paint the leaves shooting up through the snow with a larger brush.

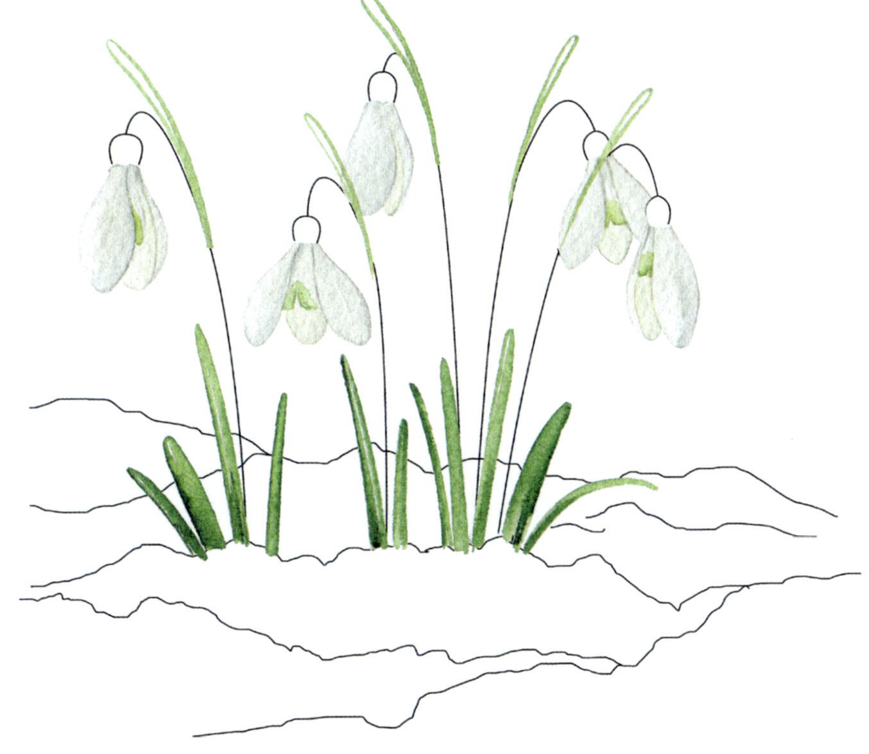

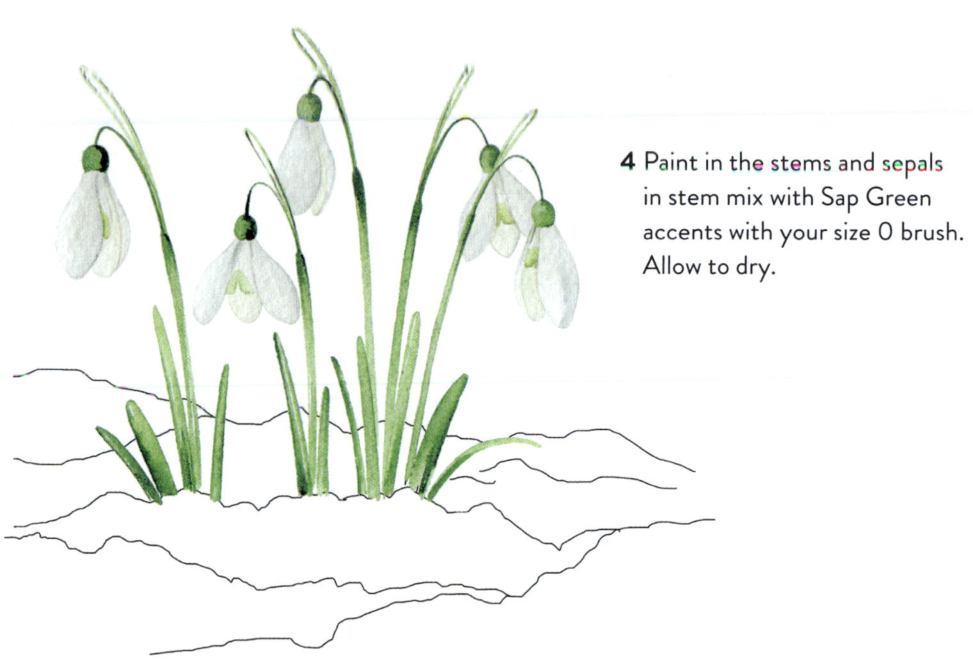

4 Paint in the stems and sepals in stem mix with Sap Green accents with your size 0 brush. Allow to dry.

5 For each section of snow, paint tea-consistency dabs of Lemon Yellow and Pyrrol Orange along the top with your size 8 brush. Clean off your brush and blend the colour down with clear water. Blend this in to dilute Payne's Grey to the bottom edge of the section. This will give the appearance of-churned up channels of snow. Add more Payne's Grey shadows to the base of the snowdrop stems.

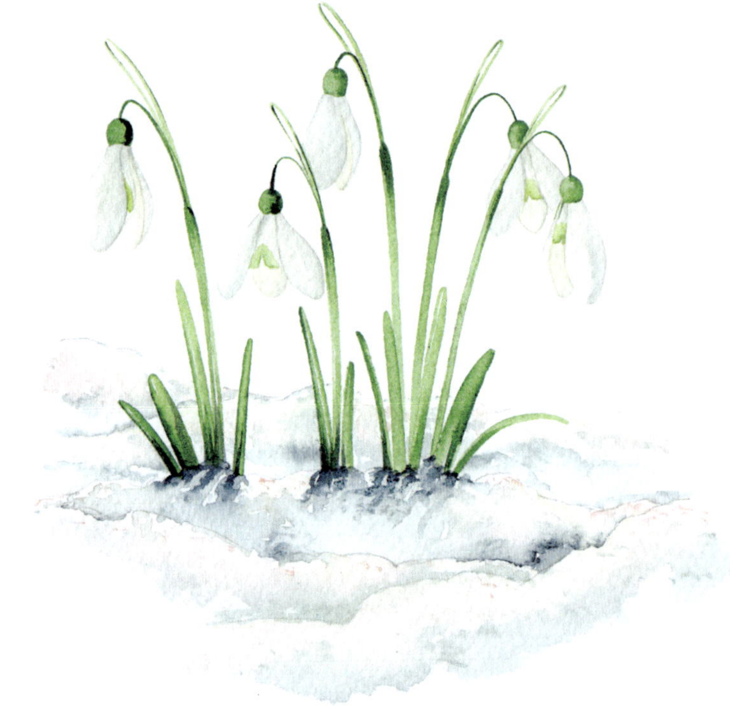

Prompt
Try incorporating other colours into your petal mix and see how it influences the overall look of the flower.

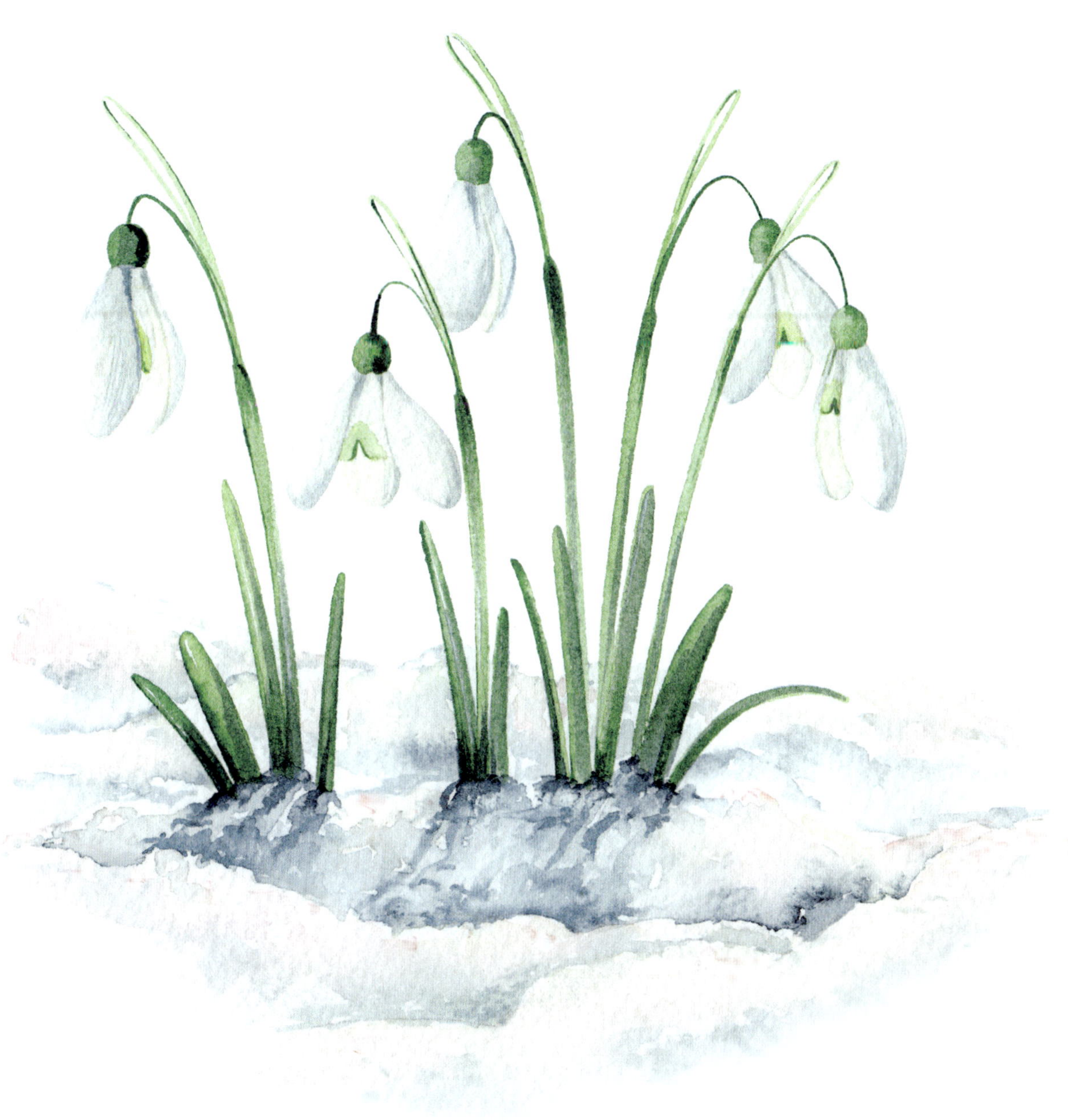

6 Add a final contrasting glaze
of shadow petal mix on the
shadowy side of the petals with
your size 0 brush in fine lines.
Paint Sap Green accents on
the central petal's green edge.
Once dry, rub out any visible
pencil with a hard eraser.

Still Life

Now, over the next few exercises, let's bring all the techniques we've practised so far together...

TUTORIAL: **Glass Vase of Kumquats**

This vase of kumquats will also teach you the new skill of painting glass effects in watercolour.

Level
Intermediate

Colours
Aqua Green
Cadmium-Free Orange
Cadmium-Free Red
French Ultramarine
Green Gold
Payne's Grey
Pyrrol Orange
Raw Umber
Sap Green
Yellow Ochre

Brushes
Pointed round sizes 8, 4, 2, 0, 4/0

You will also need
HB pencil, soft and hard erasers

Mixes
Petal mix: Green Gold (33%), Payne's Grey (33%), Raw Umber (33%) (very dilute)
Leaf mix: Green Gold (50%) and Sap Green (50%)
Underpainting mix: Cadmium-Free Orange (80%) and French Ultramarine (20%)
Leaf vein mix: Sap Green (70%), Payne's Grey (30%)

1 Draw the vase scene in pencil. Because the composition has many overlapping elements, it will be useful to draw the leaves in full. Draw circles and ovals for the flowers. Roll with a soft eraser to fade the lines.

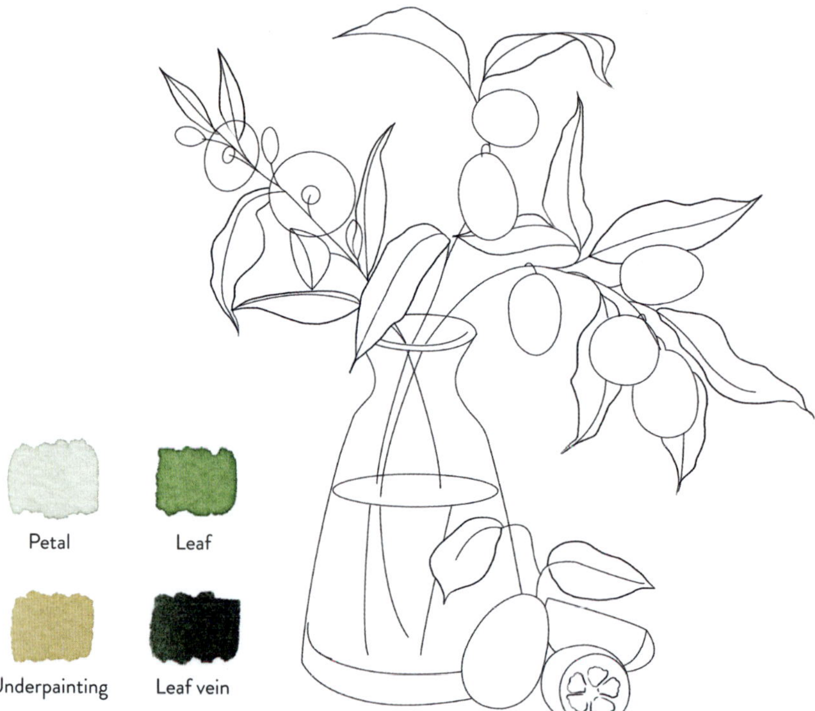

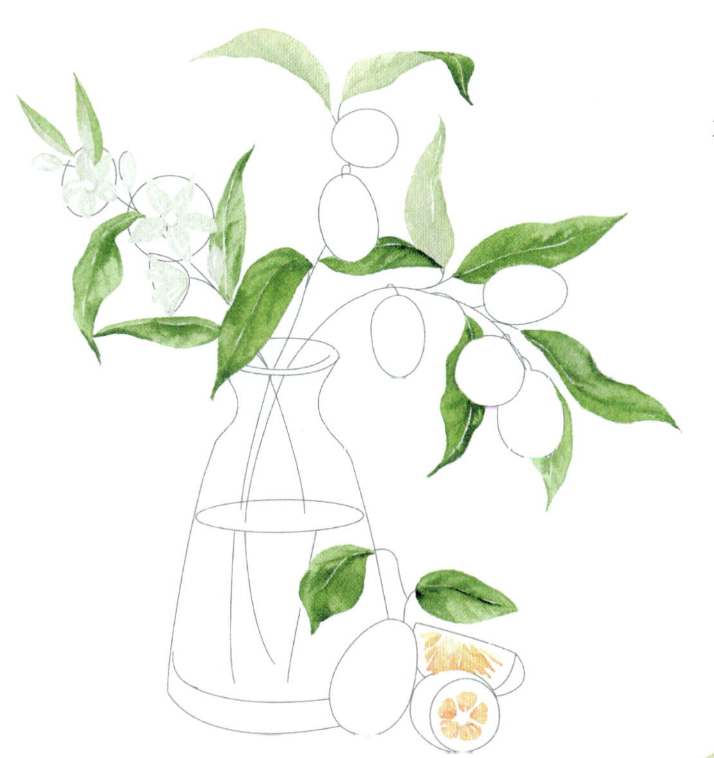

2 Dilute your petal mix to a sludgy green, then paint the visible underside of any leaves with your size 2 brush. Next, dilute the petal mix until it looks nearly clear and paint five petals on each flower with your size 2 brush.

Paint strokes of dilute Cadmium-Free Orange on the inside of the cut fruit segments with your size 0 brush.

Paint the remaining leaves in the leaf mix with some wet-on-wet fine lines of Sap Green leaf veins.

3 The underpainting mix uses the complementary colour blue to desaturate the orange. Paint a mottled edge on the shadowy side of each kumquat with your size 0 brush.

Paint in the stems and branches with a mixture of Yellow Ochre, leaf mix and Raw Umber wet on wet with your size 0 brush. Dab Raw Umber in the flower centres.

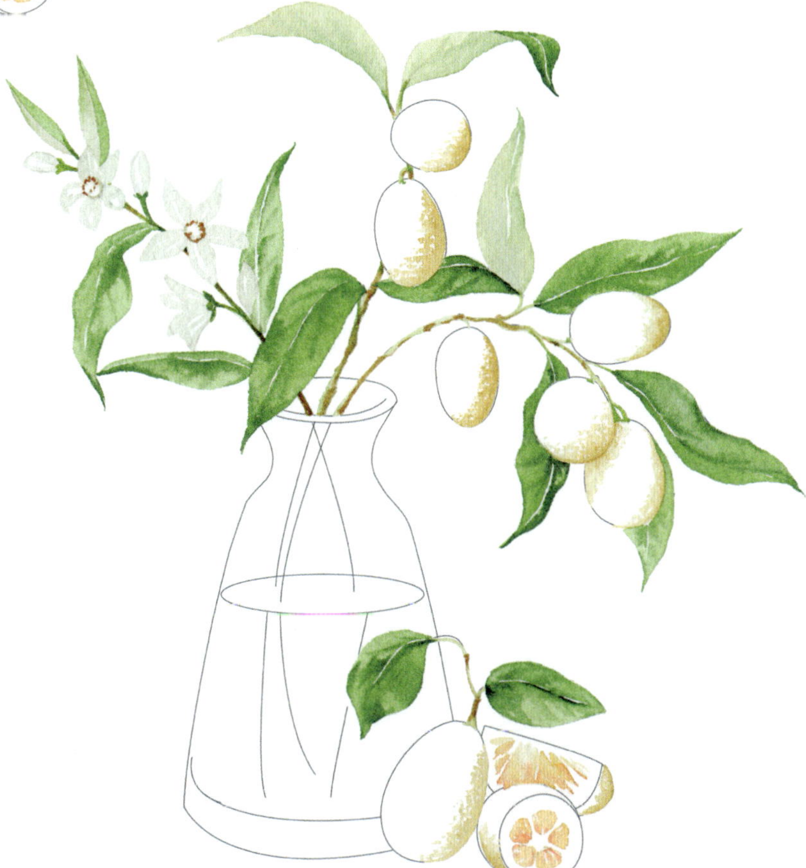

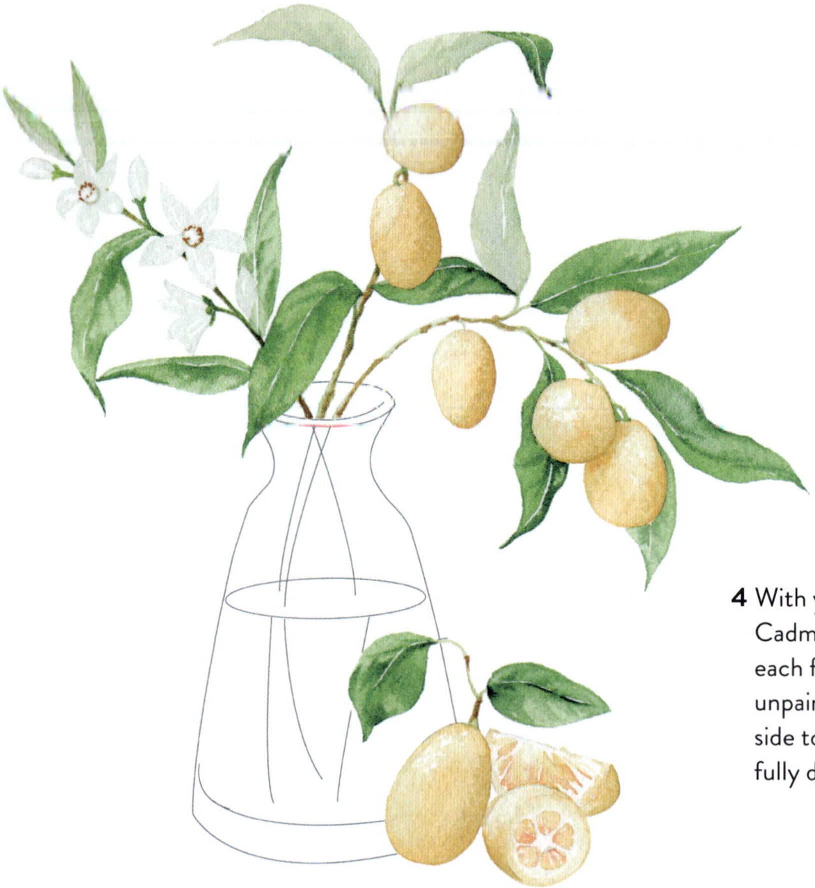

4 With your size 2 brush, glaze
Cadmium-Free Orange over
each fruit, leaving a dabbed
unpainted area on the opposite
side to your shadow. Allow to
fully dry.

5 Glaze Pyrrol Orange over
each fruit, leaving a dabbed
unpainted area on the opposite
side to your shadow. Allow to
fully dry.

Extend the stems down into the
vase with the same colours you
used before, leaving a gap at
the rim of the vase and where
the stems hit the water. Take
a clean, wet size 8 brush and
make a few horizontal strokes
over the stems beneath the
water line.

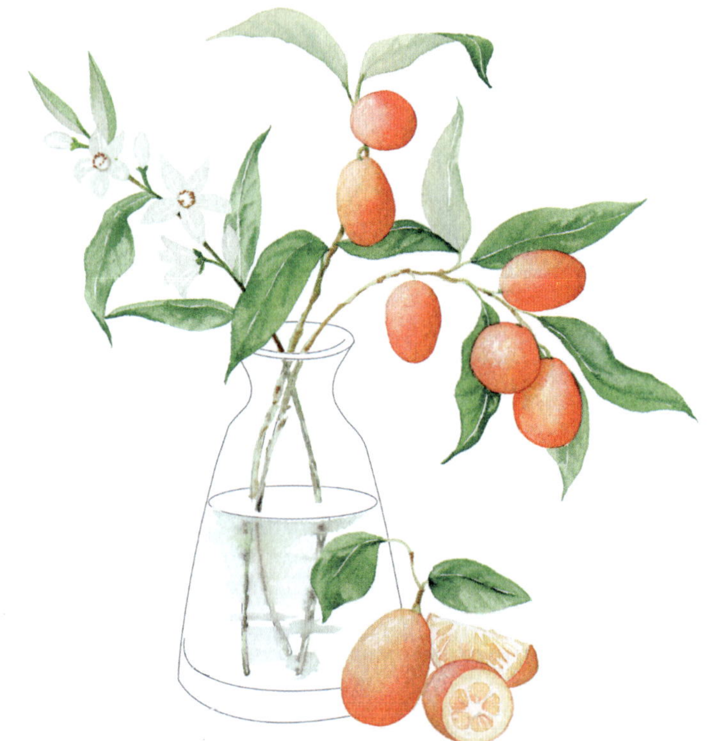

6 Vase painting is all about looking
for the quirky light and shade that
bounces off the glass (it's worth
having a close look at your own
water jar right now to see this first
hand). With your size 4 brush, paint
strokes of dilute Payne's Grey up
and down, building the vase shape.
Add accents of darker Payne's
Grey beneath the rim and round
the base. Incorporate a tiny bit of
Aqua Green to your dilute Payne's
Grey and add a few more strokes to
complete the curve of the base and
beneath the water line.

Try to leave the surface of the water
unpainted apart from a few faint
ripples around the stems. You can
also add a glaze for the reflection of
the orange fruit in the glass.

Once fully dry, rub out any visible
pencil with the hard eraser.

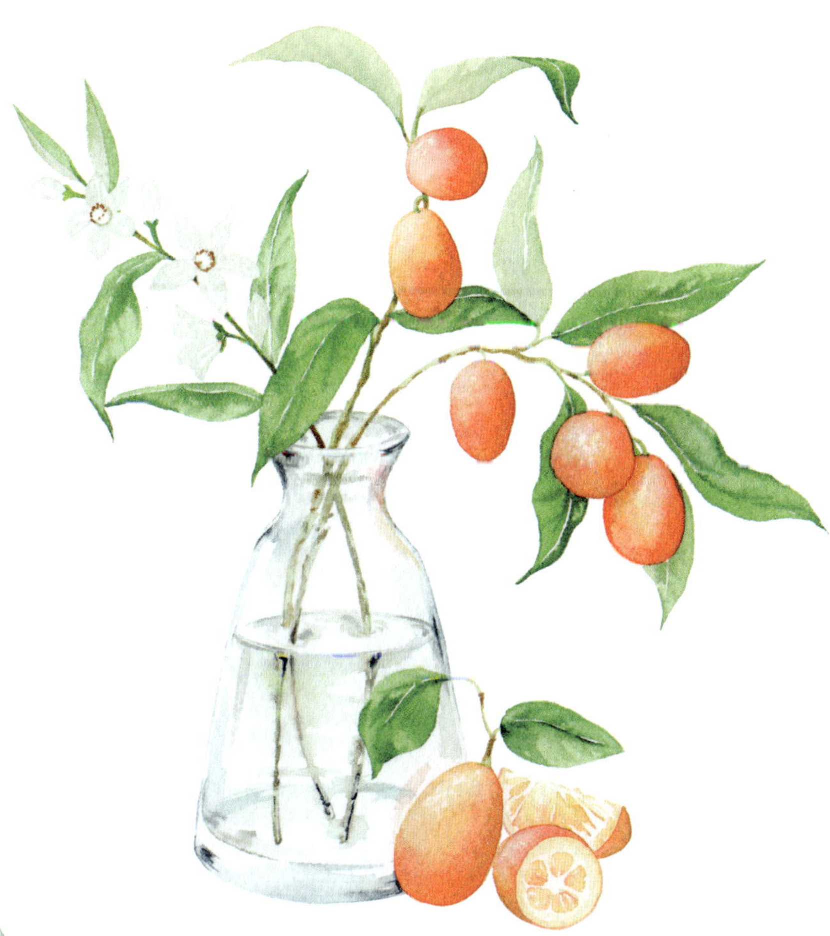

Prompt
*What if you were painting coloured
glass? Try following the steps with
a different colour palette and see
how much light and shade you can
achieve with layers, glazes and
unpainted space.*

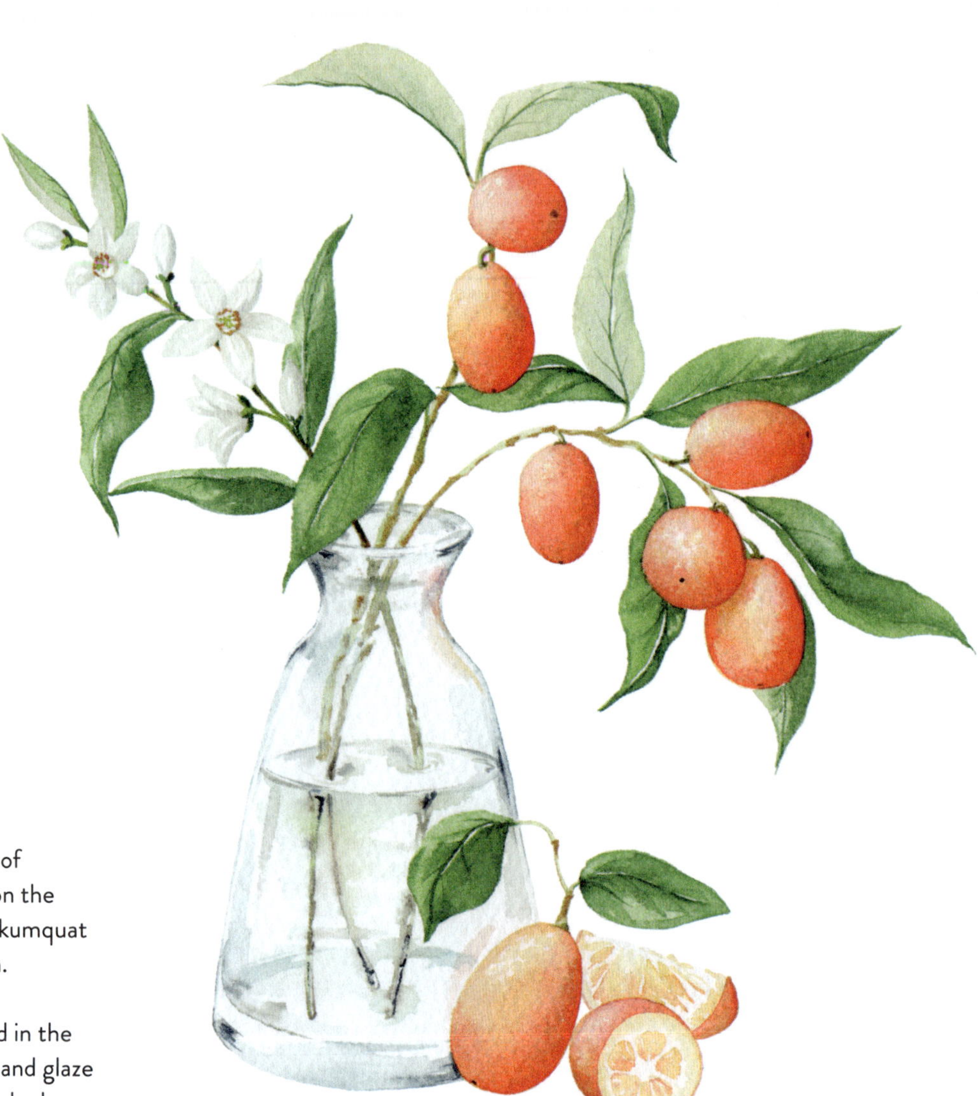

7 Glaze a mottled edge of Cadmium-Free Red on the shadowy side of each kumquat with your size 0 brush.

Dab some Green Gold in the centre of each flower and glaze a dilute Payne's Grey shadow over the part of the petals.

Paint fine-line leaf veins on the leaves with your rigger brush.

Add lowlights of Payne's Grey to the stems beneath the water and a dot on the base of each fruit.

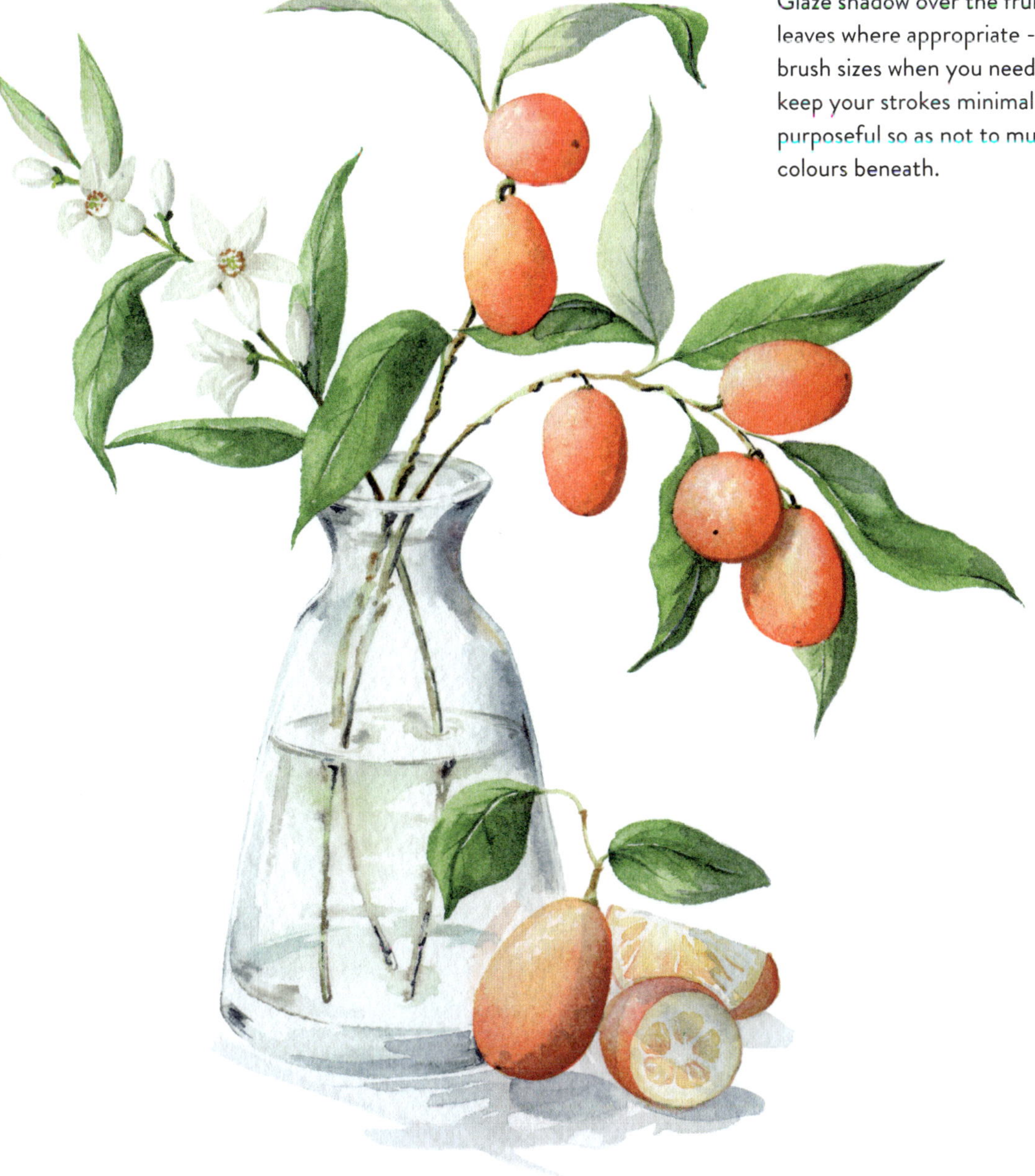

8 Continue to add lowlights to the stems with concentrated browns, greens and Payne's Grey. Let the piece dry fully and mix up some dilute Payne's Grey for shadows.

With your size 8 brush, paint a few sweeps of shadow down the shadowy side of the vase and underneath the fruit on the floor, as well as a few curving streaks of shadow from the vase (again, look at your water jar to see how light and shadow shines through it). Glaze shadow over the fruit and leaves where appropriate - change brush sizes when you need to, but keep your strokes minimal and purposeful so as not to muddy the colours beneath.

Let's put some techniques together to paint this sunny window box.

Colours
Alizarin Crimson
Buff Titanium
Burnt Sienna
Cerulean Blue
Green Gold
Opera Rose
Payne's Grey
Permanent Rose
Pyrrol Orange
Sap Green
Winsor Blue
Yellow Ochre

Brushes
Pointed round sizes 8, 2, 0, 4/0

You will also need
Masking fluid, masking fluid brush, HB pencil, set square, compass, soft and hard erasers

Mixes
Wall mix: Buff Titanium (50%), Yellow Ochre (30%), Payne's Grey (20%)
Window mix: Cerulean Blue (50%), Winsor Blue (30%), Payne's Grey (20%)
Shadow mix: Payne's Grey (50%) and Burnt Sienna (50%)

Wall   Window   Shadow

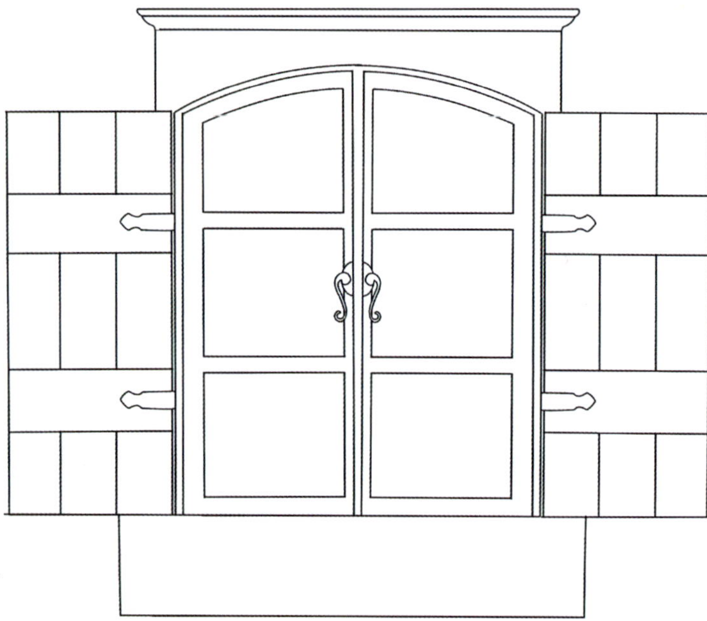

1 Draw the window box scene in pencil. Once you've drawn the neat, straight lines, add a little wobble to the lines of the shutters and windowpanes. Roll with a soft eraser to fade the lines.

2 Dab masking-fluid flowers around the window-box area and allow to dry. Paint wall mix in textural strokes with your size 8 brush around the window, dab dilute Payne's Grey in places while still wet. Once dry, paint the shutters in dilute Cerulean Blue with your size 0 brush, painting textural streaks to establish the wood grain. Keep it light so the flowers can show up on top of it later.

Use wall mix to paint the window sashes, leaving slivers of unpainted space and adding a little dilute Yellow Ochre or Burnt Sienna in places for extra depth. Leave the window frame unpainted.

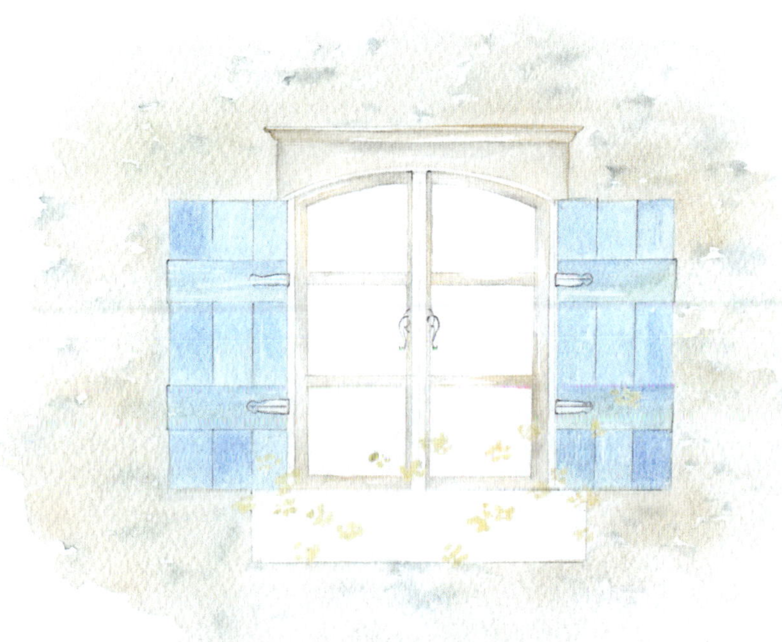

3 Use wall mix to paint the window frame, leaving slivers of unpainted space and adding a little dilute Yellow Ochre or Burnt Sienna in places for extra depth.

Use your size 2 brush to scribble dilute window mix into the windows, purposefully leaving slivers of unpainted space. (Keep it light so the flowers can show up on top of it later.) While still wet, use your size 0 brush to paint a Payne's Grey edge on the outer side and top curve.

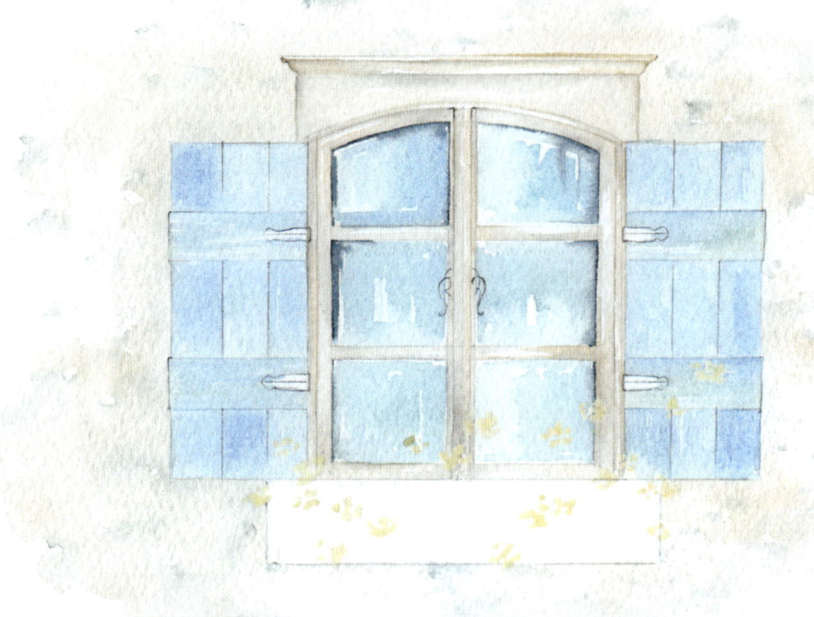

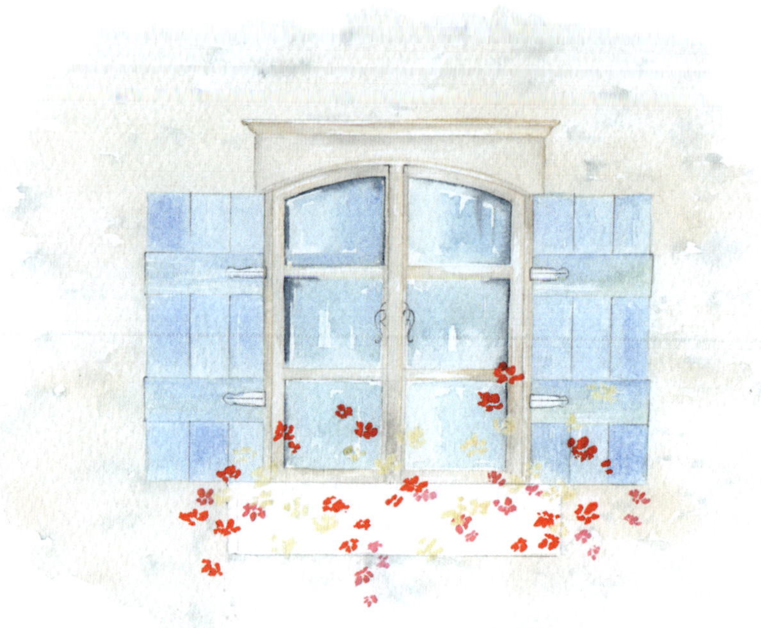

4 Paint cream consistency Pyrrol Orange and opera rose petals around the window box area with your size 0 brush.

5 With your size 0 brush, paint wet-on-wet Green Gold loops of leaves, dropping in accents of Sap Green. Keep the right-hand side of the window box lighter, adding more Sap Green to the left hand side. Paint Sap Green stems with your size 4/0 brush.

Once dry, carefully paint in a Yellow Ochre and Burnt Sienna wet-on-wet terracotta pot with your size 0 brush.

Once the painting is 100% dry, rub off the masking fluid and use the hard eraser to rub out any visible pencil.

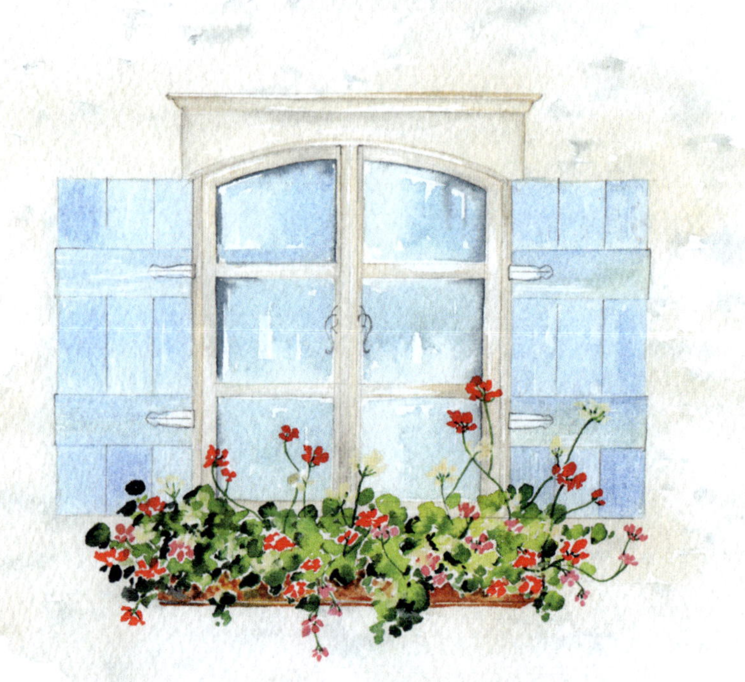

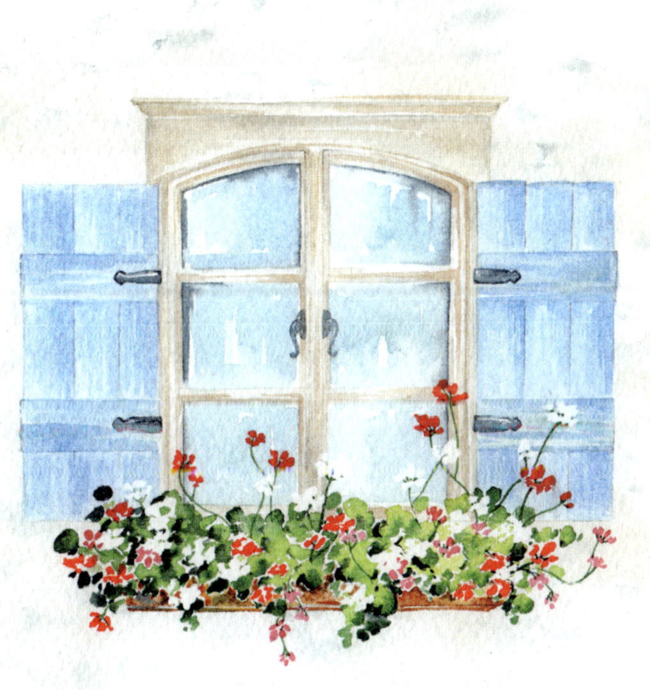

6 With your size 0 brush, glaze a textured layer of Cerulean Blue on the shutters, and wall mix on the window frame and sashes. Paint a wash of Payne's Grey on the ironmongery.

For the flowers, use your size 4/0 brush to paint alizarin crimson accents on the Pyrrol Orange petals and Permanent Rose accents on the Opera Rose petals. You can use these colours to add a few extra little flowers here and there. For the white flowers, paint dilute Opera Rose accents.

7 With your smaller brushes, layer fine lines of detail on the shutters (Cerulean Blue) and on the window (Burnt Sienna). If the lines feel too heavy, clean off your size 2 brush and smooth over them to partially blend them. Allow to dry fully.

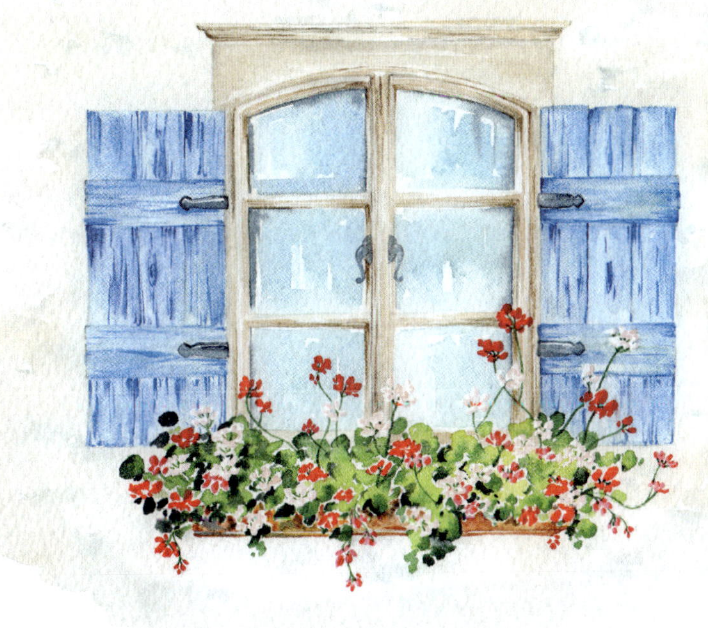

0 It can be really helpful to draw a pencil arrow just off to the side to establish the direction the light is coming from. Prepare plenty of dilute shadow in your palette and use a size 4 brush to glaze shadow on the window and shutters. Remember that your textured wall will affect how the shadow falls. For the window box use a size 0 brush to glaze in the gaps and flower and leaf shadows on the background.

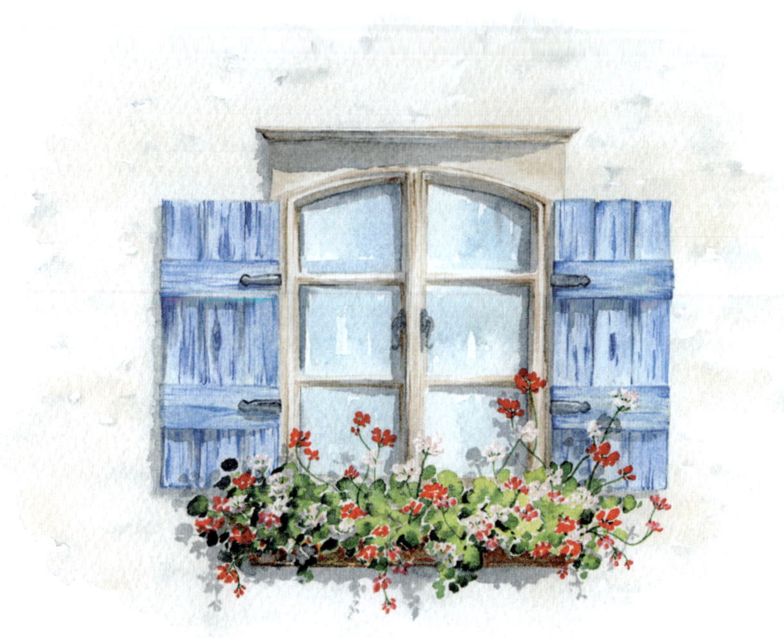

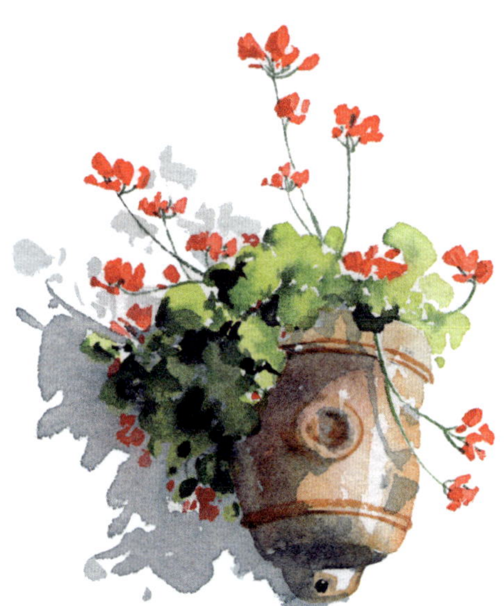

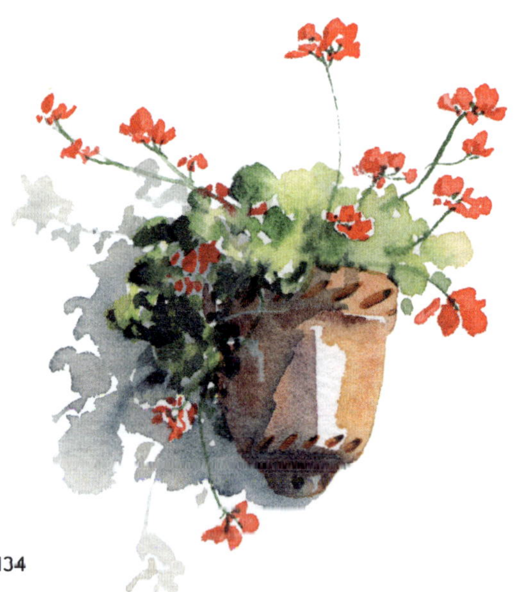

You could apply these techniques to individual plant pots. Here are two wall hanging pots that pop off the page with use of shadow glazes.

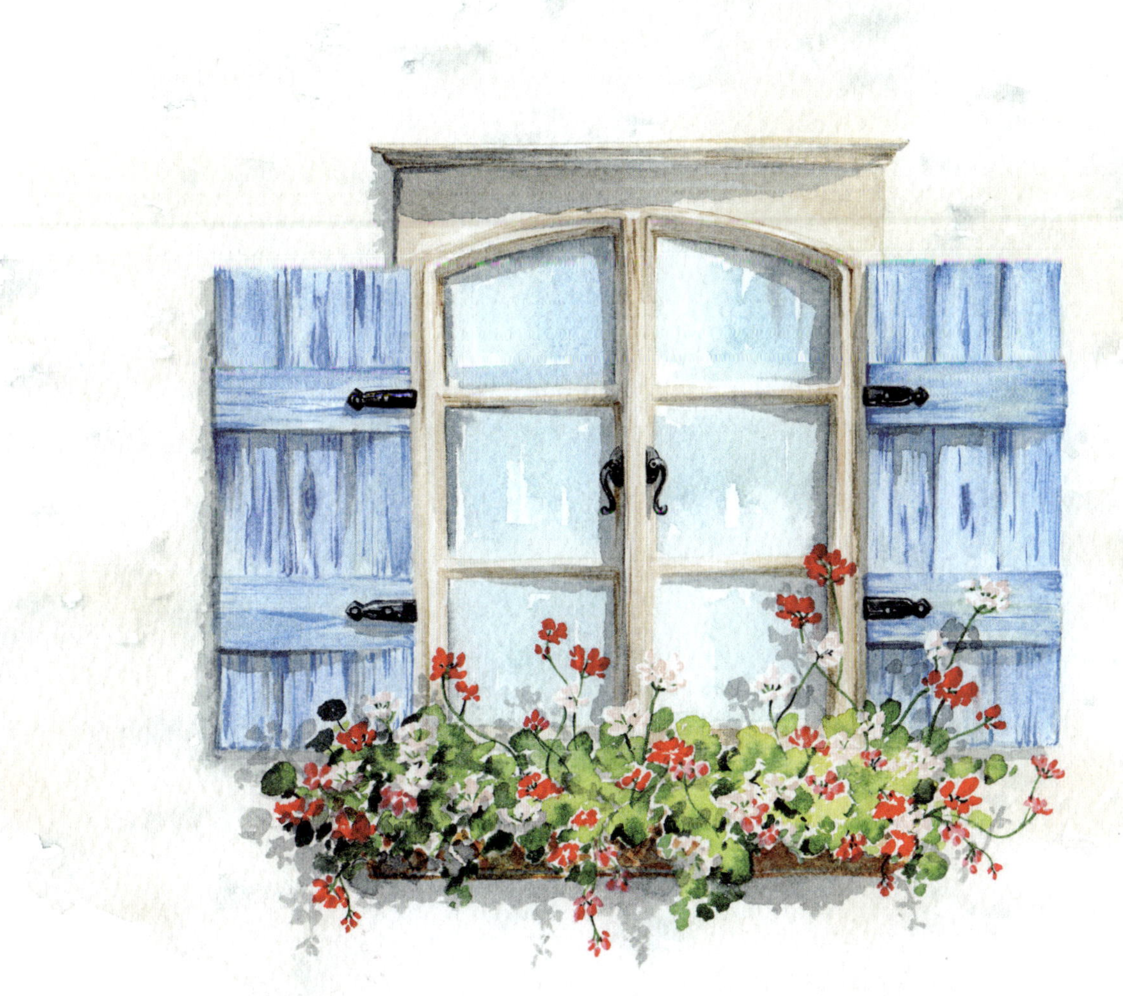

9 The shadow glaze will dry
lighter so you could add a few
extra accents where necessary.
Once dry, paint concentrated
Payne's Grey accents on the
ironmongery.

Getting Started in Landscape Painting

Landscape painting is all about creating depth and distance in your piece, here are some simple ways to achieve that through colour and texture.

Divide your piece into a foreground, mid-ground and background.

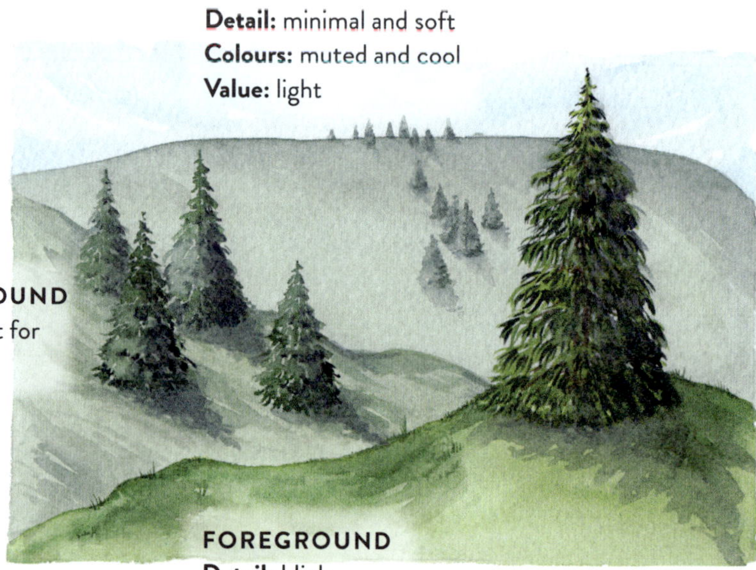

BACKGROUND
Detail: minimal and soft
Colours: muted and cool
Value: light

MID-GROUND
A midpoint for all factors

FOREGROUND
Detail: High
Colours: Vibrant, warm and saturated
Value: Dark

WHAT TO PAINT FIRST?

To work out what to paint first you can use the value scale and paint from light to dark. This translates into painting the background washes, then the mid-value shapes, and finishing up with the foreground details.

See how the pine trees change in detail, colour and value in the foreground, the mid-ground and the background.

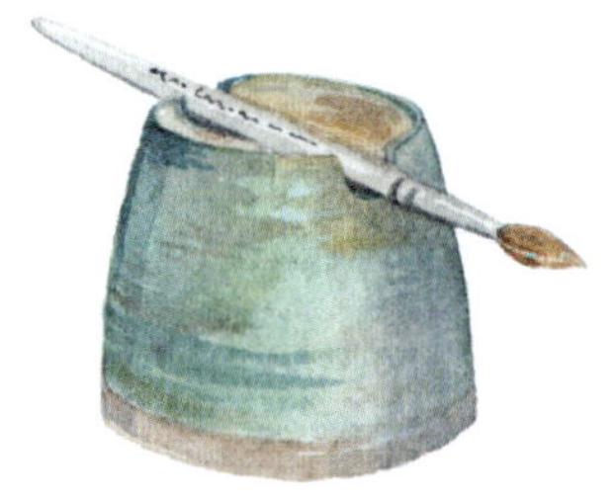

VIGNETTES

If you prefer to work on a small scale, why not try a vignette? Crop down your landscape into a manageable little window like this little lighthouse.

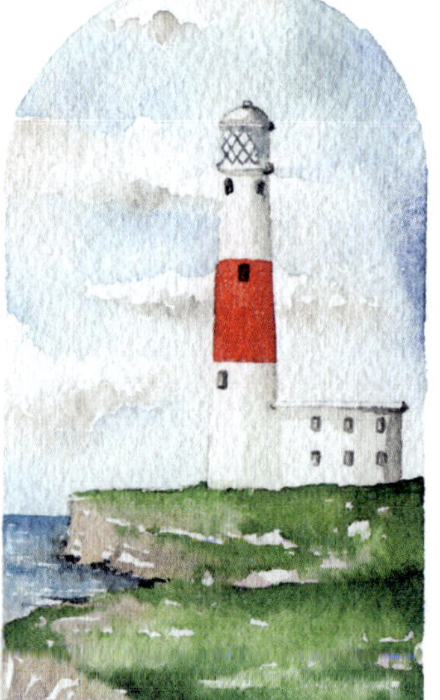

Level
Intermediate

Colours
Alizarin Crimson
Payne's Grey
Raw Umber

Brushes
Mop brush size 6
Flat size ¾ inch
Large round size 12
Pointed round sizes 4, 0
Rigger size 0

You will also need
Ruler, HB pencil, soft and hard
erasers, and masking tape

BEFORE YOU START

Prep your paints and colours
Washes require you to work fast,
have your colours ready-mixed to
the correct consistency. You could
swatch your colours, too, for a
handy reference.

Picture the scene
Are you working from a reference
photo? If you are, crop it to
feature only what you want to
paint. I like to print out the photo
and sketch onto it if I want to
change the composition or add
things.

Edges
You can tape down your page
to minimize buckling. Masking
your page gives you the option
of a neat edge or paint within the
page. Or you can leave raw edges,
as I have done.

WHERE TO START?
If you're sketching your
landscape, remember to keep it
as simple as possible. I start with
a horizon line, from there I might
use perspective lines (page 141)
or I can build up a composition in
terms of background, mid-ground
and foreground.

1 Sketch your landscape on
a separate piece of paper,
then decide how much
of it you need to draw
on your painting paper.

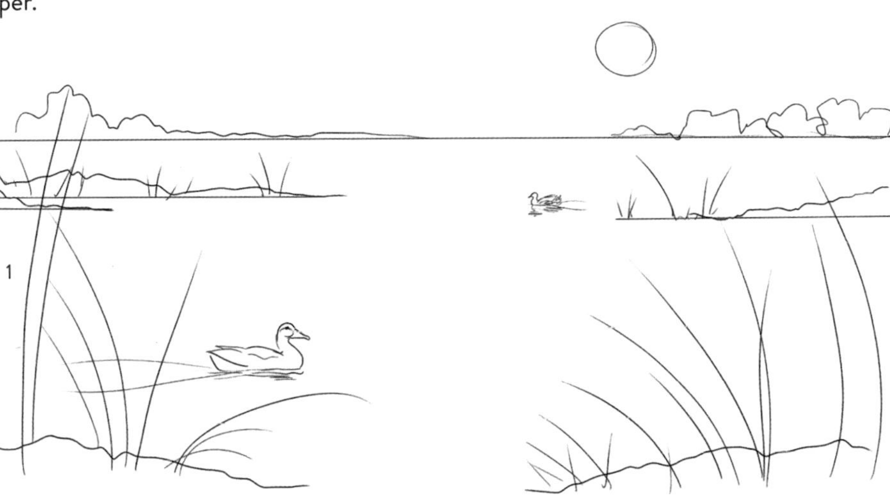

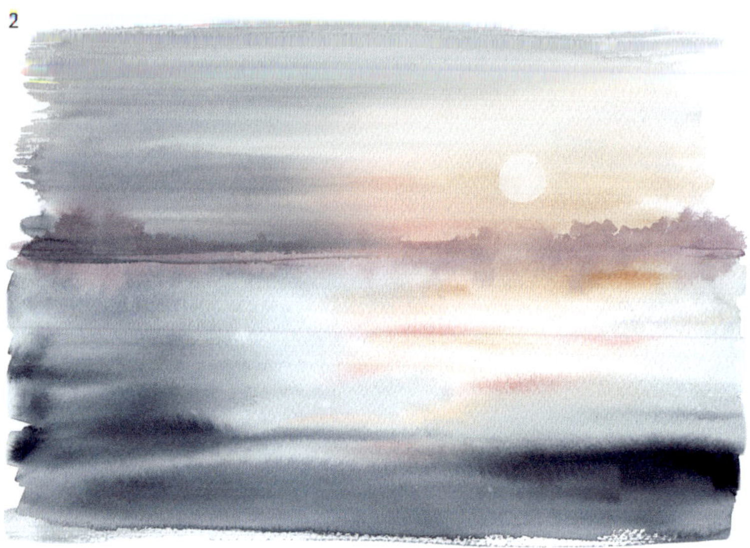

3 Once the page is completely dry, you can place in mid-ground details. Mix up a couple of variations of Payne's Grey and Raw Umber to create some dark hues. Create loose and simple foliage with your size 4 brush, making use of dry brushing for some hints of light on the scene as well as more concentrated lowlights. Either use your size 0 or rigger brush for grasses and reeds. Dilute your paint and create a shadowy reflection beneath, loosely mirroring the grasses and shapes. Clean off your size 0 brush and paint a few horizontal strokes across the reflected shapes to create a few ripples.

What else can you place in this composition to draw the eye across? Wildlife is a great way to get eye-catching items in the middle of the water or in the sky.

2 Begin by painting a circle outline of clean water; this will be your sun. Then wash clean water over the rest of the top half of the page, avoiding that unpainted circle with your mop brush. It's up to you whether you continue to use your mop for the colours, or a large round or flat brush to paint tea-consistency Raw Umber strokes of colour into the right-hand side of the piece and add streaks of Alizarin Crimson.

From the left, drag Payne's Grey across the whole page while it is still wet, to show mist. Repeat the above technique to paint the lake and sunset reflection. Mix some Payne's Grey and Alizarin Crimson and paint a line across the horizon with your size 8 brush. The variation in page wetness may result in some erratic blends, representing a hazy line of trees.

A great tip when building these washes is to take the minimum amount of colour on your brush. You can always add more but it's hard to take away. Sweep the brush over the page in a back-and-forth motion.

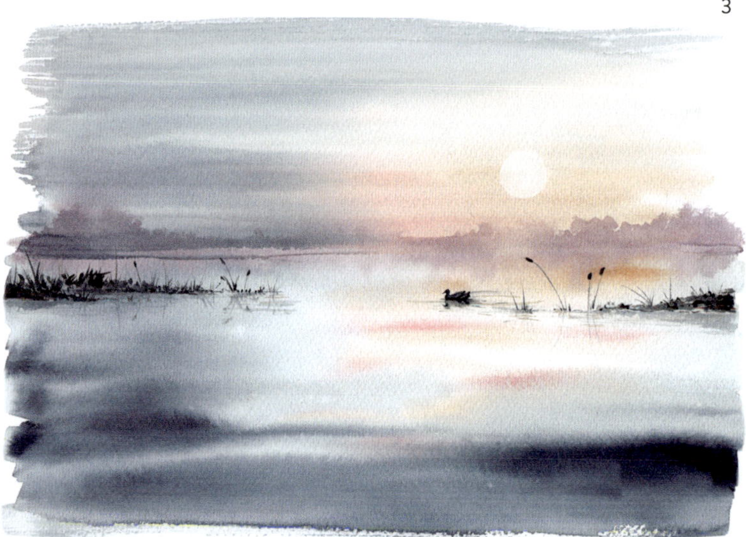

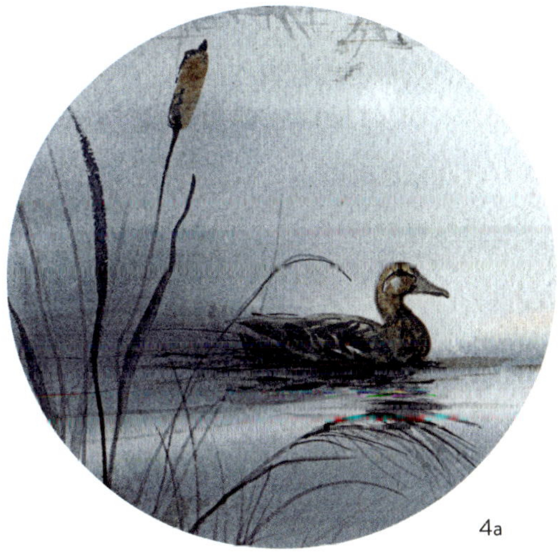

4a

4 In the foreground create statuesque reeds and grasses with more saturated Payne's Grey and Raw Umber mixes. In the foreground we can pick out more detail and colour in these shapes, so add Raw Umber heads to the reeds and some warmth to the duck's feathers (4a). Add lowlight accents of concentrated Payne's Grey to heighten the sharpness of the foreground items.

4b

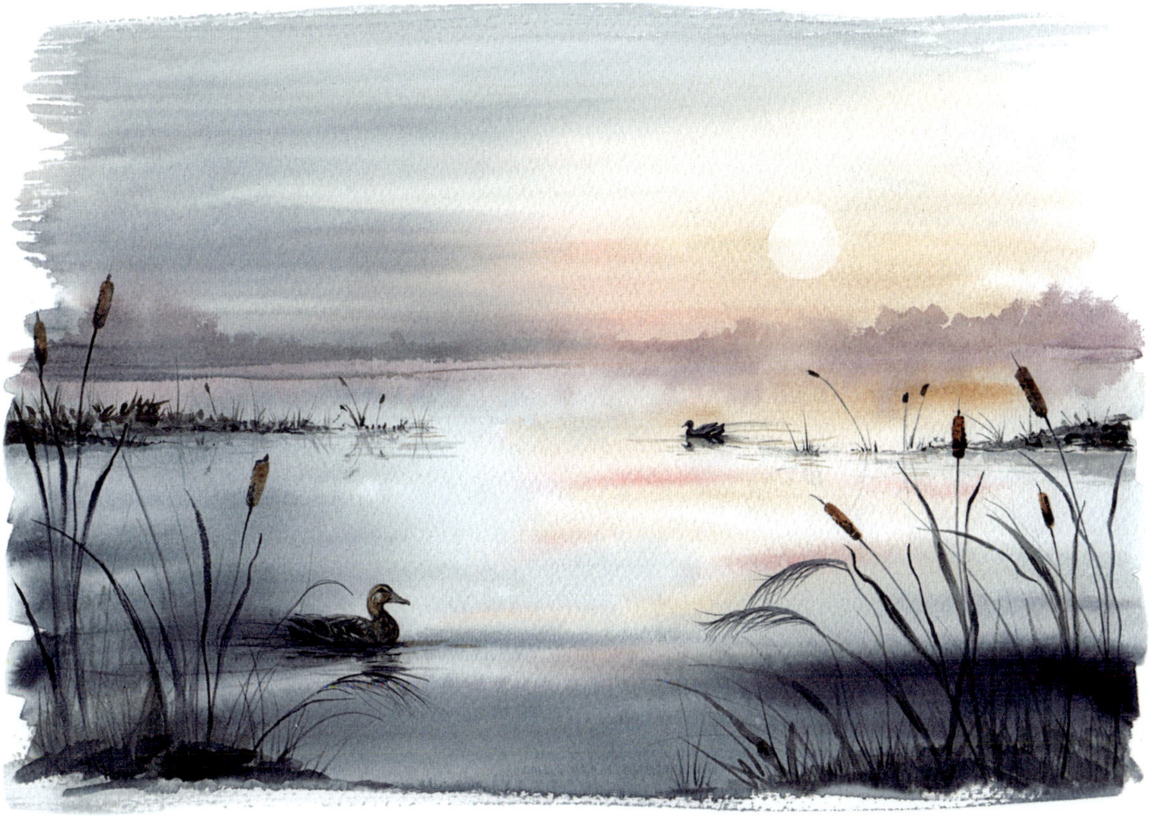

One-Point Perspective

In a one-point perspective painting, lines converge in a single vanishing point on the horizon. It can be particularly helpful to repeat a single item into the distance like streetlights or trees. Things simply get smaller the farther away they are, but the way in which we paint can also help signify depth and distance.

Prompt

Can you think of other landscape features for a one-point perspective landscape? Fencing? Pylons? Try painting the simplest one-point perspective scene you can using just one feature.

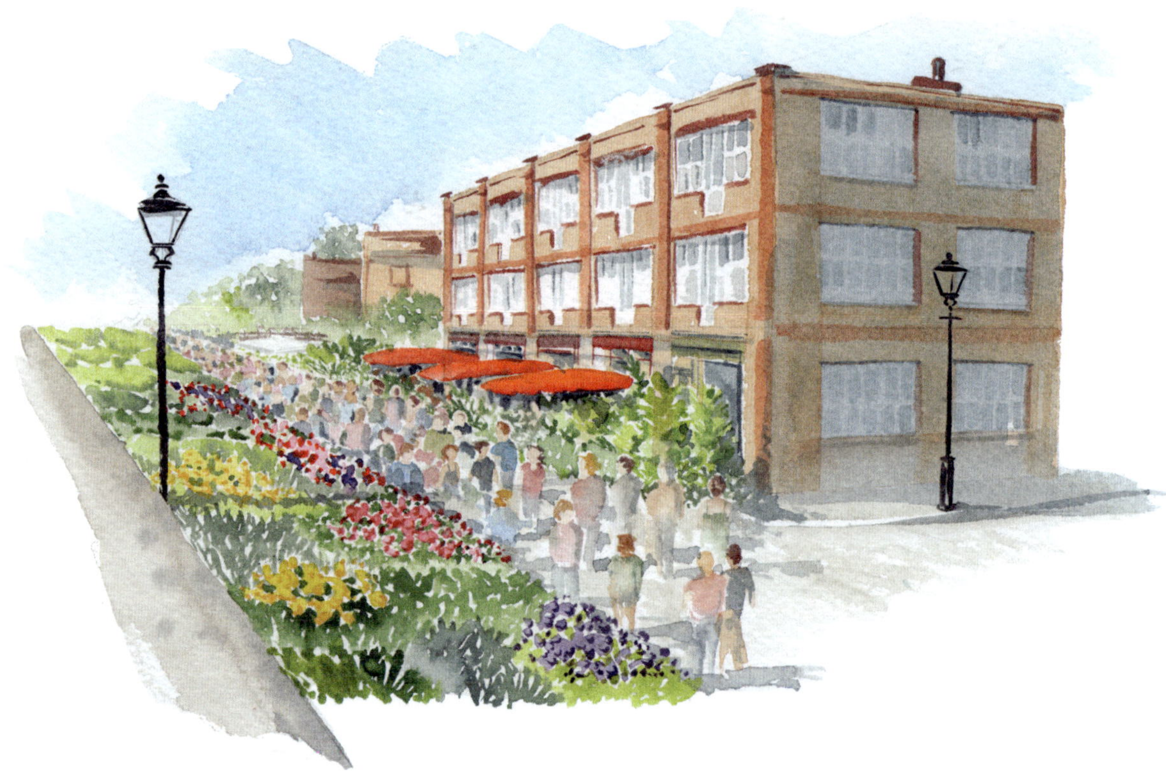

Orchard Landscape

Level
Intermediate

Colours
Burnt Sienna
Cadmium-Free Yellow
Cerulean Blue
Green Gold
Payne's Grey
Sap Green
Yellow Ochre

Brushes
Mop size 6
Pointed round sizes 8, 4 ,2 ,0, 4/0

You will also need
Ruler, HB pencil, soft and hard erasers

Mixes
Background green: Sap Green (70%)
and Payne's Grey (30%)
Foreground green: Green Gold
(50%) & Sap Green (50%)

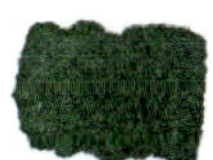

Background green

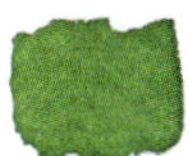

Foreground green

1 Define the horizon line and
a vanishing point. This is the
point from which you can map
out your perspective. Draw
converging lines from that
point to provide a framework
for things disappearing into the
distance. Sketch your landscape
and trees, which will get larger
in the foreground.

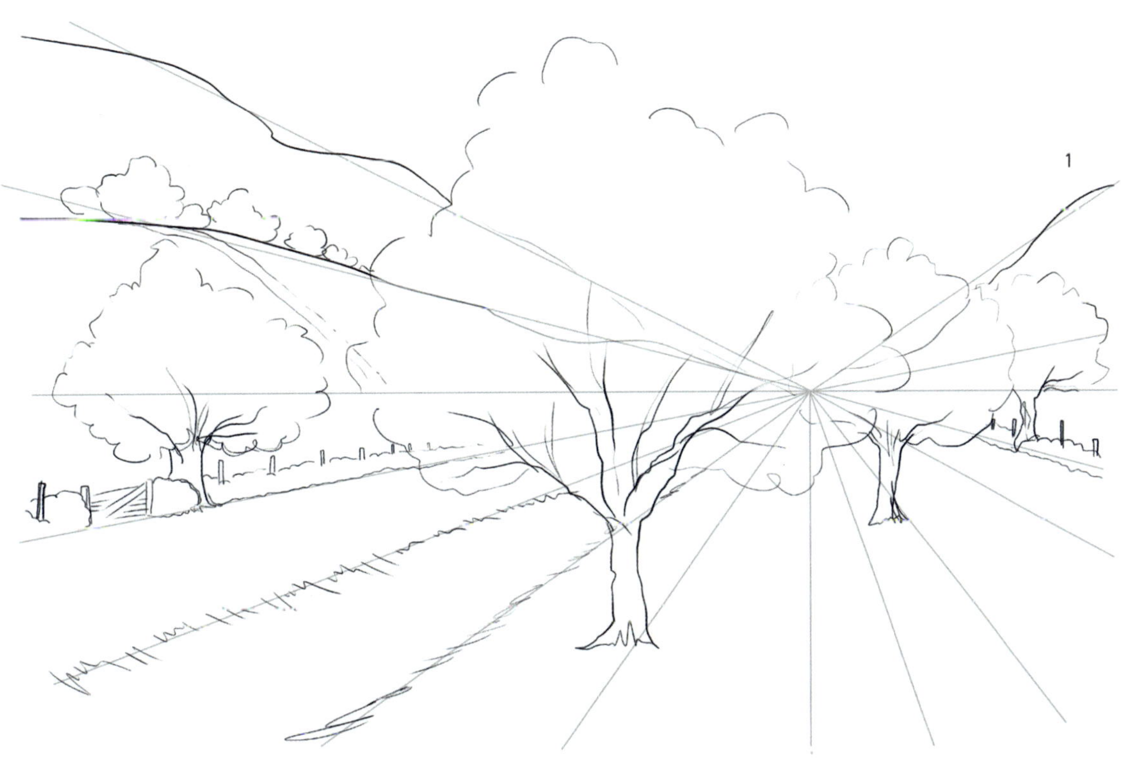

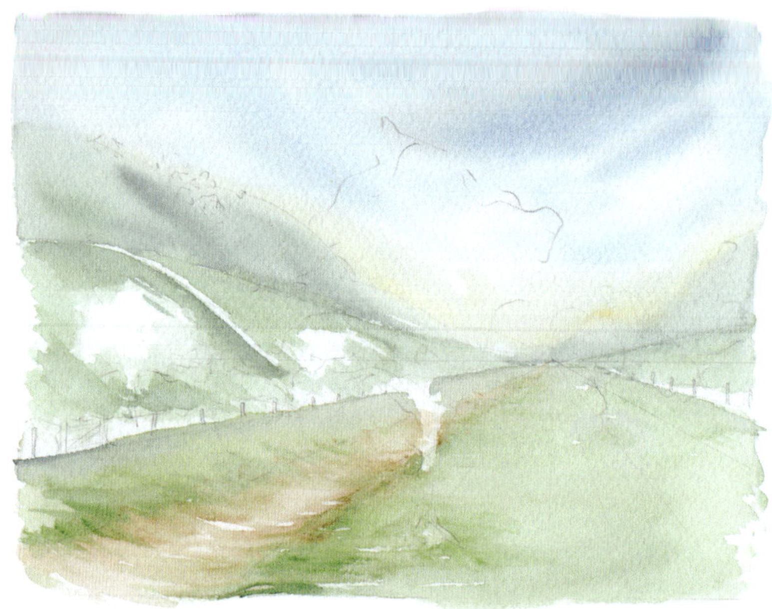

2 For this first wash, keep your colours dilute and use only a little colour on your brush. You can always build it up. Use your mop brush to wet the sky area and distant hills. Paint strokes of Cerulean Blue and Payne's Grey in the sky with a low line of Cadmium-Free Yellow and Yellow Ochre for a glow on the horizon.

Paint the mid-ground hills in a wash of Sap Green with your size 8 brush, keeping it light and leaving unpainted space for the trees. The wet page will have partially dried so paint the background hills in background green, keeping it soft and lacking in detail or hard edges.

Paint the foreground in foreground green with your size 2 brush. Create a path of curving strokes of Yellow Ochre edged with Burnt Sienna accents. Allow to dry.

3

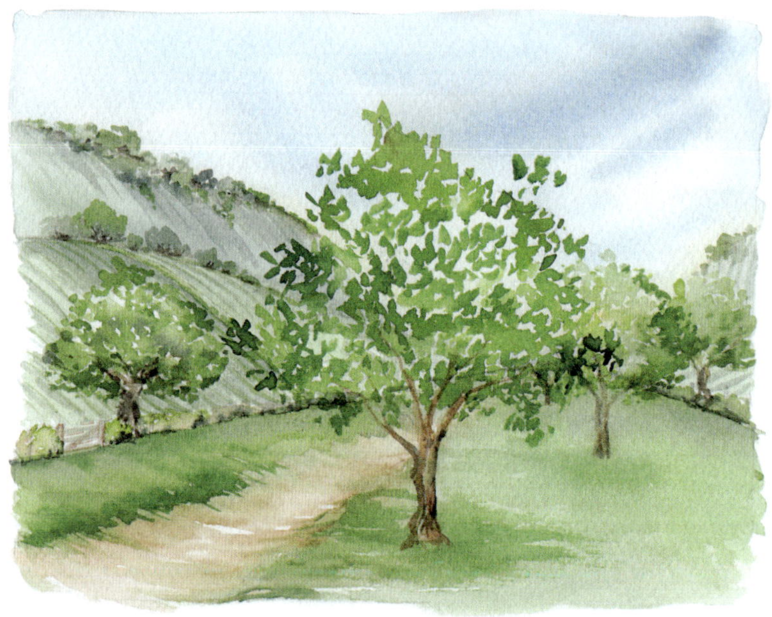

3 With your size 0 brush, paint in the basic structure of your trees with Sap Green and Green Gold leaves and Burnt Sienna, Yellow Ochre and Payne's Grey trunks. Now is a good time to erase any visible pencil with a hard eraser.

4 Once dry, add detail to the foreground with your size 0 and 4/0 brushes, deepening the concentration of colours and textures. Allow to dry fully.

5 Glaze Payne's Grey shadows, making sure to keep following the rules of foreground and background.

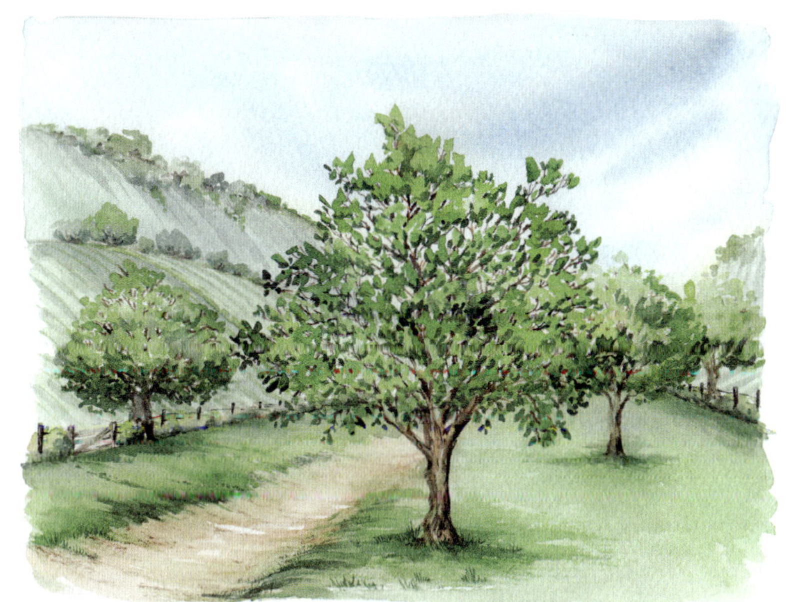

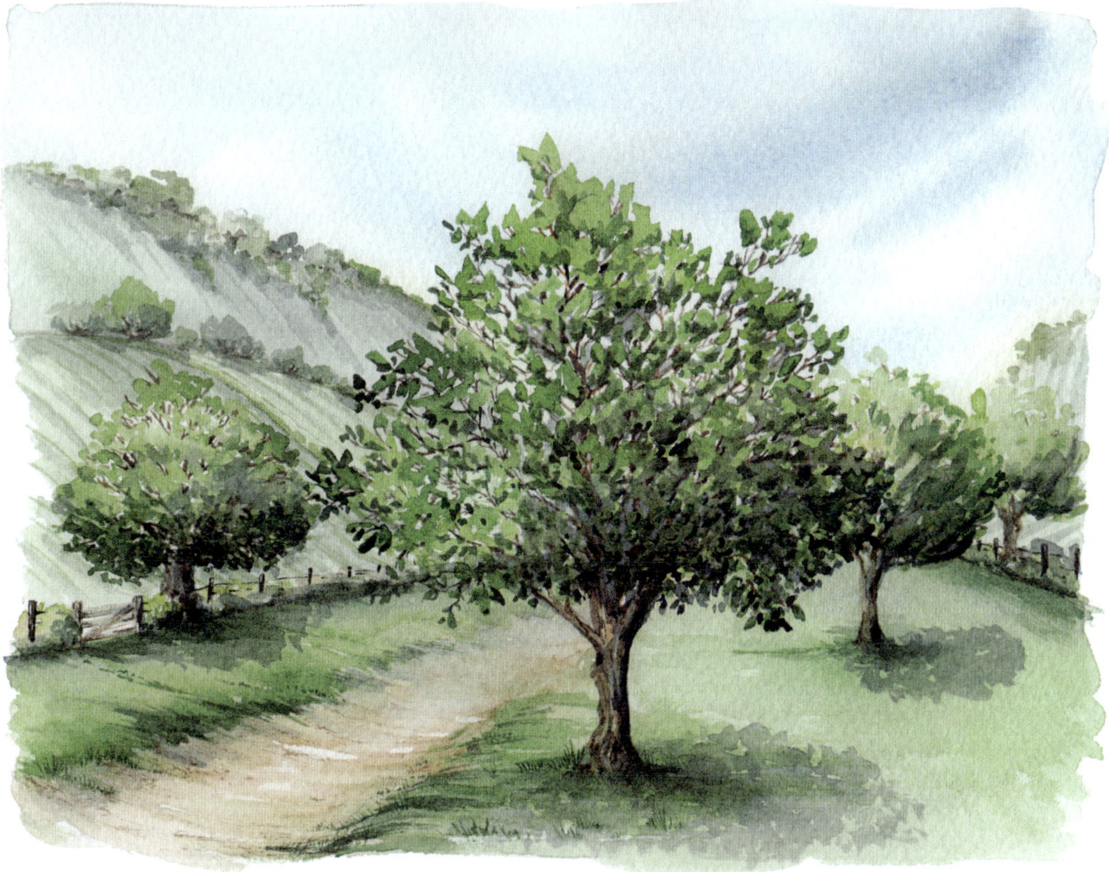

Two-Point Perspective

Horizon lines and vanishing points are the foundations for a sound structural house drawing. You can then transform it into a quirky, characterful cottage with wobbly lines and soft edges. We live in a part of the world surrounded by charming cottages like this one. Anyone who has stepped inside such a dwelling will tell you there's not a straight line or right angle in sight.

TUTORIAL: Country Cottage

Level
Intermediate

Colours
Aqua Green
Buff Titanium
Burnt Sienna
Cerulean Blue
Green Gold
Imperial Purple
Opera Rose
Payne's Grey
Permanent Rose
Pyrrol Orange
Sap Green

Mixes
Sage mix: Aqua Green (30%), Sap Green (50%), Payne's Grey (20%)
Shadow mix: Payne's Grey (50%), Burnt Sienna (50%)
Terracotta mix: Burnt Sienna (70%), Pyrrol Orange (30%)

Brushes
Pointed round sizes 6, 4, 0, 4/0

You will also need
Ruler, HB pencil, soft and hard erasers

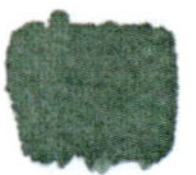
Sage

Shadow

Terracotta

DRAWING

1 Draw a horizon line and choose vanishing points at either end. Then draw a vertical line – this will be the corner of the house closest to us – and connect receding lines to your vanishing points. Draw the vertical sides of the house. Stay light with the pencil to give yourself the best chance of being able to rub it out after painting.

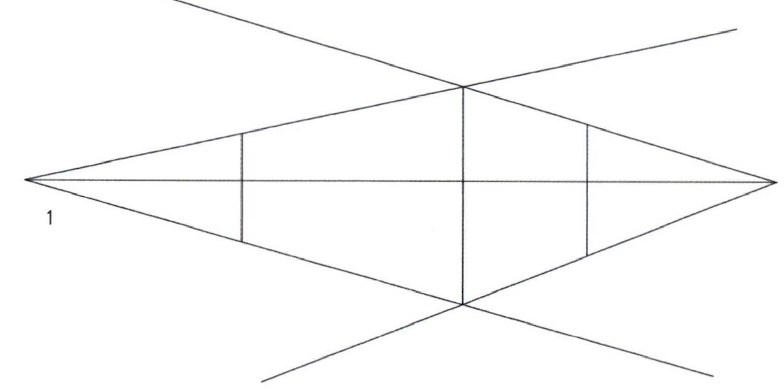

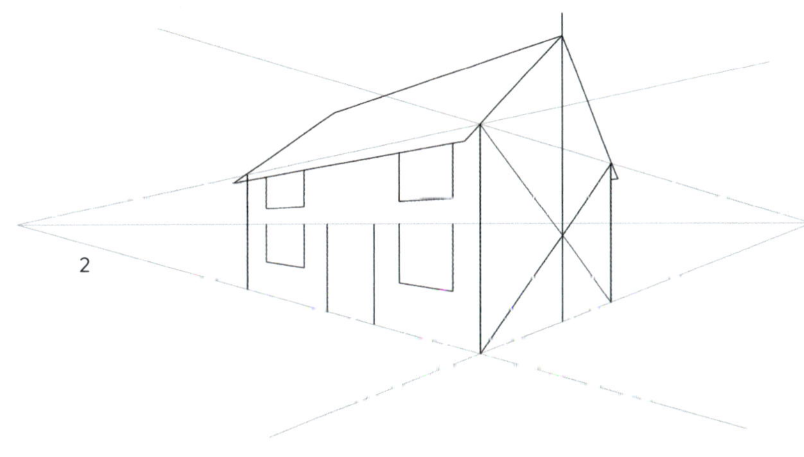

2 Draw a faint cross in one wall and use the cross-section to find the centre for your vertical line. This will help you get the roof pitch even. You can use the vanishing points as your guide for more horizontal lines on the house: the tops and bottom edges of window, doors and other details.

Adding quirky details: Draw character into the piece by wobbling the edges and adding details and surrounding trees. The way you paint will also impact the charm of the finished piece. Painting smooth colours results in a flat and lifeless finish so that the cottage seems to float in the landscape. Introducing texture through brushstrokes, wet on wet, and colour mixes will bring the piece to life.

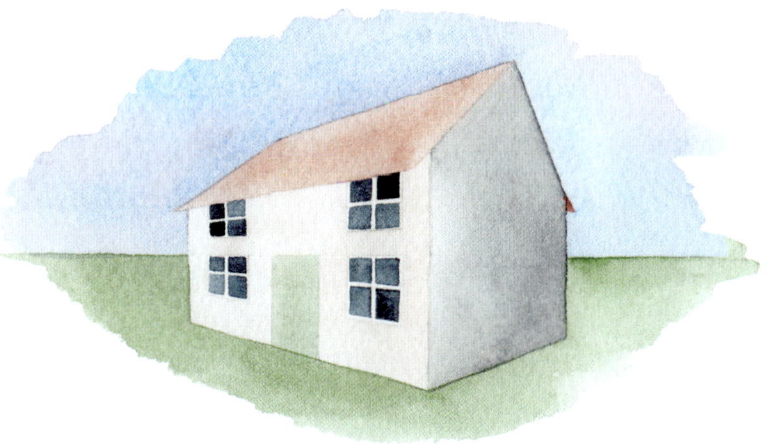

3 Once you've got those basics in place, it's time to give it a bit more character with softer edges and wobbly lines. How can you sit your house in the landscape? Can you add a tree, fence or shed? When you're ready to paint, lightly fade the pencil with a soft eraser.

4 These initial washes should be painted in a **tea** consistency. Dab Buff Titanium all over the walls of the house with your size 0 brush, leaving tiny flecks of unpainted space and dabbing diluted Payne's Grey here and there. Allow to dry.

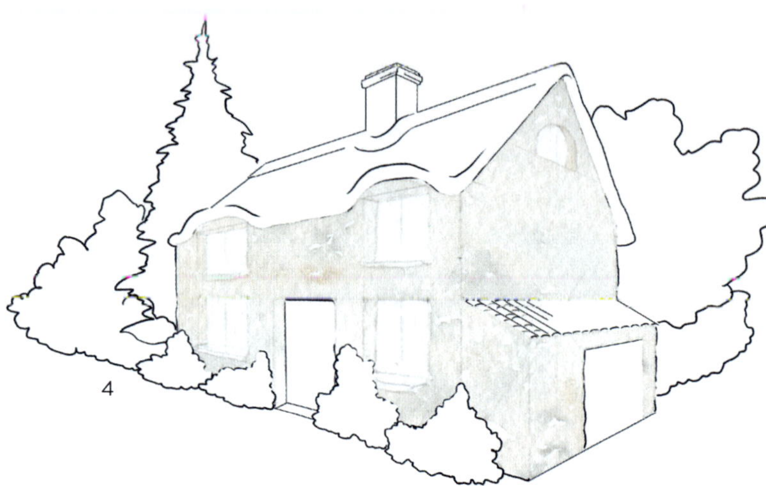

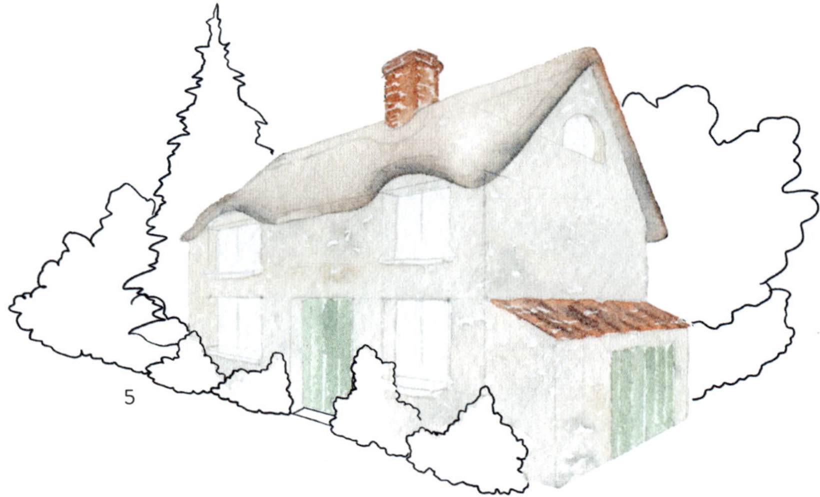

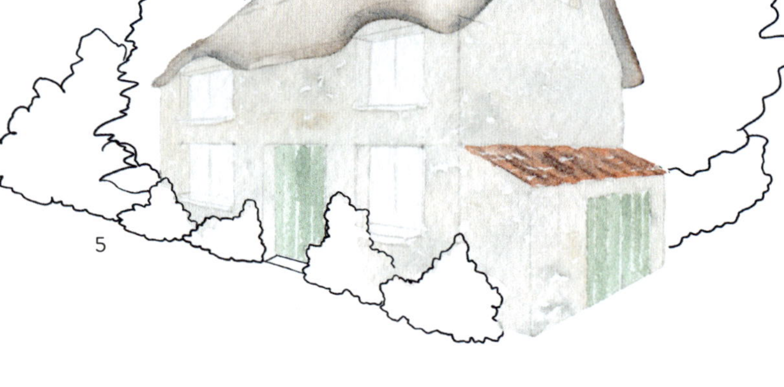

5 Still with a size 0 brush, create the chimney bricks and woodshed roof tiles by alternating strokes of terracotta mix with slivers of unpainted space (a few overlaps will lead to a more characterful piece). While the roof tiles are damp, paint fine lines of shadow mix down them. For the weathered woodwork on the doors and windowpanes, once you have sage mix on your size 0 brush, blot it on your paper towel to remove a little paint, and apply it in some dry-brushed streaks. The thatched roof starts as a tea-consistency Buff Titanium with wet-on-wet blends of Burnt Sienna and Payne's Grey in the shadier undersides.

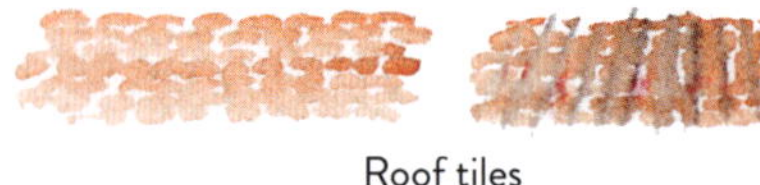

Roof tiles

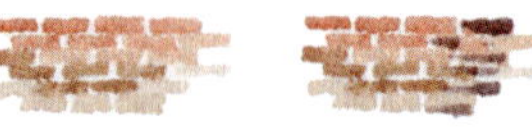

Chimney

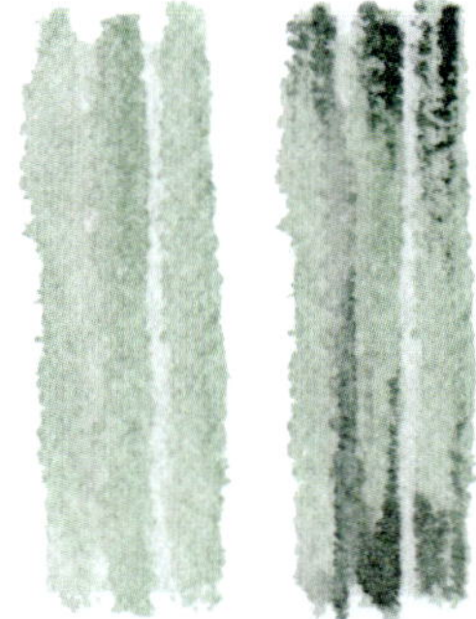

Weathered paintwork

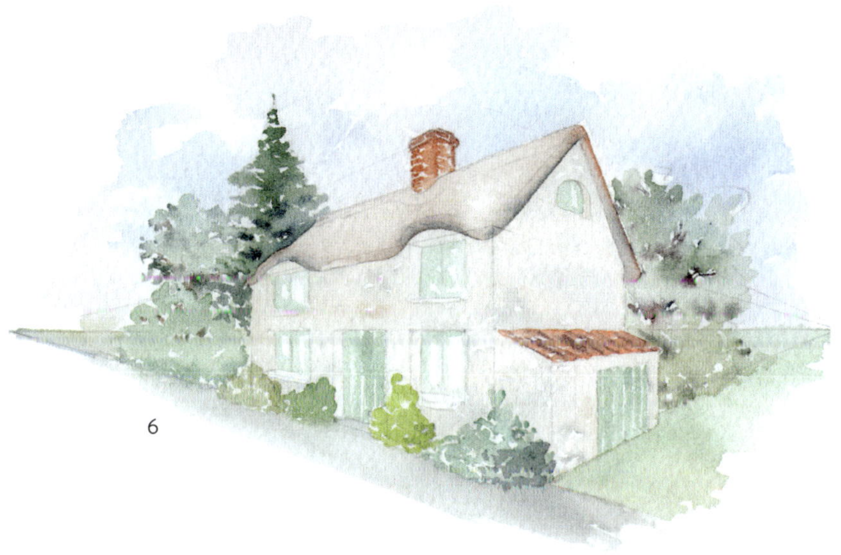

6 Use a size 6 brush to sweep a sky of Cerulean Blue with negative-space clouds. You can also blot clouds out while wet with scrunched-up paper towel. Sweep a stroke of Payne's Grey along the front of the house and then play around with mixing different greens in your palette to paint the surrounding lawn. Use a smaller brush to dab bushes and trees around the house.

7 The last tea-consistency detail to this house is a few shadow-mix bricks on the walls in clusters here and there. Now, increase your paint consistency to coffee/milk. Choose bright colours to add flowers to some of the bushes with your size 4/0 brush. Add some Payne's Grey to your greens and dab along the shadowy sides of the bushes. You can also elongate the greenery creeping up the house with this darker tone. Adding detail to the plants in the foreground creates a sense of distance by comparison with the softer trees in the background. Find lowlights on the green woodwork and chimney by simply adding touches of the same colour in heavier consistencies.

The windows are the first big leap of faith for a new painter: trust that, in one, confident dab of Payne's Grey with a size 0 brush, you'll get a good mark resembling a pane of glass. The unpainted space resembles the reflection of sunlight off the window.

8 Once dry, it's a good time to rub
out any visible pencil with
a hard eraser. Complete the
piece with a glaze of shadow. I
do this in two stages, first with
a tea-consistency shadow mix,
with a size 0 brush, focusing on
the smaller areas like the window
recesses, under the window sills,
and individual plants.

9 The second shadow stage is with
a slightly darker shadow mix
and a larger brush (I use a size
6 and size 4) for the wall of the
house in shadow. Paint this in
as few brush strokes as possible.
While still damp, dab some more
concentrated shadow mix on the
wall to emphasize its mottled
texture (which may have got lost by
now). Think about where else the
shadow will fall – perhaps under the
roof and along the ground by the
woodshed. Once dry, use a size 0
brush to paint more concentrated
shadow accents on the underside
of the roof.

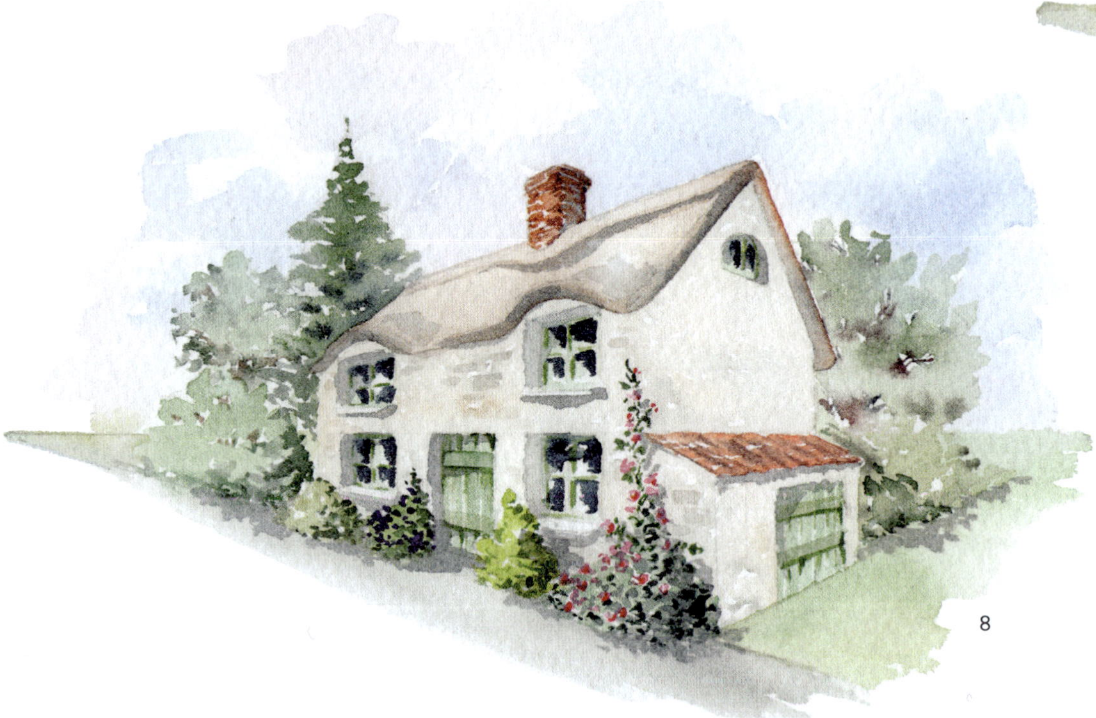

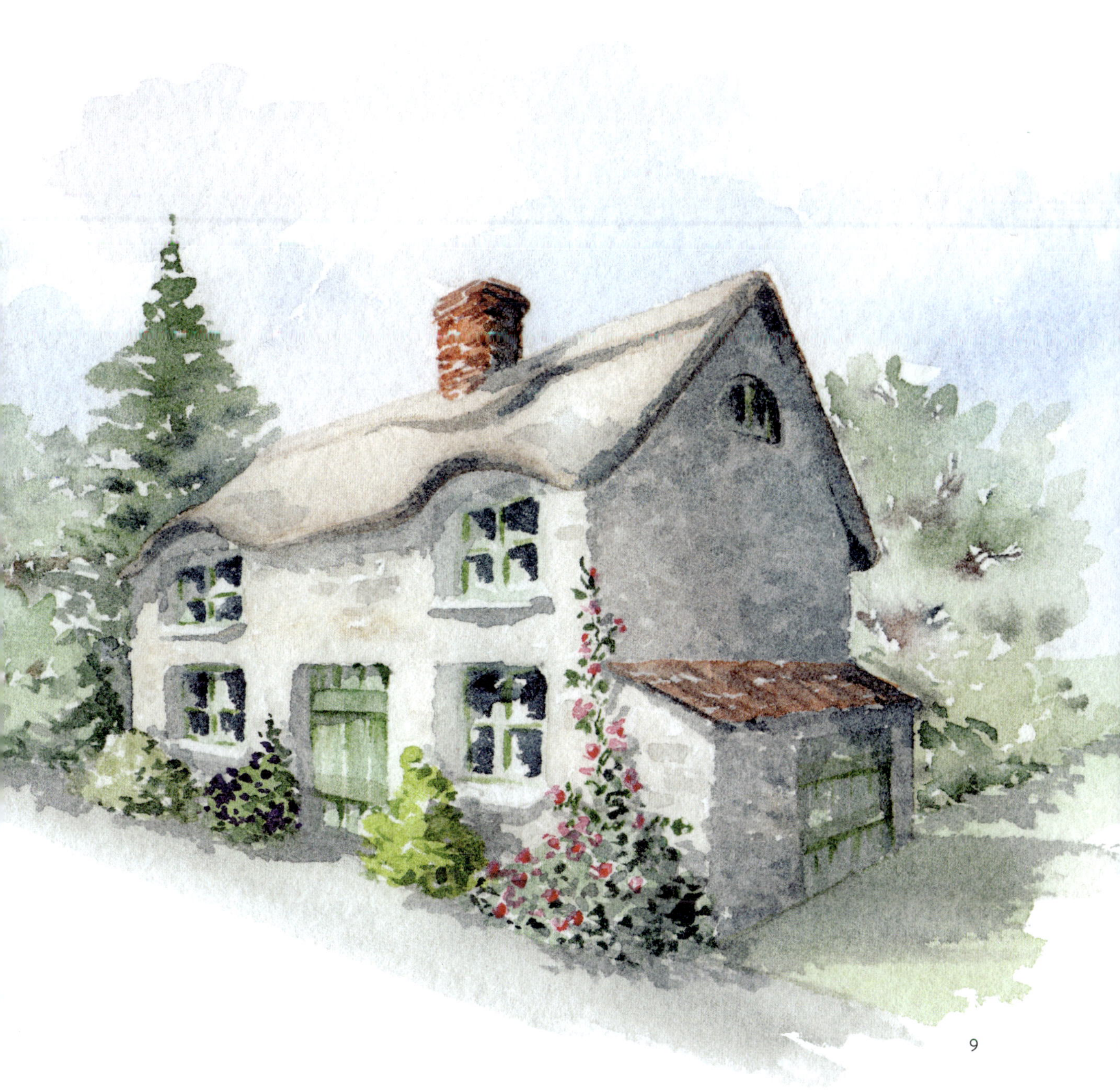

9

Negative Space

Negative space in landscapes can create all kinds of structural detail. What we don't paint can have as big an impact on a scene as what we do paint. This technique is one of my favourite ways to start a landscape painting in my sketchbook when I have limited means.

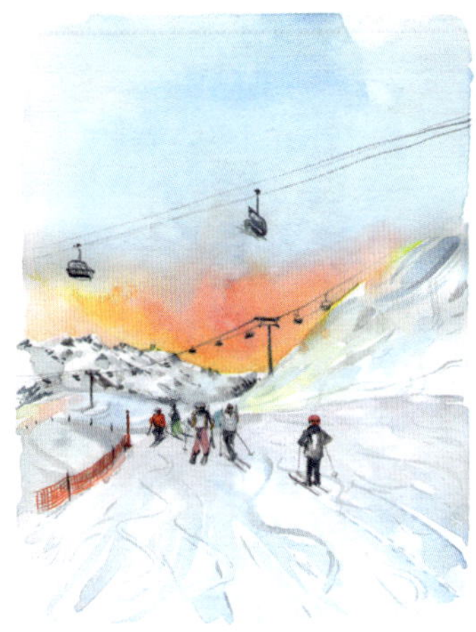 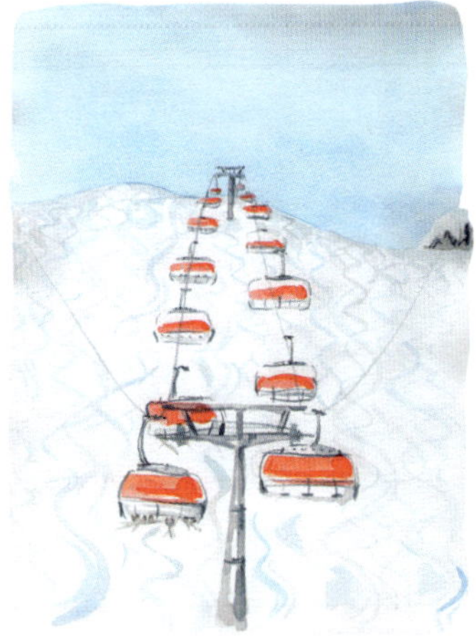

The negative space technique doesn't just apply to snowy landscapes – it's a great way to map out a piece. For example, you could mark out the sky of a city skyline with this technique even though you'll be painting in the buildings later on.

TUTORIAL: Blue-Sky Mountain Range

Level
Beginner

Colours
Burnt Sienna
Cerulean Blue
Payne's Grey
Sap Green
Winsor Blue

Brushes
Mop size 6, pointed round sizes 2, 0, 4/0

Mixes
Sky mix: Cerulean Blue (60%) and Winsor Blue (40%)
Shadow mix: Burnt Sienna (50%) and Payne's Grey (50%)
Tree mix: Sap Green (20%), Burnt Sienna (40%) and Payne's Grey (40%)

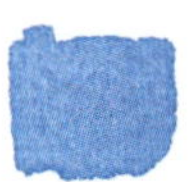  

Sky   Shadow   Tree

1 Use your mop brush to paint the top edge of your mountain range in coffee-consistency sky mix. Quickly fill the sky upwards.

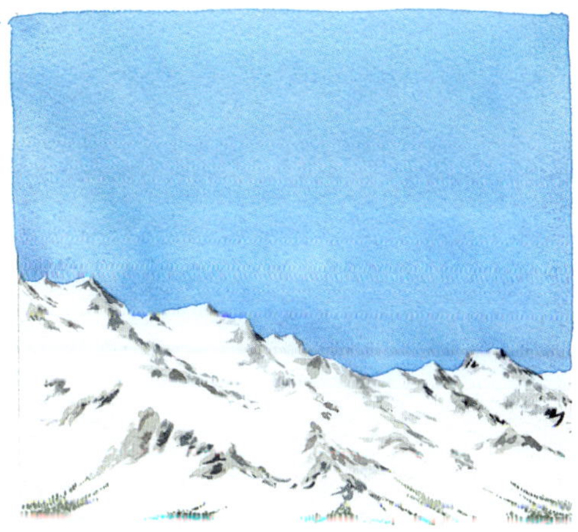

2 Allow the sky to dry for a crisp edge. With your size 2 brush, paint tea-consistency shadow-mix marks diagonally down from the mountain points to create the stony texture poking out through the snow. Allow to dry.

3 With your size 0 brush and slightly more concentrated range of shadow mixes, paint smaller and more concentrated marks into the mountains to build the texture.

Try not to overthink this part; instead, try a light scribble with the brush. Paint tiny lines of pine trees in small dabs of tree mix with your size 4/0 brush. Allow to dry.

4 With a clear blue sky the light will be bright, creating crisp shadows. Dilute your shadow mix to a tea consistency and glaze shadows down one side of the mountains with your size 2 brush.

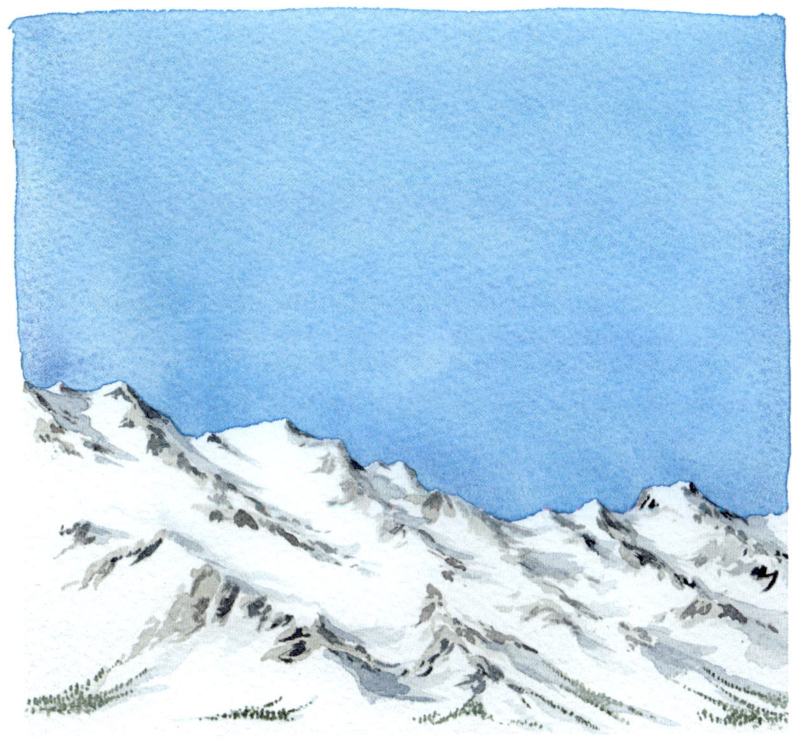

Think Like an Artist

You've come across every technique I consider necessary to be able to paint in watercolour. But what now? How do you conjure the artistic magic to paint your own pieces?

With my years of experience teaching students and meeting fellow artists, I can reassure you that everyone goes through the same peaks and troughs of creativity. There will be days where it's a struggle to make anything work and your inner critic is particularly vocal. But there are also days when inspiration flows through your veins.

Although it's impossible to bottle this fantastic feeling, I am sure it will come if you just let it. How? By giving your brain some space: go for a walk, switch off your devices, allow yourself to get a bit bored. For example, 45 minutes into a yoga class my brain bursts open with inspiration – every time, like clockwork.

It can be hard to arrange the inspiration to hit at convenient times (as a child I would wake up in the night and draw for hours). And that is why it's so wonderful to carry a sketchbook.

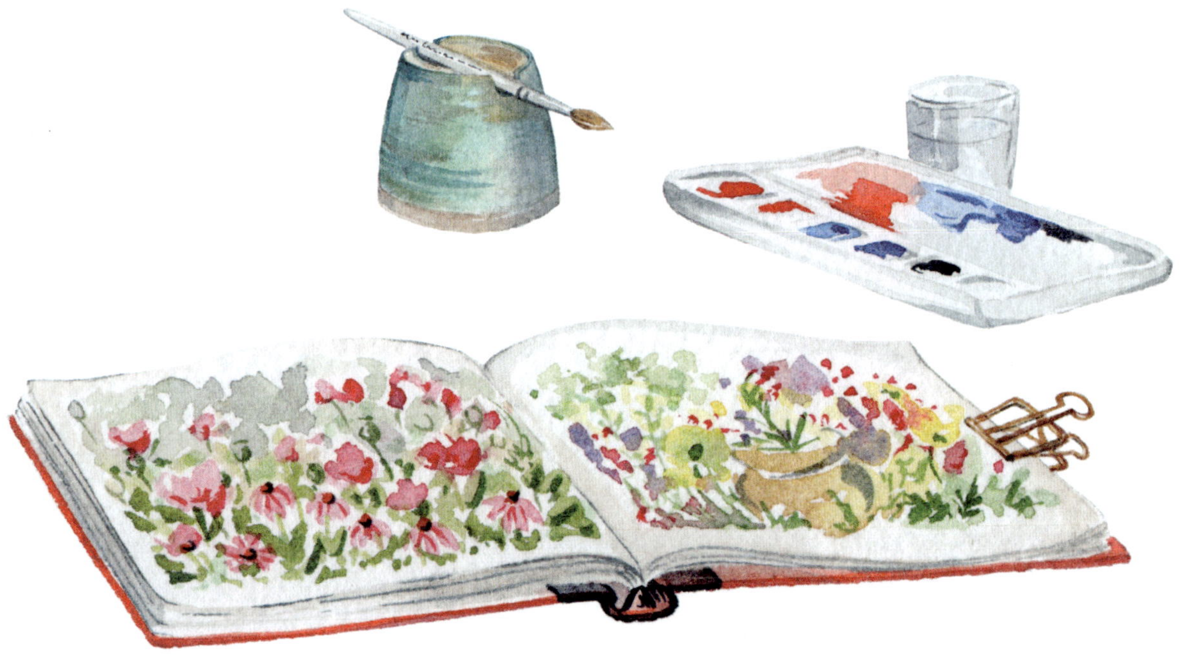

CARRYING A SKETCHBOOK

We have a bird feeder outside our
kitchen window and I watch it for
hours – it's up there with yoga for
freeing the mind. The problem with
creative thoughts that burst forth
during yoga class is that I spend the
rest of the class worried that the
thoughts will fall out of my head. No
such problem at the bird feeder!

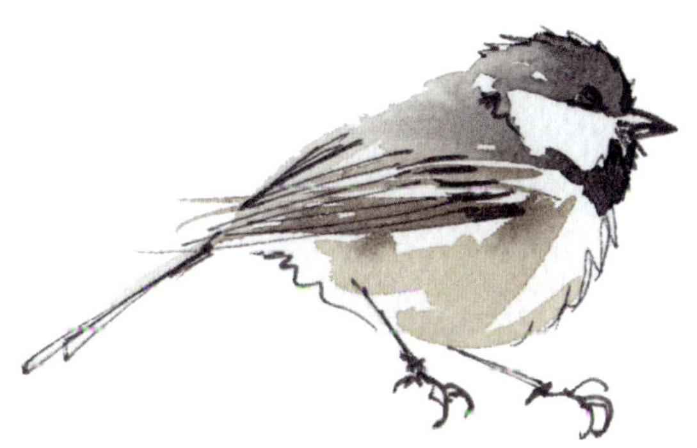

The speed at which the birds dart
in and out allows a scribble and a
swish of paint at best. I began to
capture those flashes of colour
in a sketchbook – a diary of the
comings and goings.

These line and wash scribbles
would be strange and pointless on
disparate pieces of paper but they
tell a compelling story in sketchbook
form. The succeeding blank pages are
full of promise; maybe they would
hold scribbles of birds from another
day or a development of those
initial sketches into something fully
formed.

A sketchbook shows you how far
you've come in one quick flick
through the pages. If only we
could be constantly reminded of
how far we've come in every part
of our life!

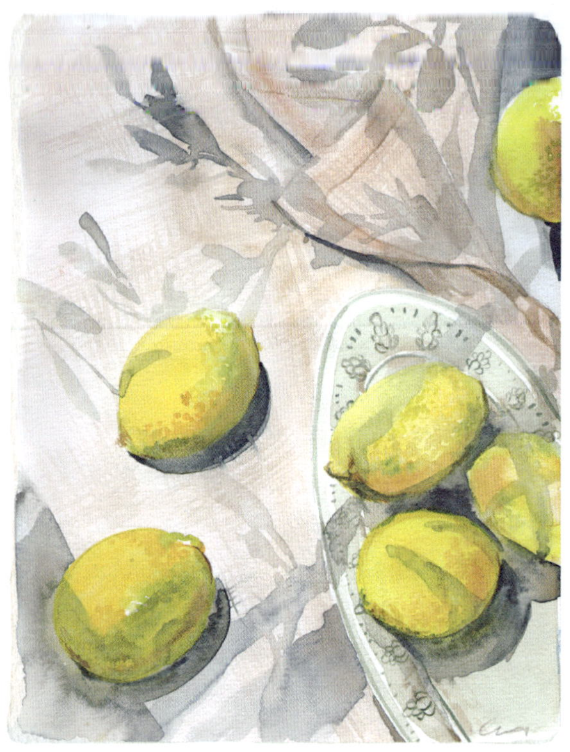

Keeping a sketchbook close by is a way of being attentive to the world around you. If you haven't tried it yet, it might be key to unlocking your creative confidence.

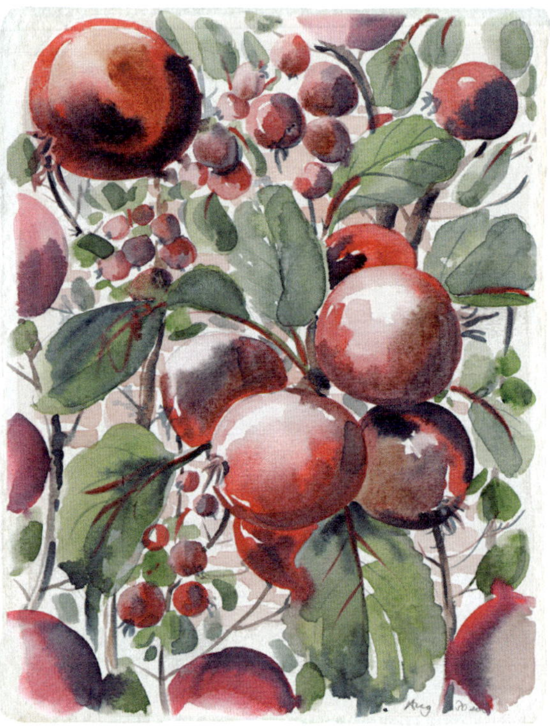

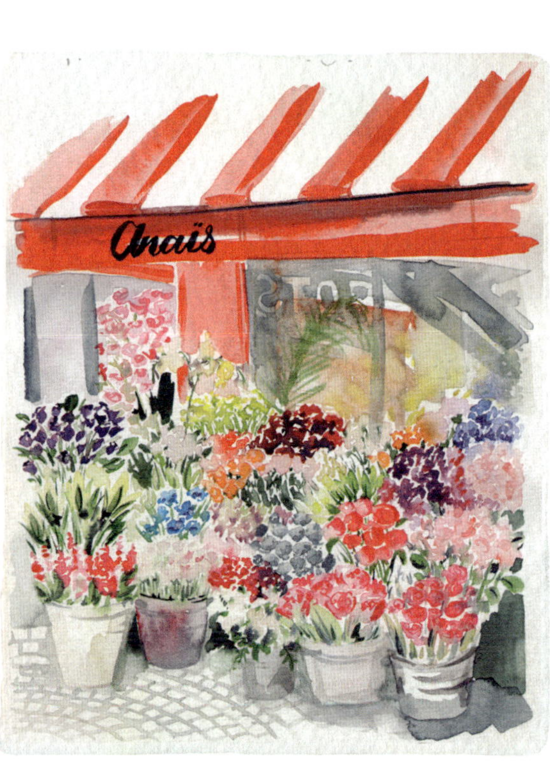
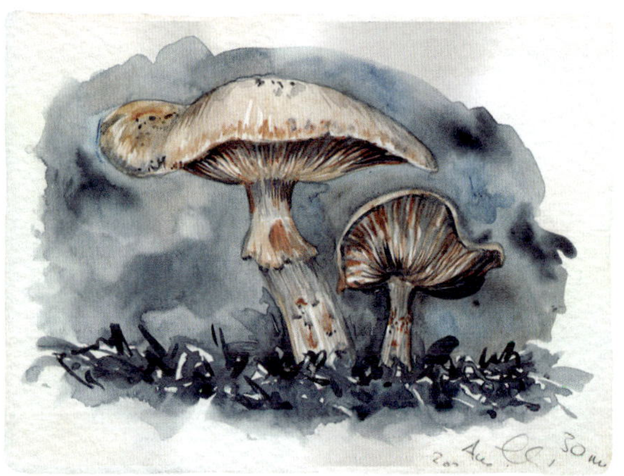

My students fret at not 'getting it right' first time. I remind them Van Gogh first made studies of all kinds of flowers before settling on sunflowers, and even then he painted multiple versions. A sketchbook is a gentle way of unlearning instant perfection and instead taking delight at documenting tiny changes in the world around you. Soon you'll have filled the pages and clutch that little book like the precious time capsule it is. In low points our Inner critic will shout loud, but don't be discouraged. The best way to silence it is to focus on the enjoyment of painting rather than the finished result. That might mean filling a page with abstract shapes and simple marks instead of painting a lifelike composition that day.

It took me a while to get on board with the idea of sketchbooks – I had always enjoyed an expansive desk space. Painting at the bird feeder showed me that the sketchbook's awkwardness is its brilliance. When I paint in a book it's often balanced on my knee, I work with a single brush, have a limited palette and am simultaneously fighting the elements! Condensing your painting space is the best way to reconnect with your raw creativity. I've never painted so expressively as when I paint in my sketchbook. Personally, a sketchbook now comes with me on holiday, to work events and any adventure I might take.

TUTORIALS

Tutorials are perfect tools for learning, and this book is full of them. However, there needs to be a point when you wean yourself off following steps and try your own versions. Instead of going cold turkey, you can make subtle adjustments to existing tutorials you enjoyed. Why not change the colour palette to one of your own choosing? Add a background if it's an object floating in space. Incorporate your own experiences and cultural references — make your painting your own.

BE READY

Whether or not you're carrying around a sketchbook, removing as many obstacles between sitting down and painting really helps. If you have a dedicated space to leave your art supplies out, it will make it so much easier to paint little and often.

HAVE NO PLAN

On page 60, I suggested it was a good idea to have a plan when starting a watercolour composition. However, it's just as important to allow yourself time to paint with no thought of the finished piece. Focusing on the process, not the result, is easier said than done, so from time to time fill a page with completely mindless marks. No plan means no failure. And it usually results in something unexpectedly wonderful.

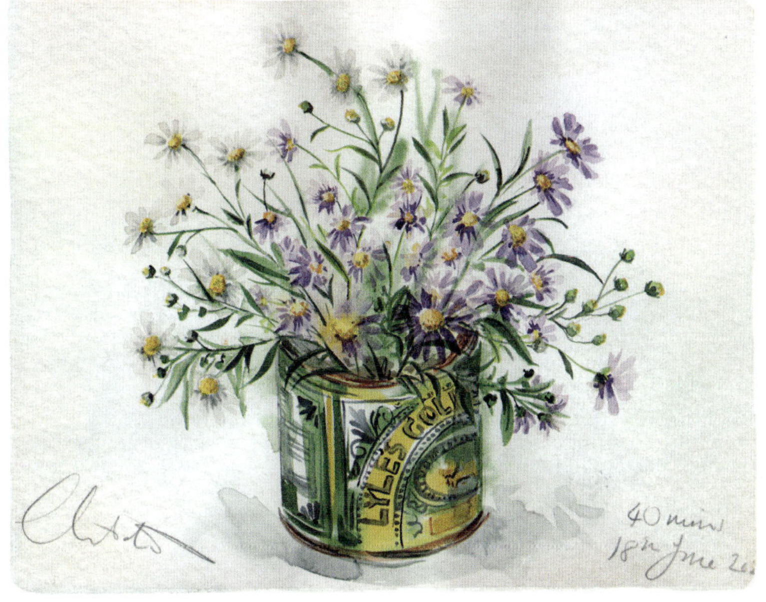

Variations

Having come through a full book of tutorials, here are some ways to start you on the path of creating your own original work.

Carving out time to create is hard. It can be even harder to get your head into an artistic mode when you've found some precious time for yourself. This exercise of choosing a familiar object and painting as many variations of it as possible is great way to effortlessly let your imagination wander.

Choose a familiar and simple object and draw a few basic pencil shapes, but no detail.

Get your paints out and have fun with pattern, colour and all the watercolour techniques you've learned throughout this book. See how many variations you can paint – soon you'll have a full page.

What starts as a basic exercise often turns into a new obsession!

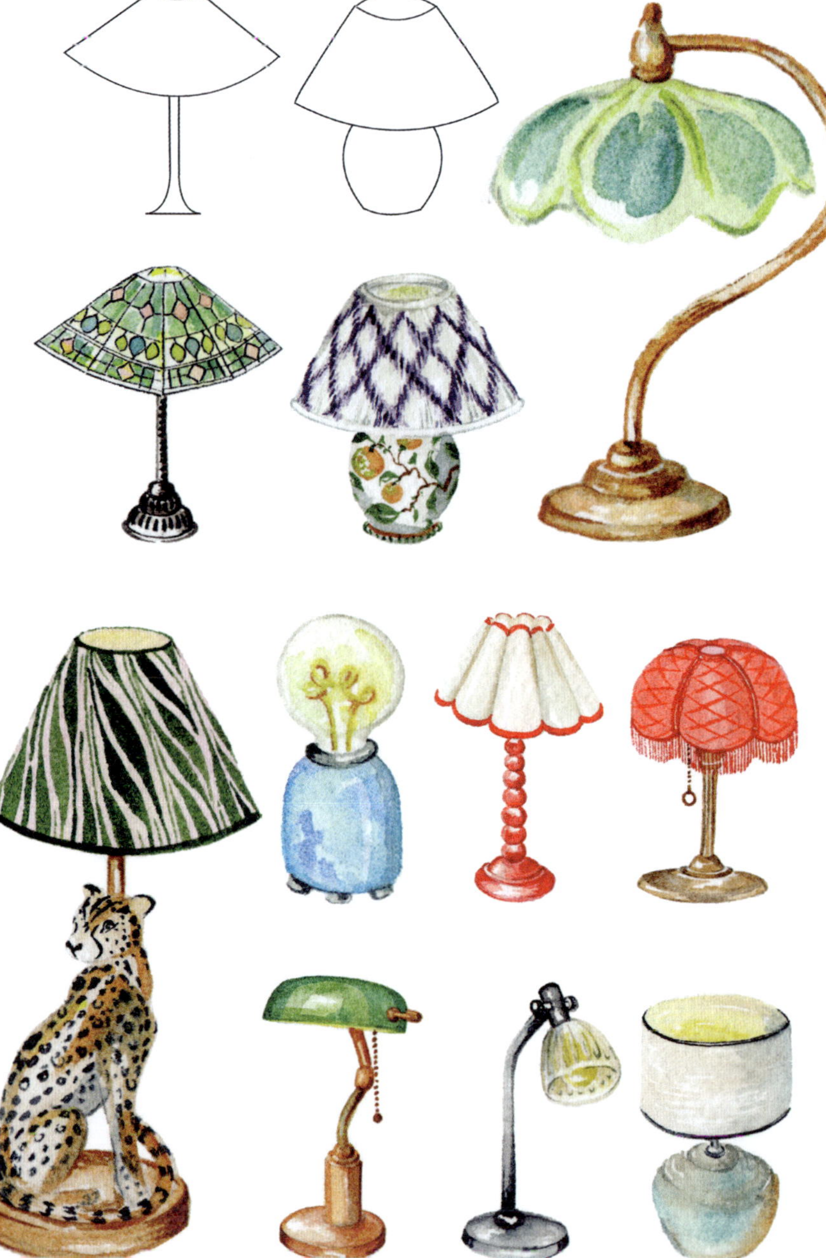

What Does Your Art Say about You?

You will be able to paint by the end of this book. What now?

Whether you're doodling in the margins of an exercise book, painting a card for a loved one or submitting a piece to a local exhibition, the art you create is sending a message to the world.

What does your art say about you? What do you like to paint?

Try writing down a few lines about what you like to paint and why you paint. Here is what I wrote:

At the moment I love to paint miniature items, vases of flowers and tile patterns. I never really understood art for art's sake; instead, I like giving my art a function and turning paintings into cards, stationery and 3D dioramas. I was a bit scared of large-scale work and landscapes, but now I'm trying to paint more of this kind of thing. I like a level of realism but am not interested in perfection. Instead, I love to capture the essence of a piece; its imperfect perfection.

Phew. Now it's your turn.

If you're not sure what you'd write, try this exercise. Choose an object and paint it in a few different artistic styles. These styles could use techniques like the ones used to create the tomato on pages 76–7 or they could relate to broader artistic movements: folk art, Impressionism, Arts and Crafts, abstraction, expressionism and so on.

Watercolour is a wonderfully diverse medium and it can adapt to all sorts of artistic styles. Painting a peacock in different ways highlighted how much I enjoy the accuracy of the detailed peacock and the blocky simplicity of the folk-art style.

We began this book with three colours and three brushes. We then pondered how to get 'better' at watercolour and here we are on the last page. These tutorials are now in the rearview mirror but return to these chapters whenever you need to be reminded of how far you've come. This is a creative journey that gets 'better' the longer we keep travelling.

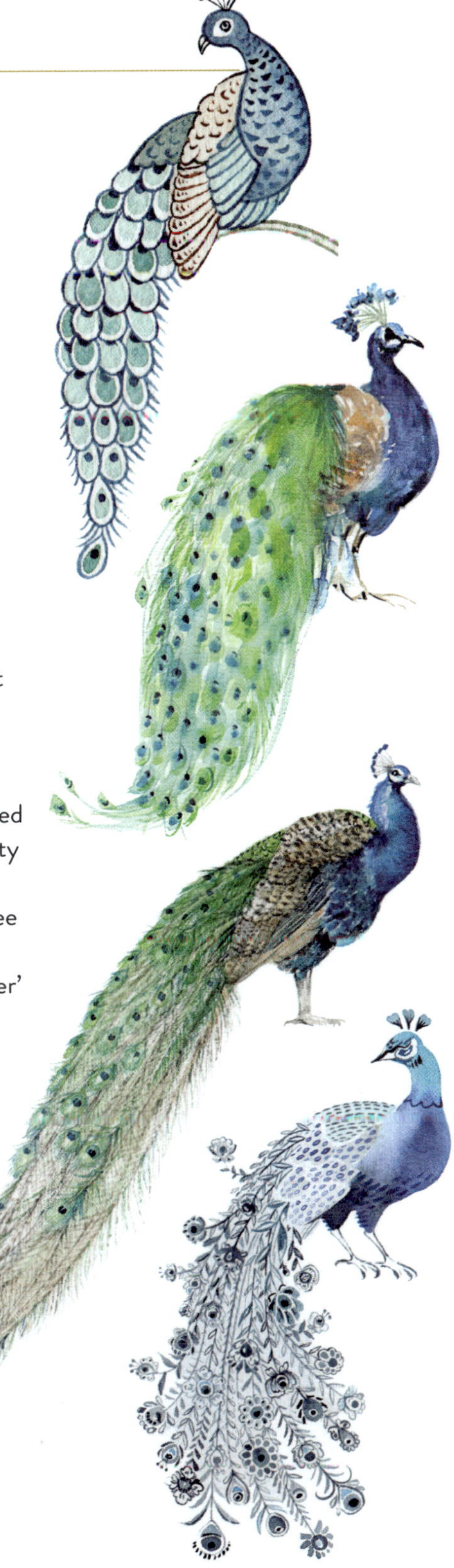

Index

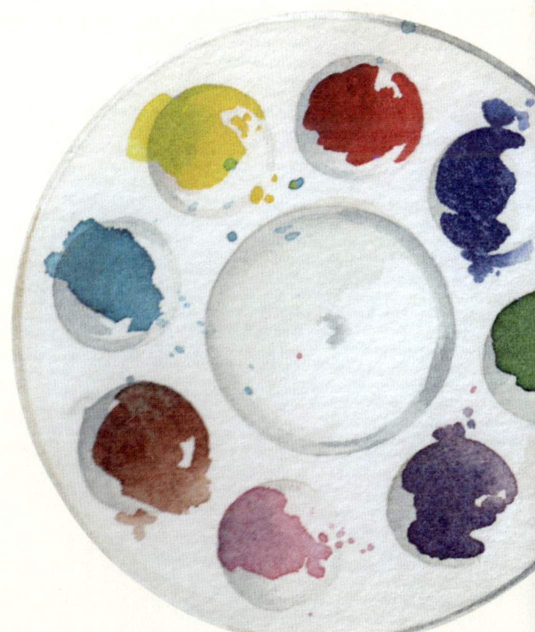

Acknowledgements

I couldn't have begun to understand how to write this book had it not been for my wonderful friend Emma Carlisle. Emma has burst open my sense of what it is to paint and teach; it was she who planted the thought of what it means to get 'better' at art – a thought that stayed on my mind throughout the writing of this book. Thanks Emma for the many creative questions and answers you give me and all of your students the world over.

Thank you so much to Ellie for five wonderful years as my Editor. I wish you all the best with your new adventures. Bonne chance! To the wider Octopus publishing team, thank you for putting together a beautiful book.

Thank you Oscar for always being there and having my back.

Thank you to my Patrons; a true global family who encourage and inspire me to make new watercolour discoveries. To anyone who was watched a YouTube tutorial, bought one of my books or attended a workshop, thank you so much for giving watercolour a go.

Thank you to my family for believing in me and encouraging me to follow my passion.

A huge thank you to Ant and Crumble who have each become watercolour experts in their own right, by my side down the many thematic paths this book travelled until reaching its destination.

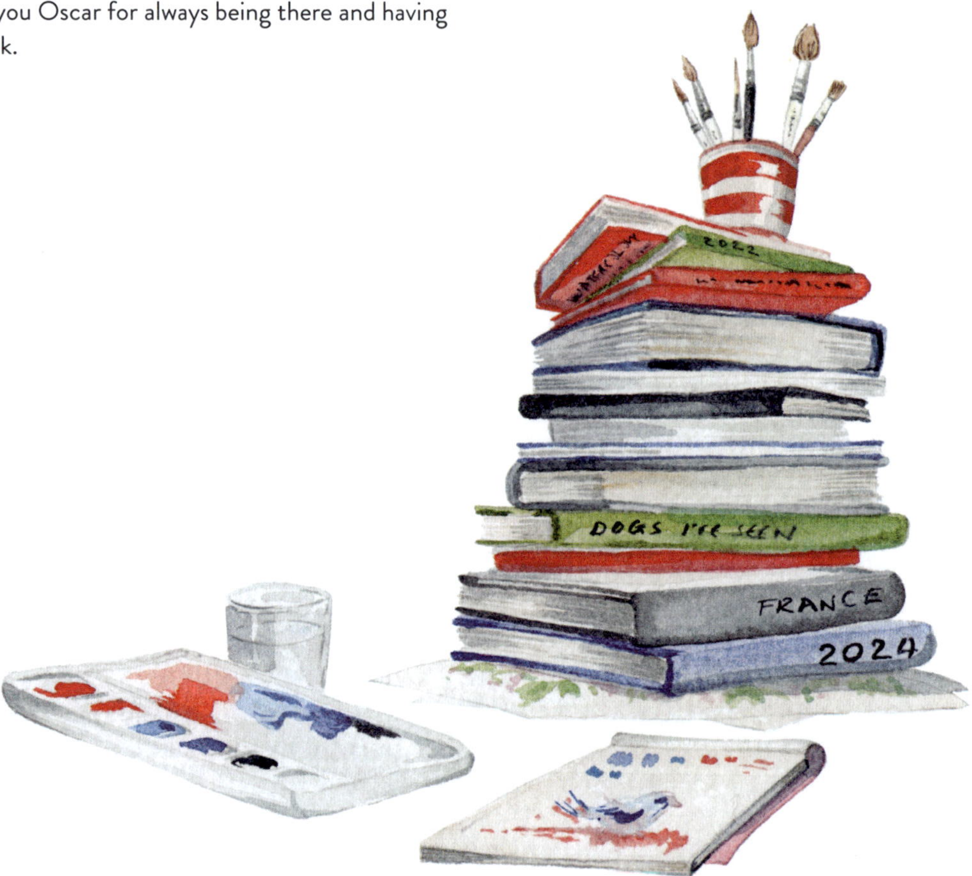